THE SPOILED SYSTEM

THE SPOILED SYSTEM

A Call for Civil Service Reform

by ROBERT G. VAUGHN

Incorporating: ***Behind the Promises: Equal Employment Opportunity in the Federal Government***

by M. Weldon Brewer, Jr.

Introduction by Ralph Nader

CHARTERHOUSE
NEW YORK

THE SPOILED SYSTEM

Library of Congress Catalog Card Number: 73-84086

ISBN 0–88327–029–3

Manufactured in the United States of America

This book is dedicated to thousands of civil servants for their daily heroism in supporting the public interest.

Preface

During this study of the Civil Service Commission, over two hundred interviews were conducted with employees, former employees, agency management and personnel officials, employee union leaders, and personnel administrators. These interviews do not include contacts with over four hundred federal employees in other agencies and departments. Three regional offices of the Commission—Philadelphia, Boston, and Dallas—were visited. Also, extensive review was made of personnel administration literature and legal materials.

Two law students, James Sneed and Weldon Brewer, studied selected operations of the Commission intensively during the summer of 1971. In each bureau studied, they first interviewed its director for a general description and explanation of its operations. They then conducted interviews with employees at all levels and, before leaving, again met with the director to discuss their findings and observations with him.

In an initial meeting on June 5, Robert Hampton, Chairman of the Civil Service Commission, offered the complete cooperation of the Commission. Much of the access which we did receive was due to his policy and the efforts of Bernard Rosen, executive director. We were never denied an interview and rarely was an interview delayed. Regional offices were also cooperative during our visits. At the bureau level, however, we encountered resistance and subterfuge. The Board of Appeals and Review and the Equal Employment Opportunity Program were particularly uncooperative.

On August 19, 1971, before leaving the Commission, we met with Mr. Hampton and Mr. Rosen to discuss our observations and findings and to recommend changes in Commission practices that we believed would be beneficial if adopted. Both men showed a commendable willingness to discuss Commission programs and performance.

Both the Civil Service report *(The Spoiled System)* and the Equal Employment Opportunity report *(Behind the Promises)* were issued in June 1972. Although in this book the reports have been edited for publication, the thrust of their recommendations remains. Initially the Commission responded to the Civil Service report with a terse paragraph to the effect that the Commission was continuing its leadership in the improvement of federal personnel policy.

During hearings conducted by the House Post Office and Civil Service Committee in September and October of 1972, Mr. Hampton termed the reports "wholly unwarranted, unfounded, unprincipled, and reprehensible." The Commission critique of the reports accompanied by a brief comment is contained in Appendix I.

Since the issuance of the reports the Commission has recommended changes in the appeals process and revised the Equal Employment Opportunity complaint procedures. These changes have been acknowledged and statistical material updated for this book.

Robert Vaughn

Acknowledgments

We should like to thank James Sneed, B.A., J.D., University of Oklahoma, for his special help in preparing this book, and Craig Kubey, for his research dealing with the President's Commission on Personnel Interchange; Richard Goldstein, for his work in updating the report; Harvey Miller, for his research concerning discrimination in the federal service; Peter J. Petkas, coauthor of the Employee Rights and Accountability Act; Mark Silbergeld, for his advice on the Fair Credit Reporting Act; and Nancy Vaughn, for her editorial review of the manuscript (and for her patience and encouragement). Thanks also to Adele Winters, Karen Klingensmith, Susan Perry, Jean Rowan, Larry MacCubbin, and Tom Quinn.

Contents

Tables

Introduction

Throughout the history of nations, both mass and elite movements have struggled over principles and policies for rearranging, in one way or another, the distribution of power. And from these frequently tumultuous cycles of change, bureaucracy has repeatedly emerged victorious. The relentless leveler of different social and economic systems, bureaucracy may be defined as the common bond of mankind—the true opiate of the people, reflecting visions of performance, and surrounded by symbols of government.

Like international chess players, political leaders from different countries and cultures use a common language and understanding in despairing over the immovability and insularity of their bureaucracies. They are not likely, however, to exchange insights as to how such seemingly endemic obstacles to the implementation of policy might be overcome. For, outside of the recent spread of the modest ombudsman concept from Scandinavia to other countries, ideas and models for making these sprawling officialdoms more open, fair, efficient, responsive, accountable, and attractive to the best talent of the land have not been forthcoming. This is no mere irritation to government. It is the core of the problem of how a complex society with many competing and conflicting interests can get things done *after* policies, directions, and funds have been decided upon by legislative councils or the upper echelons of the bureaucratic structures themselves. It is not a problem unique to government but one that plagues corporations, many unions, and other private organizations as well. As such, it is the continuous thread running through and beyond the more dramatic abuses, the scandals, and the lack of motivation and creativity which sap the potential of groups.

Bureaucratic structure develops and defends its own vested interests as ends in themselves. These vested interests include the security of tenure, the security of inevitable promotion, the security of habit, the security of sloth, and the unfettered right to stifle dissent within the ranks and block evaluation of performance from outside, whether by the public or by other governmental bodies. Such self-generating patterns of interest and inertia do not exist wholly apart from the general political and economic environment. The distribution of power and wealth in society shapes all aspects of the bureaucratic structure, from the selection of personnel to the maintenance of their status-quo orientation.

External pressure is most easily detected when a civil servant takes seriously his agency's statutory mission. Many conscientious civil servants have learned that the surest way to lose one's job is to do one's job. This report analyzes a number of cases in which a government employee stood fast to protect citizens from unsafe products, waste, or corruption, but lost his job even though proved right.

The report goes much further. In examining the federal civil service system and the Civil Service Commission, it asks several central questions. What are the ways in which the civil service, to which Congress delegated the task of administering the laws that help determine the quality of justice, safety, and power in our society, can be held accountable for the actions of agencies and individual public officials? What are the reasons for and the ways by which government employees are disciplined? What are their rights of appeal, and who makes the decisions and by what standards? What are the informal methods of retaliation against those who do not choose to get along by going along? How well does the U.S. Civil Service Commission—the oldest federal regulatory agency—carry out its responsibility to prevent the spread of a new spoils system and to advance and protect procedures for equal access to federal employment?

Within the executive branch of government, the orders and regulations regarding equal employment opportunity have become increasingly explicit. Yet the Commission has camouflaged and obfuscated its failure to cooperate to a degree that must have required considerable effort and imagination. The Commission reacts to criticism with elaborate semantic and statistical distortion—the defensive and diversionary tactics of a cornered government agency for wearing down a probing citizenry or congressional committee. When presented with the recommendations of this report, the officials in charge of the federal Equal Employment Opportunity Program replied, in vintage bureaucratese, that they have been or are considering such changes for review and adoption at some future date. These men apparently believe that criticism will go away if only it is ignored.

The federal EEO program, described in much detail in this report, is responsible for handling complaints of discrimination in the civil service, as well as for creating a climate in which employees may come forward with complaints without fear of reprisal and without great delay in receiving attention. The Commission's expressly recognized responsibility for "affirmative action" to overcome the decades of neglect has, overall, resulted mainly in public-relations tinsel. Unlike some other federal agencies, the Commission has ample authority, leverage, and disciplinary power to achieve equal employment, but it has been reluctant to use its tools. Failure is systematically assured by delegating responsibility for regulating to the subject agencies and by deliberately diffusing the lines of administrative control within the Commission. The result is de facto repudiation of the program.

The authors of this report interviewed hundreds of public officials, civil servants, and observers of the federal service over a period of nearly two years. They avoided excessive reliance on abstractions and rules by focusing on their meaning to the people of this country. They draw upon many of the documented abuses of the bureaucracy, from its selective enforcement of health, safety, and minority protection laws, to its institutionalized lawlessness, to its techniques of delay and secrecy that serve to protect the "bureaucratic flanks." To better understand what William D. Carey, former Assistant Director of the Budget, described as "arrogance of overconfidence and the shelter of ethical neutrality," they went to the victims of bureaucratic practices inside and outside government, visiting such unlikely places as the torrid steam tunnels underneath Washington, D.C., to feel, if briefly, what it is like to work there and not have anyone listen to real grievances.

The report's recommendations are directed at preventing the deprivation, fraud, and other injustices heaped upon people by monolithic, nonaccountable governmental bodies. After a number of studies on our part of federal regulatory, contracting, and service agencies, it has become clear that the Civil Service Commission's function is crucial to all these agencies. Perhaps the overriding necessity is to develop mechanisms which citizens and officials may use, and which may result in application of sanctions for malfeasance, misfeasance, and nonfeasance by civil servants and their politically appointed overseers. Insecurity of bureaucratic power or, to put it another way, exposure of the public official to the possibility of losing something of value for improper behavior, is a cardinal incentive for any policy changes and reforms.

This report is replete with specific and general recommendations for the improvement of existing structures, the refinement and enlargement of rights and remedies for citizens and dissenters within the federal service, and the formation of an Employees Rights and Accountability Board independent of the Civil Service Commission. The analysis should be pertinent to state and local governments and, in some respects, to corporate "governments." To our knowledge, this is the first comprehensive analysis of the Civil Service Commission in many years.

Public attitudes toward the bureaucracy—largely somnolent or negative in nature—must be changed also. The periodic interest which many citizens develop in political campaigns—filled, as they are, with promises of changes of direction or preservation of good old ways—should be continued beyond the campaigns. For it is in the operation of the administrative state that hopes, promises, and goals are manipulated and frustrated. However recurrent the focus is on political leadership to provide a better life for all people, when the huzzas recede, the burden of performance falls heavily on bureaucratic systems.

Ralph Nader
Washington, D.C.

THE SPOILED SYSTEM

1

Institutionalized Boredom

Our government is the potent, the omnipresent teacher. For good or for ill, it teaches the whole people by example. Crime is contagious. If the government becomes a lawbreaker, it breeds contempt for law; it invites every man to become a law unto himself; it invites anarchy.

LOUIS D. BRANDEIS

Barely had interviewing begun at the Civil Service Commission when an official commented, "How do you like studying the dullest agency in government?" Indeed, "civil service" conjures up visions of eye-shaded clerks, of a never-ending paper serpent writhing up from accumulated memoranda, regulations, and directives. Still, beneath this blanket of tedium are critical issues affecting the performance of government. For, although only a small number of people are employed by the Civil Service Commission, the Commission, as we shall see, affects every civil servant, be he a poultry inspector or a code clerk, a physicist or a presidential guard. And the functioning of civil servants affects every citizen.

While personnel policies are seen as mere techniques—their practitioners ranking low in daring and dash—once the initial yawn barrier is penetrated, important issues emerge. The primary issue is how to make civil servants perform their duties to the public.

Civil servants often hold immense power. It is they who

determine whether laws designed to protect the public are enforced. It is they who ensure the distribution of wholesome and uncontaminated meat and poultry and who determine whether metals and chemicals will be allowed in food and water, whether the Flammable Fabrics Act will be enforced, whether unsafe automobiles will be recalled, whether nuclear power plants will have adequate safeguards, whether occupational health and safety standards will be implemented, whether pesticides are safe, whether unsafe toys will be banned, whether food stamps will be properly distributed, whether nursing homes will meet health and safety standards, whether education funds will be properly awarded, whether procurement will be conducted fairly and honestly. It is they, in short, who determine whether and how well anything gets done.

Civil service reform has focused upon corruption and political patronage within federal bureaucracy. Important as these problems may be, they are secondary to the abuses flowing from the enormous power collected in the executive branch and in federal regulatory agencies. The old safeguards designed to prevent the more egregious abuses of political patronage are useless or ineffective in responding to the problems and threats posed by this power and its potential abuse. Even if consistently and conscientiously applied, the old techniques have not been sufficient to prevent the development of a new spoils system.

Examination of four duties of the Civil Service Commission illustrates the inability of the present personnel system to respond to the challenges of executive power and explains the forces which have created the new spoils system. Briefly these four duties are (1) to protect the rights of the federal employees and to administer the appeals system; (2) to regulate and enforce and, to that end, inspect federal agencies' efficacy in enforcing personnel regulations; (3) to conduct the federal Equal Employment Opportunity program; (4) to conduct investigations into the suitability for employment of present or potential government employees. The effective and imaginative performance of these duties could do much to provide a climate in the federal service in which employees are inclined to perform their public duties.

Early in his career the civil servant learns that the statutory goals of his agency—usually stated in terms of the public good—are rarely invoked and never used to evaluate his performance. He learns to consider other variables, outstanding among them the power of special-interest groups.

For many civil servants, dedication to professional or scientific ethics brings them into conflict with the management of their agencies: an analyst is dismissed after refusing to endorse a report distorting and misrepresenting research data about the antiballistics missile; a Food and Drug Administration physician who questions the safety of a vaccine loses his secretary, his laboratory, and his phone; a Department of Agriculture scientist who attempts to protect his experimental animals from being moved into an inadequate building is dismissed and his carefully bred animals are destroyed.

In each of these cases, personnel rules and regulations are used to "discipline" an errant employee. Personnel rules are often selectively enforced, and personnel administration becomes a means of mollifying and diffusing concern about the performance of government, rather than generating solutions and rectifying ills. Common candor thus becomes uncommon courage, and job security is tied to maintaining the status quo.

It is just such areas for which the Commission is responsible—the protection of the civil servant. But the role of the Commission as policeman is more and more disparaged, whereas an advisory role is seen as more consistent with its expertise. The agencies themselves, or the President, come more and more to be seen as the Commission's clientele, a situation well illustrated in the case of John Macy.

While serving as chairman of the Civil Service Commission, Macy also advised President Johnson on personnel matters, and was responsible for obtaining the greatest political advantage from presidential appointments. At the same time, as the chairman of the Commission, he was responsible for preventing the undermining of the career service. While there were duties of both positions that overlapped, many, surely, were incompatible. This dual appointment is a vivid example of the attitudes of the Commission and of its relationship to the White House. Commission employees work closely with the White House, with the Office of Management and Budget, and with the management of executive agencies. While the Commission's present chairman, Robert Hampton, is not a formal advisor to the President, his service at the White House makes him sensitive to the views of the executive. (For several months in 1961 before joining the Commission, he served as a special assistant on presidential appointments; he is in constant contact with the Office of Management and Budget.)

A premium is placed upon cooperation with the agencies, which is justified by regarding personnel management as a difficult and complex area in which cooperation is necessary. Cooperation is also highly valued because the Commission sees itself as lacking in political clout and financial resources. ("What would happen if we disagreed with Defense?") A self-fulfilling prophecy, the Commission's view of its own powers eventually circumscribes and limits it.

A part of the Commission's rationale for its present role and perspective is that the vast federal establishment requires decentralization of efforts.[1] But decentralization of either organization or program requires a clear view of goals and purposes. Without clearly shaped goals and a highly developed review mechanism, decentralization can create more problems than it solves. Decentralization without controls becomes abnegation.

Functionally, the Commission has become a purveyor of technical services to the management of the federal agencies. Politically, it has become a servant of the administration in power at the moment, defining itself as the "President's Personnel Office."

As "bureaucracy's bureaucrat" the Commission has done well by bureaucracy and badly by the public. After examining its appeals system, one doubts whether it is an adequate guardian of employees who place the public mission of an agency over the temporary interests of its managers.

In the federal Equal Employment Opportunity program (EEO), the Commission has been given the mandate, the power, and resources to create a major change in the federal environment. Its failure indicates the inability of its present methods to change behavior in the federal service.

An effective Commission inspection program can be used to implement and enforce its policies. Yet, the present program emphasizes self-evaluation by the agencies and assumes that the responsibilities of the Commission to employees and the public are identical with the interests of agency management.

The Commission's personnel investigations influence what kind of person government agencies hire, yet its Bureau of Personnel Investigation is its most agency-oriented bureau and seems directed primarily toward distributing the government's vast stockpile of intelligence data.

A government can only be as good as the people who work for it. The Commission is not an obscure agency dealing with classification and examination—it is potentially a powerful agent for change. This report is not only a study of the Civil Service Commission, but a presentation of suggestions for dealing with bureaucratic lawlessness as well.

In the nineteenth century, the cry, "To the victors belong the spoils" was born; public employment became a reward for political service rather than a duty based upon qualification, and corruption grew until offices were openly sold in the daily columns of Washington newspapers. In 1883 the Civil Service Commission was established out of public concern, and to a large degree it succeeded in vitiating the ills of the spoils system.

But a new spoils system exists today, created by the new regulatory state and based upon economic and political influence. Rather than responding and adapting to the new problems of huge growth and the encroachment of private interests, the Commission has allowed personnel management and administration to become a technology separate from the public goals it should be pursuing, which is the effective management of federal agencies.

Two internal trends have helped to create the new spoils system. The first is the tendency to see industry as a model for efficiency, to be emulated by government—a tendency reinforced by the close ties between government and industry. Little consideration is given to the view that government can be efficient and still fail to serve the public. The second is what one Washington attorney categorized as the "You will obey" syndrome. Supreme Court Justice William H. Rehnquist, then assistant attorney general, expressed this viewpoint well in an article on "Public Dissent and the Public Employee" in the January–March 1971 *Civil Service Journal.*[2] Rehnquist commented that factors in the background of every dismissal action are discipline, personal loyalty, and harmony. This attitude is illustrated, as we shall see, by the Commission's response to the most moderate attempts of its employees to raise and discuss the Commission's role.

The Commission presents a placid if not staid image; some former employees speak of it affectionately as the "old lady," a sometimes severe grandame, but one who takes care of her own. Only four actions against employees—three of which involved demotion—have occurred in the Commission in the last five years. Two of these employees accepted demotion; the third appealed through administrative channels to the executive director, who upheld the demotion; the fourth action involved the removal of an employee who appealed unsuccessfully. Placidity, however, does not always mean peace nor does silence always mean agreement. There has, in fact, been growing concern with the Commission's attitudes among younger, talented officers. Clearly the Commission's disregard for the open discussion of issues, its sensitivity to any conceivable controversy, and its reluctance to antagonize federal agencies prevents it from serving effectively as a guardian of the career service.

When Congress established the Civil Service Commission, it hoped that the commissioners would have the authority, the expertise, and the independence to guard the public's interest in fair and honest government service, and to this end Congress introduced safeguards. The appointment process required confirmation of each commissioner by the Senate, terms were staggered, and it was stipulated that no more than two of the three commissioners be of the same political party. However, the Commissioners serve at the pleasure of the President. The absence of independent terms is one major factor reducing the regulatory effectiveness of the Commission.

Four persons served as Civil Service Commissioners in the course of this study. James E. Johnson, appointed in 1969 as a Republican member of the Commission, resigned in 1971 to become assistant secretary of the navy for administration and was replaced by another Republican, Jayne B. Spain. Robert Hampton, a Republican, is chairman of the Commission, and Ludwig U. Andolsek is the Democratic member.

Facts emerged at the Senate Confirmation hearing of James Johnson—the first black Civil Service Commissioner—that cast doubt on whether his attitudes and background were desirable in that position. While he was Director of the California Department of Veterans' Affairs under Governor Ronald Reagan, Johnson issued a memorandum to his aids ("Implementing the Administration's Creative Society Philosophy and Policy") that stated, "In order for the 'creative society' to flourish, all persons in state government must think this way. . . . The Director will inform career employees of the Administration's philosophy and policy and in so doing allay fears and combat resistance to change. . . . The performance and execution of the Governor's policy is the job of our department."[3]

The newest member, and vice-chairman of the Commission, Jayne B. Spain, has had extensive experience in private industry as a member of the board of directors of Litton Industries. Ms. Spain displayed a sincere desire to discuss her impressions of the Commission, and indicated that once she learned the ropes, she intended to do some recruiting of women for top government positions. Her staff, however, consists only of a secretary and the administrative assistant, Mr. James Spry, who also serves the other two commissioners.

In January 1973 Congressman Jerome Waldie, a member of the House Post Office and Civil Service Committee, commented on the impropriety of Ms. Spain receiving $7,500 in consulting fees in 1972 from Litton. Congressman Waldie believed that this relationship with Litton violated that section of the employee code of conduct which says that federal employees shall avoid any action which might result in or create the appearance of losing complete independence or impartiality. (A potential for such conflict was illustrated by the transfer of Gordon Rule, a navy procurement official, who had criticized Litton's performance as a defense contractor. If Rule had sought Civil Service Commission assistance, the relationship of Ms. Spain with Litton would cast doubt upon the impartiality of the decision.)

The minority (Democratic) member of the Commission is Ludwig J. Andolsek, a Commissioner since 1963. The walls of his office are covered with memorabilia: gavels, tomahawks, and certificates. Andolsek commented that everyone was welcome in his office. The employee might not be welcomed the second time, but the first time Andolsek would listen to whatever complaints anyone had, regardless of his grade. Some employees mentioned Andolsek's willingness to see them. One former employee said, "He was the only one there who was interested in me or my problem." A former high-level Commission employee commented, "Andolsek's heart is in the right place."

Andolsek summarized his service as a commissioner. When he was younger, he was "full of piss and vinegar," but now he is "mellowing like good booze." As an example of this mellowing process, Andolsek said that when he entered the Commission he supported "100 percent, hearings in every case" and unannounced inspections, but his opinions had changed. Concerning the dearth of black regional directors in the federal Equal Employment Opportunity program, Andolsek explained, "It takes twenty to twenty-five years to get there." His comments about women were hardly more encouraging. He thought that they were "inners and outers" who wanted supplementary income. He felt that employees were the cause of delay in the complaint process.

The chairman of the Civil Service Commission is Robert Hampton, whose prior experience in government was primarily in the Department of State and in the air force, where he served as assistant deputy for manpower, personnel, and organization. Hampton has served as commissioner since 1961 and as chairman since 1969. His position gives him administrative powers, and his experience and personality make him the dominant member of the Commission.

Hampton's personal staff is small. In addition to Mr. Spry, there is an administrative assistant, a secretary, and a staff assistant. Thus, Hampton relies heavily upon the executive staff and on executive director Bernard Rosen for both information and administration. The complex relationship between the Commissioners and the executive director makes Rosen often the most influential man within the Commission.

The executive director is more than an advisor; he is the chief administrative officer of the Commission, carrying out the chairman's role as administrative head of the Commission. These functions ensure that he will have a voice in the implementation and enforcement of policies and decisions concerning implementation of a program that will effect its direction, priority, and success. The executive director's control over internal administration may give him the power to shape the opinions of others within the Commission. At the very least, it may cause other Commission career officials to pause before becoming too vigorous in opposing his views.[4]

This power is not, of course, monolithic or unrestrained. The executive director must operate within the broad framework of Commission policy. A director is most effective in defending the status quo because such defense is least likely to upset working arrangements with others in the Commission. A director who desires to consolidate and protect his influence will be inclined to become primarily a defender of Commission programs.

The power and influence of the executive director and the interplay of personality and policy are exemplified by the two men who served as executive director during the span of this study—Nicholas Oganavic and Bernard Rosen. Oganavic had been an employee of the Commission since 1943, serving as deputy regional director, regional director in St. Paul and Denver, and then in Washington as director of the Bureau of Departmental Operations. In 1960 he became deputy executive director of the Commission and in 1965 he became its executive director.

Oganavic was considered a powerful director. In discussing promotions and upgradings, Commission personnel spoke of the "O factor." He showed a great concern for minor administrative details, once directing employees not to take their coffee breaks in the Commission cafeteria because visitors might think they were not hard workers.

To many government employees, Oganavic seemed the ultimate bureaucrat. In an interview with Elizabeth Drew in 1969 about "the misunderstandings between him and the young dissenters," he said:

> I don't think that the end of the war is going to stop it. God hoping, the war should have been over a long time ago. They will pick on something else. There was a certain class of people in the thirties who behaved just like these people. The Communist Party was trying to organize these kids, but I don't think that exists here. It may be here and there, but I'd be the last one to say these kids would knowingly be pawns.

In the summer of 1970, Oganavic issued a memorandum to "Commissionettes" indicating the programs in which women throughout the government might participate. Among the projects he suggested were:

> preventing high school dropouts—girls; assisting one girl a year who is in difficulty; assisting children by working with Camp Fire Girls, Scouts and other girls' organizations—especially in the inner cities; promoting occupational health in Government for early detection of female diseases; assisting in eradicating venereal disease and prostitution—80 percent of venereal disease is due to "free premarital sex relations."

The present executive director, Bernard Rosen, who has served as a regional director and deputy executive director, is intelligent and articulate. He is a member of Phi Beta Kappa and holds a master's degree in public administration. Within the Commission, Rosen's power rests in part upon his reputation as a hard fighter who has the ability to mold the system to his own uses. Because of his ability, personality, and position, he should be a powerful executive director.

Except in those few instances in which the Commissioners exercise their discretion to reopen a case, the Board of Appeals and Review (BAR) is an employee's last opportunity for justice in the civil service appeals process.

The Board of Appeals and Review at the time of this study consisted of five members: William P. Berzak, chairman; Leon S. Mapes, deputy chairman; Edward H. Bechtold, Jr.; John O. Hardesty; and Peggy S. Griffiths. Virgil Jefferies, a BAR examiner, served as a substitute member of the BAR when there was a temporary vacancy.

The newest member of the Board at the time of the study was Peggy Griffiths, a member for three years. Ms. Griffiths, an attorney with a master's degree in labor relations, and the youngest member of the BAR, was the only black member, the only woman member, and the only member with experience outside the federal personnel establishment.[5]

All members except Ms. Griffiths had spent their careers entirely within the Commission—and they have been long careers (averaging twenty-seven and one-half years). So many years in the Commission can lead to inflexibility and rigidity, and we shall see later in this study how the perceptions and personalities of the BAR members and of the Commissioners are replicated in less highly placed employees of the Commission.

These are just a few hints that the Commission stands atop a personnel system that is not performing the functions for which it was conceived. The following chapters discuss the need for reform and the directions it might take.

2

The Management Monopoly

> The speed of exit of a civil servant is directly proportional to the quality of his service.
>
> RALPH NADER

After Ralph Nader announced that the Public Interest Research Group would be mounting a study of the Civil Service Commission, hundreds of federal employees were heard from. The complaints seemed to indicate not simply individual dislocations, but structural faults in the ways in which employees are disciplined.

The civil servant finds himself in an unpleasant position in which his relationship with his agency is marked by a lack of substantive rights. It is a relationship between superior and subordinate in which the superior has many opportunities to make discretionary judgments of considerable importance to the subordinate. The exercise of legal rights in such a relationship is often difficult and restrained.

Few organizations stress superior-subordinate relationships more than the federal government. Status differentiations are made clear by the general service (GS) ratings. The GS scale establishes the rate of pay for employees in the federal service. As of January 1974 salaries range from approximately $5,000 for a GS-1 to $40,000 for a GS-18 with several years of service. The system provides precise differentiation between grades one through eighteen and ten salary step levels within each. (As one indication of status, lower-grade employees are given small metal desks while higher-grade employees receive larger wooden desks. Even space is an indication of station; a GS-5 is allowed 60 square feet of work space while a GS-15 supervisory employee is allotted 225 square feet.)

All communication is made through layers of intermediaries. Each employee must be given performance and appraisal ratings for purposes of retention and promotion. Such appraisals are always made by superiors, and the goodwill of one's supervisor therefore becomes paramount. The work environment may be made friendly or hostile, open or repressive, tolerable or intolerable by the superior, who is equipped with a finely honed and calibrated set of sanctions to be used against subordinates. The granting of leave and the assignment of duties may be effective tools of discipline in the hands of the superior. We found that employee after employee believed that an agency could "get" any employee. Some of the personnel officers with whom we spoke believed that it was always possible "to remove an irritant." Several methods are available by which agencies may remove or restrain a troublesome employee.

The Direct Approach

One of the myths surrounding federal employment is that it is difficult or impossible to remove a federal employee. Initial restraints upon removals—the reluctance of managers to confront employees and the time and effort required to build a case—may cause a manager to reassess what would be an arbitrary decision, but these restraints may not serve the purpose for which they are intended; they may discourage management from removing a marginal employee who, while inconvenient, poses no real threat to the perpetuation of the status quo within the agency, but they do not prevent moving against outspoken or unorthodox employees who do pose a threat.

In actuality, a removal is easy if one takes the proper procedural steps, and even procedural safeguards against unfair use of removal mechanisms are susceptible to manipulation. (One personnel director noted, "Thirty days notice is required for a dismissal, but no notice is required for a suspension. We give the removal notice and a thirty-day suspension notice at the same time.")

Finding grounds presents little difficulty for motivated management. If the difficulty of building a case against an employee is too great, or if the agency does not want to risk the review of the grounds of removal, other methods are available. When it is not possible to build a case on nonperformance, management has the discretion of selective enforcement of regulations.[1] Consider, for example, that almost all federal employees occasionally violate the thirty-minute lunch rule; indeed, many employees regularly take an hour. But management can select employees to be punished for this violation. Similarly, many employees are late for work and escape with impunity, yet lateness can be selected as grounds for dismissal.

Love It or Leave It

Rather than bringing formal charges against an employee, an agency may choose to use the threat of charges to force his retirement or resignation.[2] Even when the threatened charges are improper or not clearly supportable, an employee may be tempted to capitulate. If he fights and loses, he has a dismissal on his record and loses his pension and insurance rights. If he feels that his appeal will not be evaluated fairly, he may decide to resign. The legal process appears lengthy and, if there is a possibility that the case may be appealed ultimately in court, expensive, during which time the employee is out of a job and the psychological pressures on him are great.

Some officials argue that the opportunity to resign or retire is an act of mercy to protect an employee's record. Such protestations, however, are belied by the behavior of many agencies. Rather than ending the matter, many an employee has found that his resignation only began a new ordeal. The resignation that goes into his personnel folder, to be referred to by potential employers, is marked "resigned under charges of dismissal." (Bernard Rosen indicated that this practice is no longer tolerated, but nothing prevents management from providing this information when consulted by potential employers.)[3]

Lost in a RIF

When an agency is required by budget restraints or by reorganization to reduce its staff, it follows a process known as a Reduction in Force (RIF). A dismissal by RIF carries with it no stigma of nonperformance or inadequate performance, for it is the job that is being eliminated, and not the jobholder. Management can and does use RIFs to rid itself of employees against whom dismissal actions would not be sustained.

In theory, who will lose his job in a RIF is based on objective principles that center on retention ratings. (Retention ratings are based in large part upon length of service; veterans receive special consideration, and additional retention points are given to employees who have received awards for superior service.) An employee's right to challenge a RIF is limited to questions of whether his retention rating has been properly computed, whether his job was in the proper category, whether he has been placed in the proper competitive area, and whether certain procedural requirements have been followed. An employee whose job is abolished in a RIF may take over the job of another employee in the same competitive category, who then loses his job instead. While this "bumping" is done on the basis of retention points, management has considerable discretion in establishing the competitive categories. Thus, an employee with several years of service and with high performance ratings may find himself in a category where his seniority and performance count for little.

One of the more famous examples of RIFing was that of Ernest Fitzgerald. Mr. Fitzgerald, an air force civilian employee who exposed before the Joint Economic Committee in the fall of 1968 a $2.5 billion cost overrun on the C-5A transport plane, was shortly thereafter removed in a Reduction in Force, which the air force described as an "economy move." His retention rights were mooted because he was the only man in his competitive category—his was the one job abolished and no similar jobs existed in which he might exercise his retention rights. An air force memorandum of January 6, 1969 suggested a RIF as one of three ways to get rid of Fitzgerald. Fitzgerald appealed to the Civil Service Commission. After court action, he won in 1972 the right to an open hearing. The Commission's Appeals Examining Office recently ordered Fitzgerald's reinstatement. However, the Commission failed to find that Fitzgerald's dismissal was in retaliation for his congressional testimony but was rather the result of an "adversary relationship" which had been allowed to develop between Fitzgerald and the air force. Fitzgerald commented that he made the appeals system work only because he had received approximately $200,000 in donated legal services from the American Civil Liberties Union to wage his lengthy battle.

Reduction in force can prove an effective tool to silence troublesome employees as the following case shows:

Oscar Hoffman, a government inspector of pipe welds on combat ships being built for the navy, troubled his superiors by finding a great many defects. When he resisted pressure to ease up, he was threatened with a reprimand. When he filed a grievance against this threat, he was reprimanded and transferred shortly from Seattle to Tacoma, Washington, where he was RIFed in 1970 soon after his arrival. (Accidents involving faulty welds have occurred since on some of the ships about which Mr. Hoffman had expressed concern. Although his superior has been promoted, Mr. Hoffman has been unable to secure another job as a government inspector.)

Those who appeal RIF actions are not notably successful. In 1970, 62,720 Reductions in Force occurred. In 1971, 2,241 RIF appeals were processed at the Commission's first appellate level. The appellant was defeated in 90 percent of the actions. Statistics do not indicate precisely how many of the remainder were reversed on grounds of faulty procedure, but the Commission's ultimate appeals level, its Board of Appeals and Review, processed 1,147 RIF appeals in 1971.

The examples of Fitzgerald and Hoffman do not begin to exhaust the possibilities inherent in RIFing. An employee may, for example, be downgraded to a position soon to be abolished; an employee may be RIFed on the basis of lack of work, and a temporary employee hired soon after; an employee may find that employees he might "bump" have been placed in special training programs where they are not subject to RIF. A variant of RIFing gets the employee down to get him out—to exercise bumping rights he may have to accept a reduction in grade or a reassignment. In 1970, 25,890 employees were downgraded and 17,350 were reassigned through reductions in force. Management has considerable discretion in determining what positions will be offered an employee who is RIFed, and many employees will leave rather than accept the offered job. Such rejection ends all rights that the employee has to appeal the RIF. Of course, demotion or reassignment may itself be an effective sanction, even if the employee does not leave.

Exiled to Siberia

Some agencies have a Siberia—an unpleasant or professionally unproductive duty station, to which rebellious employees may be reassigned. Faced with Siberia, an employee may, of course, resign, but even if he accepts exile, he is effectively removed from the position in which he caused difficulty.

Reassignments may be either to a different geographical location or to a different division within the agency. Since the decision to reassign is considered to be a management prerogative, an employee may have difficulty proving that the reassignment is unnecessary or retaliatory.[4] Because an employee must accept reassignment in order to file a grievance challenging reassignment, he may have to go through the trouble and expense of relocating his family before he can begin his appeal.[5]

"You'd be surprised how many resignations we had when people discovered they had been reassigned to Anchorage," said one former Federal Aeronautics Administration official. A Colorado-stationed research scientist for the Agricultural Research Service who expressed concern about consultants for private industry using laboratory facilities found himself exiled to Alabama. H. Battle Hale, the Department of Agriculture official who questioned the propriety of the activities of Billy Sol Estes, was sent to Louisiana for a nonexistent "key job" before he was eventually reassigned to Kansas City. What is exile for a New Yorker is, of course, not necessarily exile for a Texan. Management is, however, able to tailor the geographical Siberia to the individual. In 1970, 1,960 employees were separated for refusal to relocate geographically.

But it is hardly necessary to send an employee far away to convince him to resign. For many government employees a rewarding and stimulating job assignment is important, and transfer to an agency dumping ground creates, particularly for a professional, great pressure to resign or retire. (Within the Federal Trade Commission, for example, the Division of Wools and Textiles functions as Siberia.)

In regulatory areas, these reassignments directly affect the consumer, since they either incline an aggressive employee to resign or, by discouraging aggressive behavior, they weaken an entire regulatory program. The consumer's "cops on the beat," such as meat and poultry inspectors, are particularly susceptible to this type of harassment.[6]

But perhaps the best example of the use of Siberia to leave the consumer out in the cold is found in a case within the Food and Drug Administration.

Crucial to the FDA's ability to protect the consumer from unsafe or inadequately tested prescription drugs are the medical officers within its Bureau of New Drugs. The medical officer must determine whether clinical trials of new drugs on animals are adequate to justify tests on man. Based on his evaluation of their safety and effectiveness, he must determine whether new drugs should be marketed and whether proposed labeling contains truthful claims and adequate directions. The history of John O. Nestor, M.D., board-certified in pediatrics and board-eligible in cardiology, shows that it is often the most diligent civil servant who is marked for Siberia.

In 1961, Dr. Nestor was enjoying a lucrative practice as a pediatric cardiologist in Arlington, Virginia. In the same year that the FDA was excusing its ineffectiveness before the Kefauver Committee by pleaing an inability to attract specialists, Dr. Nestor, who himself had been the victim of an adverse drug reaction because of a faulty label warning, volunteered to work part time for the FDA. When the FDA indicated that it would not accept part-time work, Dr. Nestor agreed to give up the greater part of his practice in order to work full time for the FDA.

Immediately after joining, Dr. Nestor attacked his job with a dedication and intensity that should, although it does not, characterize all those who hold a public trust. He was responsible for the withdrawal from the market of Entoquel, a White Laboratories product for the systematic treatment of diarrhea, after he uncovered erroneous test data submitted to the FDA. Dr. Bennet A. Robin, who had submitted the data and who had "tested" approximately forty-five drugs for twenty-two firms, pleaded no contest to charges of submitting erroneous reports. Dr. Nestor was instrumental in helping to block the marketing here of Thalidomide, a drug that caused hundreds of deformed babies in Europe. He was also responsible for the withdrawal from the market of MER/29, a cholesterol-lowering drug that posed a significant risk of producing cataracts in patients, while having doubtful therapeutic efficacy. Three officials of Richardson-Merrill, the manufacturers of MER/29, after pleading no contest to charges of withholding information concerning the drug, were placed on probation.

In the wake of the MER/29 scandal, Dr. Nestor raised issues of general FDA policy before congressional committees and in the form of memoranda to FDA officials. In March 1963, testifying before Senator Hubert Humphrey's Subcommittee on Reorganization, Dr. Nestor criticized the fact that there was "no internal appraisal to determine how a drug was allowed to clear New Drug Procedures."

Rather than being rewarded for his record of public service, Dr. Nestor's tenure at the FDA has been one of trial. At one point, when he questioned a supervisor about not having received a pay increase, he was asked, "Why are you acting the way you are acting?" After a session with the grand jury investigating the MER/29 incident, Dr. Nestor returned to find his office empty; without consulting him the FDA had reassigned Dr. Nestor to the Surveillance

Division of the Bureau of Medicine, an undesirable post. This was not to be the last undesirable reassignment Dr. Nestor would receive. In 1965 he was transferred to the Case Review Branch of the Division of Medical Review, which collects evidence for prosecution. Some eighteen months later, as the result of White House inquiries, Dr. Nestor was returned to the Bureau of New Drugs.

On June 11, 1970, Dr. Nestor directed a special memorandum to Charles Edwards, commissioner of the Food and Drug Administration, warning him of the risks involved in existing FDA testing procedures. Although Dr. Henry Simmons, director of the Bureau of New Drugs, did not approve of this communication, Dr. Nestor used the FDA Critical Problem Report System, ostensibly established to cut red tape in communicating with top officials. In July, Dr. Nestor again wrote Commissioner Edwards discussing the morality and ethics of human experimentation encouraged by the FDA and reiterating the gravity of the situation.

Early in the week of August 17, 1970, Dr. Nestor was called into the office of Dr. Marian Finkel, the deputy director of the Bureau of New Drugs, and asked if he would be interested in working in the Division of Drug Advertising. Dr. Nestor responded that he was not at all interested and left, believing the matter closed. On September 1, 1970, however, Dr. Nestor was informed that he was being transferred to the Division of Drug Advertising.[7] He had not been consulted prior to the decision and it was not until September 4 that he learned from Commissioner Edwards that he would be detailed to the division for only four months. The detail placed Dr. Nestor, a GS-15, under the supervision of a GS-14 whom he had formerly supervised. Dr. Nestor believed that the action was a retaliatory one, motivated by his use of the Critical Problem Report System and by a desire to remove him from the sensitive drug applications with which he was dealing. He feared that he would be placed on other undesirable details when this one was completed or would eventually be reassigned from the bureau entirely. Dr. J. Marion Bryant, a fellow medical officer, commented in 1970 on Dr. Nestor's reassignment. "A large segment of the medical officers, including myself, are of the opinion that it *is* retaliatory and intended to silence Dr. Nestor."

Articles by Morton Mintz in the *Washington Post* of September 7, 1970, and by Reginald W. Rhein in *U.S. Medicine* of September 15, 1970, and continuing congressional inquiry and support for Dr. Nestor may have aided his return to the Cardiopulmonary-Renal Division of the Bureau of New Drugs. Once back, he proceeded to pursue his responsibilities with his customary zeal. Along with several other doctors, including Dr. John W. Winkler, acting division director, Dr. Nestor had turned the Cardiopulmonary-Renal Division into one of the most effective units within the bureau, an effectiveness that distressed the drug industry and, apparently, the hierarchy of the FDA.

On March 14, 1972, Dr. Nestor was called to the office of Dr. Henry Simmons, director of the Bureau of New Drugs, and told that he was being reassigned to the Bureau of Compliance—effective in six days. Neither Dr. Nestor nor his supervisor had been consulted about the reassignment. When asked the reason for the transfer, Dr. Simmons answered that Dr. Nestor had done such a good job with other investigations that the Bureau of Compliance wanted him to work on Laetrile, an anticancer drug. Dr. Nestor pointed out that he was not a cancer specialist and that one drug investigation hardly justified a reassignment, since he could work on loan for that. The reassignment, furthermore, would be to a nonspecialist position and would remove Dr. Nestor from important current drug investigations. Dr. Nestor became more concerned about the reassignment when he spoke the next day with the director of the Bureau of Compliance. The director told of a conversation with Dr. Simmons the week before in which Dr. Simmons said that he intended to move Dr. Nestor, and asked if he could be used in the Bureau of Compliance. The director had responded by saying there were some problems, such as Laetrile, on which Dr. Nestor could work.

Dr. Nestor filed a formal grievance with the FDA and an appeal with the Civil Service Commission, contending that his assignment to a general medical position not requiring a specialty was an improper reduction in rank. According to him, much of the work he had been assigned could be handled by "a competent first year medical student."

Dr. Nestor had been reviewing an application for the proposed new use of a cholesterol-lowering drug, which had been reviewed previously and approved for use in human investigation by Dr. Finkel. At the time of his transfer he was raising serious questions about the adequacy of the previous tests. He was also raising embarrassing questions about the propriety of the FDA's use of medical consultants to review drug applications who had tested or were testing drugs for private industry.

Dr. Nestor's formal grievance to the Food and Drug Administration was ultimately denied. Today, Dr. Nestor remains in the Office of Compliance. His assignments have become more substantive and, as he put it, "There is always something a concerned individual can find to do."

Not all reassignments, of course, are punitive or coercive, but present policies provide management with a means to suppress and punish dissidents that poses dangers for the effective enforcement of regulatory programs.[8]

The Deep Freeze

Sometimes an instant Siberia can be created without moving the objectionable employee at all. Separation from contact with other employees, physical isolation, and boredom are part of the deep freeze treatment.

One GS-13 employee in the Department of Agriculture was assigned nothing but the task of organizing departmental beauty contests. A GS-9 employee in the Department of Labor was deprived of a telephone and given no work assignment for several weeks. At first he found the resemblance to solitary confinement amusing, but after a while the lack of anything to do became distressing. He began to bring magazines to work with him, a diversion that was ended when a supervisor told him that he was not allowed to read magazines while working. When the employee had the temerity to ask what he was to be working at, his supervisor responded, "What you are assigned." This technique is particularly useful when the employee has violated no regulation.

The deep freeze is also particularly valuable when an employee has been complaining about agency malfeasance, and it appears that an attempt to remove the employee would lead to uncovering the mess. A scientist who worked for the National Institutes of Health complained about the safety of vaccines and found himself placed under "house arrest." First, his secretary was reassigned and not replaced. Then his phone was removed. Eventually, he was moved into an isolated office, the physical access to which was monitored by the agency.

The technique is not always so severe. Often an employee will simply be denied information about what happens to his work or whether his memoranda are accepted or rewritten. One high-ranking HEW employee described these practices as "being sent to Coventry." Rather than a deep freeze, a merely chilly reception is provided. Many employees simply do not like the cold and resign.

Forced Acculturation

It is important to keep in mind that dismissal is not only

a means to get people out, but a means to keep people in line.

Probationary employees—those who will be appointed to or who have served for less than a year in career civil service positions—are particularly vulnerable to manipulation. If the employee is being removed for unsatisfactory performance, he need only be notified in writing of the effective date of his separation and the agency's very brief statement of his inadequacies. In 1970, 9,680 probationary employees were thus removed.

The probationary period can and does serve a valuable purpose, but the lack of standards and the lack of requirements for a meaningful statement of the reasons for removal means that removal can be made on emotion or caprice. Since almost any basis will support a removal, an employee must be very careful not only to perform adequately, but also to refrain from extensive criticism of the agency's performance. This procedure tends to breed timidity and to deny the agency the benefit of a fresh and unbiased perspective.

The histories of the immediate victims of unjustly applied sanctions—the psychologically and morally wounded, the economically and physically destroyed—do not tell all that needs to be told. The coal miner dead because of a failure to enforce safety regulations is a victim of the same lack of external accountability within the management structure of federal agencies. But even if unfair disciplinary actions had no impact beyond the affected personnel, the individual injustices themselves would require that the system of discipline be examined.

For every Ernest Fitzgerald—who had the intelligence and luck to marshal and direct his resources, who had the active support of congressmen, who survived the investigation of his personal life and the attempts to destroy his reputation—there are hundreds who have not survived. Of course, the employees who have chosen to resign rather than to be cast into the agency mold are those who find it easiest to get another job—the most able.

3

Behind The Promises

> I am determined that the executive branch of the Government lead the way as an equal opportunity employer.
>
> RICHARD M. NIXON

The present federal Equal Employment Opportunity program is the result of many recent attempts by the federal government, spurred by citizen and legislative concern, to redress the problems of discrimination in the civil service. The number of employees potentially affected by the EEO program is great. Out of approximately 2.5 million federal civilian employees (May 31, 1972) covered by the program, about 400,000 are blacks, about 76,000 are Spanish-surnamed, about 21,000 are Orientals, about 20,000 are American Indians, and 700,000 are women (statistics for women are for "white-collar" employment).

However, only 5.4 percent of the positions at GS-12–13, only 4.5 percent of the positions at GS-14–15, and only 3.4 percent of the positions at GS-16–18 are held by all minorities, including blacks, Chicanos, American Indians, and Orientals. Only about 12,000 minority-group members are at grades 12–13, only 3,400 at grades 14–15, and only 195 at grades 16–18. As of November 1970, about 13,000 women (5.8 percent of those at grade) were at grades 12–13, only 2,600 women (3.4 percent) were at grades 14–15, and only about 150 women (1.6 percent) were at grades 16–18. These figures include women who are members of minority groups.

The Civil Service Commission has been given a broad, unambiguous mandate under Executive Order 11478 to eradicate discrimination in federal employment. The Commission is charged with the duty and responsibility "to promote the full realization of equal employment opportunity through a continuing affirmative program in each executive department and agency." It is also charged with the leadership of the federal Equal Employment Opportunity (EEO) program, and has the authority to issue the regulations, orders, and instructions it deems necessary. It must ensure that each agency devotes sufficient resources to EEO. Few regulatory programs are as tough, and failures of the EEO program therefore cannot be excused for lack of power or resources. The obligations to redress, to reverse, and to remedy previous discriminatory policies and programs potentially places the Commission in conflict with the agencies it regulates; its performance as a regulatory agency shows its unwillingness to oppose the interests of federal managers and offers a telling case study of the regulatory process within the federal government.

One of the offices principally responsible for carrying out the Commission's powers and duties is the federal Equal Employment Office, located in the office of the Executive Director of the Civil Service Commission. The staff of the Federal Equal Employment Opportunity office is dependent on many employees of the Commission for information, expertise, and implementation, which creates a diffuse organizational scheme and hampers the EEO's functioning.

Briefly, EEO responsibilities are distributed among the bureaus in the following fashion:

Bureau of Policies and Standards (BPS): responsible for the development, modification, clarification, and improvement of EEO regulations and Federal Personnel Manual guidelines, and for the preparation of EEO proposals for legislation and executive orders. The BPS reviews job designs, occupational entrance levels, and written test requirements to facilitate the employment of minority-group members who have substantial potential. The BPS does not provide a formal hearing process open to the public on proposed EEO regulations.

Bureau of Personnel Management Evaluations (BPME): responsible for most of the enforcement of EEO regulations, through its periodic "evaluation" of the EEO programs of agencies. The BPME writes recommendations to an agency after evaluating its personnel policies and operations, including those which are EEO-related, at one or more installations of that agency. Neither the evaluation findings nor the BPME's recommendations are made available to the public, even on request. Sometimes a "special inquiry" into the EEO programs of a particular installation will be made. EEO evaluation shares the inadequacies of the Commission's general evaluation program.

Bureau of Recruiting and Examining (BRE): responsible for the development of entry requirements and tests which will lessen discriminatory hiring and enhance the employment of minority-group members. The BRE also administers the Merit Promotion program, with obvious equal employment implications.

Bureau of Management Services (BMS): responsible for the compilation of governmentwide minority-group statistics.

Bureau of Training (BT): responsible for coordination and development of government employee training programs, including those intended to enhance the job skills and promotion potential of minority-group employees.

In 1971, James Frazier, a GS-16, was the highest-paid black in the Civil Service Commission and was, theoretically, the director of the Office of federal Equal Employment Opportunity.[1] Before reaching this position, Frazier had been director of EEO (communications), and Irving Kator, a white GS-16, was director of EEO (operations). On May 21, 1970, a Commission news release elevated Mr. Frazier to the directorship:

> On May 21, 1970, CSC announced a further reorganization of its civil rights office. Mr. Frazier was promoted to GS-16 and named as the *sole* Director of the Office of Federal Equal Employment Opportunity. He will assume *all* of the duties of the office *which had previously been shared with Mr. Kator* and will continue to *report directly* to Mr. Oganavic. Mr. Kator was named Assistant Executive Director and will work with Mr. Oganavic on a variety of special assignments not necessarily relating to civil rights.[2] [emphasis added]

Kator, however, retained direction for portions of the EEO program, and, if not de facto control, a significant role in the Commission's relations with Congress on EEO matters, often representing the Commission in testimony before Congress.[3]

During this study, Kator was spokesman for the EEO program and expressed views rather different from Frazier's, who was considerably more critical. Concerning the lack of blacks in upper grades of the Commission's Bureau of Personnel Investigation (BPI), for example, Kator gave the standard explanations. Frazier, however, sighed, "You should ask them [the staff of the BPI] about that and come back and tell me what they say." (As of February, 1971, there were three blacks among 89 employees of the BPI in grades 10 to 12.) Their most important disagreement concerned the effectiveness of the discrimination complaint system: Frazier believed that job applicants did not know of their rights and that reprisal was a continuing and troublesome problem.

In January 1972, Frazier resigned to become director of civil rights in the Department of Transportation. According to a newspaper account, his reasons for leaving were that the new job offered him a wider scope of duties and a higher salary. Another black, Gerald K. Hinch, labor relations officer in the Commission's Chicago office, replaced him. This time, however, Kator's overall powers and responsibilities were clearly acknowledged. Claiming it would be inappropriate to place a black, Indian, or Spanish-surnamed person over a program including other minorities, the Commission named Kator director of the federal EEO program.

This lack of concern is reflected throughout the program—although all of the Commission's ten regional EEO representatives are minority-group members, rather than reporting directly to the EEO office in Washington, they report through the Commission's regional directors or deputy regional directors, who are, invariably, white.[4]

Self-regulation

The Commission is the mirror image of those agencies it regulates. As a government agency the Commission faces the same personnel and management problems that confront other agencies; it has many of the same problems in implementing its EEO programs that other agencies have. The Commission must regulate the federal EEO complaint system, and it must handle its own internal complaints. The Commission must review and judge the performance of agency EEO affirmative-action plans, and it must implement its own plan. The Commission must evaluate federal accomplishments in improving the status of minority groups and women, and it must compile its own record. It is thus fair to say that the Commission's internal performance reflects its ability and willingness to solve similar problems within other federal agencies.

In October 1971 Walter E. Fauntroy, delegate to Congress from the District of Columbia, testified candidly before Congress about the Commission's internal status in EEO: "We should have little reason to expect [EEO] results from the Civil Service Commission when it cannot even keep its own house in order. The Commission's record in employing minority-group members at the decision-making level is far from exemplary." Let us look at that record.

The Civil Service Commission employs approximately 5,200 employees. Of these about 1,500 are minority-group members and 3,000 are women. The Commission's overall internal black employment at each grade level on the General Schedule is shown in Table 1. (Complete figures for minority-group members other than blacks are not available.)

TABLE 1
Black Employment in the Civil Service Commission (from Minority Group Employment in the Federal Government prepared by the Civil Service Commission)

	Number of Employees		
Grade	Total	Black	% Black
GS-9–11			
November 1969	1,126	78	6.9
November 1970	1,124	104	9.2
May 1971	1,101	99	9.0
May 1972	1,023	98	9.6
GS-12–13			
November 1969	686	33	4.8
November 1970	760	36	4.7
May 1971	819	44	5.4
May 1972	806	44	5.5
GS-14–15			
November 1969	291	11	3.8
November 1970	338	12	3.6
May 1971	363	17	4.7
May 1972	379	17	4.5
GS-16–18			
November 1969	47	0	0.0
November 1970	53	1	1.9
May 1971	57	1	1.8
May 1972	51	1	2.0

Note that in the eight highest grades, GS-11 through -18, the Commission's own staff ratio does not even approach the proportion of blacks in the United States, who make up 11.1 percent of the general population. Of the fifty-three supergrade (GS-16–18) positions in the Commission, only one was held by a minority-group member (James Frazier) as of November 30, 1970, and Mr. Frazier's subsequent resignation left the Commission without a single minority supergrade. Of the twenty-five blacks at GS-13, seven were regional EEO representatives. Two Spanish-surnamed employees and one of the two American Indians at GS-13 were regional EEO representatives.

Except for a gratifying performance at grade levels 9-11, the Commission did not make significant progress in appointing and promoting blacks to higher grade levels and even showed some slippage in the period between November 1969 and November 1970.

None of the Commission's ten regional directors or ten deputy directors belongs to a minority group, and none is a woman.

Table 2 shows the number and percentage of blacks and other minority-group members at GS-10 or above for each of the Commission's ten regions, compared to the number and percentage of nonminority-group members at the same grade levels, with an indication of the percentage of blacks in the general population of that region.

The Commission's bureaus in Washington also have poor EEO records. Table 3 shows the number and percentage of blacks and other minority-group members employed at GS-10 or above in each Commission bureau, compared to the number and percentage of nonminority group members at the same grade levels.

Since 40 percent of its GS employees work in its central office in Washington, where the general population is 71 percent black, the Commission should have proportionately higher minority employment levels than many other federal agencies whose personnel is more dispersed.

TABLE 2

Commission Minority Employment at GS-10 or Above by Region
(from an internal EEO record, prepared by the Civil Service Commission, February 4, 1971)

Region	Percentage Blacks in Population	Number and Percentage				
		Blacks	Spanish-Surnamed	American Indians & Orientals	Nonminority	Total
Atlanta	22.9	4 (3.1)	1 (0.8)	1 (0.8)	124 (95.4)	130
Boston	3.3	1 (2.6)	0 (0.0)	0 (0.0)	38 (97.4)	39
Chicago	9.5	3 (1.6)	0 (0.0)	0 (0.0)	179 (98.4)	182
Dallas	15.9	1 (0.7)	9 (6.5)	0 (0.0)	128 (92.8)	138
Denver	2.4	1 (2.2)	5 (11.1)	0 (0.0)	39 (86.7)	45
New York	11.7*	6 (3.8)	1 (0.6)	0 (0.0)	150 (95.5)	157
Philadelphia	12.1†	10 (10.4)	0 (0.0)	0 (0.0)	86 (89.6)	96
Seattle	1.6	1 (2.2)	0 (0.0)	1 (2.2)	43 (95.6)	45
San Francisco	7.3	6 (2.6)	2 (0.9)	6 (2.6)	213 (93.8)	227
St. Louis	4.3	5 (10.9)	0 (0.0)	1 (2.2)	40 (87.0)	46

*Percentage of blacks in population is only an approximation since the New York Region includes New York, New Jersey, and the Virgin Islands, and neither the black nor nonblack population of the Virgin Islands was considered in computing the percentage of blacks in the New York Region:

†Percentage of blacks in population is only an approximation. Philadelphia Region includes Delaware, Maryland, Pennsylvania, Virginia, and West Virginia, but excludes those counties and cities in Maryland and Virginia which are part of the Washington, D.C., Standard Metropolitan Statistical Area. Both the black and nonblack populations of the *entire* states of Maryland and Virginia were considered in computing the percentage of blacks in Pennsylvania Region.

TABLE 3

Commission Minority Employment at GS-10 or Above by Bureau

(from an internal EEO record, prepared by the Civil Service Commission February 4, 1971)

Bureau	Number and Percentage				
	Black	Spanish-Surnamed	American Indians & Orientals	Nonminority	Total
Recruiting and Examining	1 (1.5)	1 (1.5)	0 (0.0)	66 (97.1)	68
Retirement, Insurance, Occupational Health	9 (8.7)	0 (0.0)	1 (1.0)	93 (90.3)	103
Personnel Investigations	3 (3.4)	0 (0.0)	0 (0.0)	86 (96.6)	89
Executive Manpower	1 (3.6)	0 (0.0)	0 (0.0)	27 (96.4)	28
Personnel Management Evaluations	2 (3.8)	3 (5.8)	0 (0.0)	47 (90.4)	52
Policies and Standards	4 (3.4)	0 (0.0)	0 (0.0)	113 (96.6)	117
Management Services	3 (4.2)	1 (1.4)	1 (1.4)	66 (93.0)	71
Manpower Information Systems	6 (11.5)	0 (0.0)	0 (0.0)	46 (88.5)	52
Training	11 (11.2)	3 (3.1)	1 (1.0)	83 (84.7)	98
Staff*	12 (9.2)†	3 (2.3)	0 (0.0)	116 (88.5)	131

*Office of the Commissioners, Office of Personnel Interchange, Board of Appeals and Review, Office of the General Council, Job Evaluation Review Project, White House Fellows, Federal Executive Institute, Office of the Executive Director, Appeals Examining Office, Office of Labor-Management Relations, Office of Public Affairs, Office of Federal EEO, Federal Labor Relations Council.

†This figure, from a computer print-out provided by the Commission, unaccountably includes one black at GS-17. Since no black is of such a high rank on the Commission's staff, apparently this GS-17 is in some temporary status on the staff—or the Commission's statistics are inaccurate.

Wide variation in minority employment among the different Commission bureaus is evident. Regarding the Bureau of Personnel Investigation, one regional director remarked: "It looks like the Alabama Highway Patrol."

In the Commission, women constituted less than 10 percent of those employed at GS-14 through -16 as of October 31, 1971, and less than 20 percent of those employed at GS-11 through -13. On November 18, 1970, Helene Markoff, director of the Federal Women's Program in the Commission's federal EEO office, noted in a speech that "Secretary Volpe is becoming quite aware that there is a problem in the Transportation Department. At a recent regional directors' meeting he looked around and noticed—no women!" Ms. Markoff also pointed out that the Department of Transportation had only one female supergrade.

On October 21, 1966, 4.6 percent of the employees in the Commission at GS-15 were women. In October 1970 the percentage had dropped to 3.6 percent. In both 1966 and 1970 the Commission had one female supergrade, who retired in 1971.

On October 31, 1966, seven, or 5.2 percent, of 135 Commission employees at GS-14 were women. Four years later, on October 31, 1970, the percentage had risen to 5.8 percent, with eleven women of the 191 employees at GS-14. The Commission had filled the additional fifty-six positions at GS-14 with four women and fifty-two men. Women were available for promotion during this four-year period, since eighty women were employed at GS-12 and -13 in October 1966.

The Commission does not even give major policy-implementation authority to those few minority-group members who have risen to high rank. The Commission's three highest ranking minority-group members are Peggy Griffiths, a member of the Board of Appeals and Review; Anthony Hudson, internal personnel director of the Commission; and Clinton Smith, internal director of EEO. Each holds a position in which authority is limited. Hudson and Smith possess little actual appointment or promotion authority since the bureau directors and regional directors who outrank them are the final arbiters of personnel decisions, and Ms. Griffiths is only one of five members of the BAR.

The Commission's management intern programs, which prepare promising employees for federal careers in the upper grades, have shown a discriminatory pattern over the years. There are three intern programs. The Administrative Intern Program is a special program developed by the Commission for its particular needs and usually draws from present Commission employees. The Commission's Management Intern Program is similar to the intern programs of the same name found in other federal agencies, and is principally for new recruits. The less prestigious and less rigorous Federal Personnel Intern Program is a small program operated by the Commission and a few other agencies. Table 4 provides a breakdown of the minority-group composition of the intern programs in recent years. The showing is hardly impressive. The Commission's record is better in the Management Intern Program—perhaps because that program, unlike the Administrative Intern Program, was not specially designed by the Commission for the Commission. The very small Federal Personnel Intern Program (FPIP) shows a particularly good record for selecting women. However, Claudia Cooley, the Commission's internal Federal Women's Program coordinator, stated in an interview in July 1971, that the FPIP did not provide promotion opportunities comparable to the other programs.

In its own EEO affirmative action plan, the Commission has failed to meet several of the target dates. The following quotations from the Commission's own internal "1971 EEO Action Plan" are given, along with commentary on the Commission's failures to comply.

The Commission's own action plan called for the distribution of a Career Planning Handbook to supervisors by

TABLE 4

Intern Programs

Fiscal Year	Interns Selected	Black Men Selected	Spanish-Surnamed	American Indians	Orientals	Women	Black Women
Administrative							
1966	10	0	0	0	0	0	0
1967	11	0	0	0	0	0	0
1968	16	0	0	0	0	0	0
1969	No Program						
1970	10	0	1 (10%)	0	0	0	0
1971	10	1 (10%)	1 (10%)	0	0	1 (10%)	0
1972	14	3 (21%)	0	0	0	8 (57%)	2 (14%)
Total	71	4	2	0	0	9	2
Management							
1967	26	2 (8%)	1 (4%)	0	0	9 (35%)	1 (4%)
1968	28	3 (10%)	0	0	1 (4%)	9 (32%)	1 (4%)
1969	42	3 (7%)	1 (2%)	0	0	10 (24%)	2 (4%)
1970	52	7 (16%)	0	0	0	16 (31%)	2 (4%)
1971	44	6 (14%)	4 (9%)	0	0	13 (35%)	3 (7%)
Total	192	21 (11%)	6 (3%)	0	1 (.005%)	57 (30%)	9 (5%)

Federal Personnel							
1968	5	0	0	0	0	2 (40%).	0
1969	5	0	2 (40%)	0	0	4 (80%)	1 (20%)
1970	4	0	0	0	0	2 (50%)	0
1971	5	3 (60%)	0	0	1 (20%)	1 (20%)	1 (20%)
Total	19	3 (16%)	2 (11%)	0	1 (5%)	9 (47%)	2 (11%)

February 4, 1971, a goal not accomplished until March 1972. The Commission's plan placed continuing "emphasis on recognition of significant contributions toward promoting EEO in the Commission through the CSC awards program." However, in 1972 according to Clinton Smith, head of the Commission's Complaint Office, "there have not been any awards in the last year or two."

The Commission's own performance in EEO suggests why the Commission has not been more successful in its regulation of other agencies. Perhaps it is afraid to cast the first stone, for its own EEO record is dismal. Let us look now at the EEO picture in the government as a whole and the Commission's reporting of that situation.

A Biased Rendition

One of the Commission's favorite ploys is to make small gains in minority employment seem large by presenting them in terms of percentage increase. Its statistical compilation, *Minority Group Employment in the Federal Government* of November 1970, for example, includes the following summary of information under the title, "Highlights of the Study": "The percentage rate increase for minorities in the middle and upper levels (grades GS-9 and above) far exceeds that for nonminorities. By grade grouping, relative increases (or decreases) were:

Grade Groupings	Minorities	Nonminorities
GS- 9–11	up 3.3%	down 1.8%
GS-12–13	up 13.7%	up 2.5%
GS-14–15	up 21.8%	up 4.3%
GS-16–18	up 34.0%	up 4.5%

The Commission used a similar approach in its 1972 report, in which information on nonminorities was not tabulated.

Grade Groupings	Minorities
GS- 9–11	up 61.9%
GS-12–13	up 25.6%
GS-14–15	up 23.7%
GS-16–18	up 19.4%

But the Commission's figures and graphs are misleading—the long history of discriminatory employment makes even minor gains look dramatic. To reflect what is actually going on, the Commission's chart of figures might be translated into Table 5.

Between November 1969 and November 1970 the percentage of minority representation at grades 5–8 increased by only about 1 percent, from 16.7 percent to 17.8 percent. Between May 1971 and May 1972 the percentage increased by about 1 percent, from 18.4 percent to 19.1 percent. From 1971 to 1972 the actual numerical increase in grades 16–18, for example, was only 43—from 151 to 194.[5] The total increase during the same period for nonminority employees at those grades was 90. The actual percentage increase in black representation among GS-16–18 employees was only 0.4 percent, from 1.9 percent to 2.3 percent.

In actuality in 1972: of the 317 supergrade positions (GS-16-18) in six major regulatory agencies—Federal Communications Commission (49 supergrades), Federal Power Commission (47), Federal Trade Commission (37), Interstate Commerce Commission (105), Civil Aeronautics Board (46), and Securities and Exchange Commission (33)—only one employee, an Oriental in the FPC, belongs to a minority group.

The Department of the Army has only 4 minority-group members—3 blacks and 1 Spanish-surnamed—among 241 supergrades. The Department of the Navy has 1 minority-group member (black) among 321 supergrades. The Department of the Air Force has one minority member (Spanish-

TABLE 5

Analysis of Changes in Minority Representation

	November 1970		November 1969		Change 1969–1970		Commission's Characterization of Change
Grade	Number of Employees	Percent of Total	Number of Employees	Percent of Total	Empl.	Percent	
Minority							
9–11	26,293	8.3	25,462	7.9	+ 831	+0.4	up 3.3%
12–13	10,511	4.8	9,245	4.3	+1,266	+0.5	up 13.7%
14–15	2,691	3.7	2,210	3.2	+ 481	+0.5	up 21.8%
16–18	130	2.3	97	1.8	+ 33	+0.5	up 34.0%
Nonminority							
9–11	290,427	91.7	295,678	92.1	−5,251	−0.4	down 1.8%
12–13	209,123	95.2	204,016	95.7	+5,107	−0.5	up 2.5%
14–15	70,617	96.3	67,727	96.8	+2,890	−0.5	up 4.3%
16–18	5,456	97.7	5,222	98.2	+ 234	−0.5	up 4.5%

surnamed) among 169 supergrades. The remainder of the Department of Defense, including the Office of the Secretary, has 227 supergrades, of whom only 4 are minority-group members—2 blacks, 1 Spanish-surnamed, and one Oriental. In the entire civilian defense establishment there were only 8 minority-group members out of 1,031 supergrades in November 1967. Three years later, in November 1970, there were only 7 minority-group members out of 1,048 supergrades. In 1971, there were 8 out of 987 and, in 1972, 10 out of 979.

Irving Kator defended the record in the defense establishment's supergrades when he testified before the House General Subcommittee on Labor of the Committee on Education and Labor on March 18, 1971:

> . . . There is no simple solution. For example, 76% of the GS-16 through GS-18 positions in the Department of the Army are in scientific and engineering fields and require an expertise which can usually be obtained only through long experience in agency programs. In the Department of the Navy, 83% of the GS-16 through GS-18 positions are scientific or engineering. Most of the other positions at these levels are in such areas as budgeting and procurement and also require in-depth knowledge of agency operations. In fact, 90% of all GS-16 through GS-18 career positions are filled from within the service. Therefore, *to increase the number of minority employees at the upper levels, we need to have minorities in the senior level positions which comprise the pipeline to GS-16 through GS-18 jobs. This means continued emphasis on upward mobility. The accelerated rate of movement of minorities into senior level positions sets the stage for significant future gains in GS-16 and above.* We are assuring maximum opportunity for minority employees to participate in executive development programs to assist in upward mobility [emphasis added].

One wonders how Kator accounts for the fact that in November 1967 the Department of Defense had 233 minority-group employees at GS-14 through GS-15 but that three

Grade	November 1972		November 1971		Change 1971–1972		Commission's Characterization of Change
	Number of Employees	Percent of Total	Number of Employees	Percent of Total	Empl.	Percent	
Minority							
9–11	29,383	9.2	27,311	8.6	+2,072	+0.6	up 61.9%
12–13	12,347	5.4	11,224	5.0	+1,123	+0.4	up 25.0%
14–15	3,469	4.5	2,953	3.9	+ 516	+0.6	up 23.7%
16–18	194	3.4	151	2.7	+ 43	+0.7	up 19.4%
Nonminority							
9–11	189,653	90.8	288,708	91.4	+ 945	−0.6	Information not tabulated in CSC report
12–13	216,916	94.6	214,124	95.0	+2,702	−0.4	
14–15	73,597	95.5	72,457	96.1	+1,140	−0.6	
16–18	5,589	96.6	5,499	97.3	+ 90	−0.7	

years later, the number of minority supergrades had declined from 8 to 7, while the number of supergrade positions increased from 1,031 in 1967 to 1,048 in 1970 (in the intervening year, 1969, there were 1,093 supergrades).

At grades 14 and 15, moreover, the percentage of minorities in the Department of Defense increased from 0.6 to 2.2 percent (a 1.6 percent increase) during the five-year period 1967 to 1972. The Commission would probably prefer that this increase be trumpeted as a dramatic 398.1 percent increase in the last five years, since black employees jumped from 110 to 432 at grades 14 and 15 while nonminorities, the Commission would be equally glad to point out, showed an insignificant increase of only 11.7 percent, from 18,648 to 21,887. By maintaining this improvement rate (0.1 percent per year) blacks will achieve a representation of 11.1 percent in 100 years.

At grades 14 and 15, the number of blacks in the Department of Defense (DOD) increased from 431 in 1971 to 432 in 1972. In percentages, blacks represented 2.0 percent of the total DOD workforce at GS-14–15 in 1971, and 2.2 percent in 1972. The comparison of black and nonminority employment in the DOD is summarized in Table 6:

TABLE 6

Department of Defense Nonminorities at GS-14–15

Year	Total Nonminorities	Percent of Workforce
1971	21,588	98.0
1972	21,877 increase = 287 (1.34%)	97.8

Blacks at GS-14–15

Year	Total Blacks	Percent of Workforce
1971	224	1
1972	257 increase = 33 (14.7%)	1.1

Throughout *all* agencies EEO progress in the upper grades has been *very* slow since 1967, as shown in Table 7.

The script that the Commission has been following in its enforcement of EEO has been poorly conceived and has clearly resulted in a poor performance. One hears again and again of the need for cooperation with the management of other federal agencies. Cooperation, however, has often become cooption.

TABLE 7

EEO Progress in Upper Grades

	Grade Grouping			
	9–11	12–13	14–15	16–18
1967: Percentage black employees	4.3	2.1	1.2	1.2
1972: Percentage black employees	5.9	3.2	2.4	2.3
Percentage increase Nov. 1967–Nov. 1972	1.6	1.1	1.2	1.1
Years needed to reach parity with 11.1% black population	16	36	39	40
1967: Percentage Spanish-surnamed employees	1.2	0.6	0.6	0.2
1972: Percentage Spanish-surnamed employees	1.7	1.0	0.8	0.5
Percentage increase Nov. 1967–Nov. 1972	0.5	0.4	0.2	0.3
Years needed to reach parity with 5.0%* Spanish-surnamed population	33	50	105	75

*A 1969 Census Bureau sample estimated the percentage of Spanish-surnamed Americans at 4.7 percent. The Cabinet Committee on Opportunities for the Spanish-Speaking places the figure at 5.8 percent. A Civil Service Commission release places it at "approximately six percent."

Perhaps one reason the Commission stresses cooperation with federal agency management is its feeling that it is most powerful when protecting the status quo. Yet the Commission can be a powerful agency for the good. In addition to its special powers in EEO, the Commission can withdraw delegated personnel functions from the agencies, continue those powers on condition, or conduct some agency personnel functions on a reimbursable basis. The Commission wields informal power to chastise an agency that has displeased it. The influence of Commission recommendations concerning congressional allocations of supergrades is only one example. Like every regulator, the Commission has the power of selective enforcement of rules and regulations. Its concern with classification accuracy, for example, can fluctuate, depending upon the behavior of an agency.

The Commission has used its informal power and clout. Unfortunately, however, rather than acting as a force for change, it has used its influence to protect and defend its own interests and the interests of federal managers as shown in the following example.

In November 1969, the Office of Management and Budget (OMB) assembled an interdepartmental task force to review and revise federal administrative requirements in federal grants to state and local governments. A "Tentative Report and Recommendations on Personnel Policies of the OMB Task Force on Federal Grants to States and Local Governments" had been prepared as of April 14, 1971. Among the OMB task force recommendations was one calling for a provision that every federal grant, loan, or contract providing funds to state or local government require the recipient to have an affirmative action plan for equal employment opportunity. The task force also made major recommendations modifying the "merit system" and "political activity" requirements.

Executive director Rosen prevailed upon the OMB to

hold up distribution of the task force recommendations to agencies and interested parties for review and comment, which they did for about two months. Then on July 14, 1971, OMB agreed to change its recommendations *before* they were sent out for comment. Changes included an EEO recommendation that deleted the requirements of goals and target dates. The OMB's recommendations on "merit system" requirements were rescinded and principles desired by the Commission were adopted. The OMB's proposed changes in "political activity" requirements were also withdrawn, at the Commission's request, from the draft of its tentative recommendations.

President Nixon's "Sixteen-point Program for the Spanish-Surnamed," announced November 5, 1970, included as its fourteenth point an order that the Commission, "with the Department of Labor, explore the feasibility of establishing an Intergovernmental Training Facility for upward mobility and skills training for federal, state, and local careers in the Southwest, probably in San Antonio."

Among the Department of Labor's recommendations in regard to the center were the following: that the Commission train "new" entry-level employees and not just work on "upgrading" present employees; that special provision be made in the Commission's plan for the recruitment of Spanish-speaking students, faculty, and administration for the center; that the Commission's plan should include a requirement that the referring agency must have a commitment or agreement for upgrading its trainees referred to the program before the center accepts referrals from that agency; that the Commission plan lacks sufficient foresight on how the center proposes to relate to ongoing manpower programs in the same geographic area; that a "needs survey" should be conducted on the skill needs in the San Antonio area to which the center should plan to be responsive; that the center's own staff, without the participation of outside consultants, should develop all of the curricula; that the

Commission should select trainees on the basis of criteria mentioned in the recommendations. In addition to these just listed, the Department of Labor made eight other recommendations—all were ignored by the Commission.

Although the Commission proposed that the Department of Labor grant $431,843 for the establishment and first-year operation of the center, it did not even reply to Labor's fifteen recommendations. Mr. Rosen went to the top of the Labor Department, which decided to fund the center, without pressing the recommendations. Thus, the Commission got its money without having to budge on a single policy point.

It should be added that the President's program was itself a public relations ploy to capture the votes of Spanish-surnamed Americans in the 1972 elections. According to the *New York Times* (October 10, 1971):

> White House aides concede that the recruiting efforts [for Spanish-surnamed federal employees] are designed primarily to win more Latin votes in upcoming elections—mainly in New York, Texas and California, where many Latin-Americans reside. The President issued his first order [the "Sixteen-point Program"] after discovering that he had received only 10 percent of the Latin vote in the last election.

According to the *Washington Post* (January 21, 1972), President Nixon "has directed the Office of the Management and the Budget to pressure department heads to hire more Spanish-speaking persons."[6]

Accompanying President Nixon's announcement of his Sixteen-point Program was an enthusiastic assessment by the Civil Service Commission reported on the same date. The Commission reported that "while it is clear that the sixteen-point program has gotten off to a running start, we are only beginning to make progress."

The Commission was correct in its assessment that much

remained to be done. Of particular importance in the administration's "Latin strategy" were the key electoral states of California and Texas. In California 14.9 percent of the population is Mexican-American and in Texas approximately 15.1 percent. Yet the federal government's record of employing Chicanos in California and Texas in higher-grade positions has been particularly dismal, and progress is slow, as indicated by Table 8.[7]

TABLE 8
Percentage of Employment of Spanish-surnamed Employees
California—(14.9 percent of population)

Grade	1967	1970	1971
GS- 9–11	2.2	2.8	3.3
GS-12–13	1.0	1.6	1.8
GS-14–15	1.0	1.1	1.4
GS-16–18	0.0	.5	1.1

Texas—(15.1 percent of population)

	1967	1970	1971
GS- 9–11	7.6	9.0	9.5
GS-12–13	2.4	3.8	4.0
GS-14–15	1.6	2.6	2.4
GS-16–18	0.0	1.1	3.2

Mexican-Americans were rarely found in policy-making jobs even in those areas most directly affecting their group. Although 70 percent of the agricultural work force in California is Mexican-American, none of the top 500 employees in the Department of Agriculture in California was Mexican-American and no Mexican-Americans were employed by the Federal Trade Commission in California. Public Advocates, a firm employed by the Mexican-American Legal Defense and Education Fund, estimated that if Mexican-

Americans in California were employed in proportion to their population, 27,265 would have jobs, with the salaries totaling almost a quarter of a billion dollars.[8]

It is the policy of the federal government to hire "disadvantaged persons," and since "disadvantaged persons" are often minority-group members, the Commission's performance regarding its own employment has obvious EEO ramifications.[9] A General Accounting Office report found that the Commission had no governmentwide reporting system enabling it to evaluate the extent to which federal agencies have carried out the federal policy to hire the disadvantaged. "Statistics have not been maintained on the number of jobs created and filled as a result of operation MUST (Maximum Utilization of Skills and Training),"[10] and "data is not available on the number of worker-trainees who meet the Department of Labor definition of a disadvantaged person."

Although 45,133 worker-trainees were hired in 1969, 1970, and 1971, no information is available on how many were actually disadvantaged because the family income and family size of the person hired was not obtained by the Commission. "The Department of Labor defines as 'disadvantaged' a poor person who does not have suitable employment and who is either (1) a school dropout, (2) a member of a minority, (3) under 22 years of age, (4) 45 years of age or over, or (5) handicapped." (A person is considered "poor" who is on welfare or whose annual income is defined as "poor" according to the Office of Economic Opportunity Guidelines.) Questions on family size and income had been included on a proposed form but they were deleted by the Commission's Office of General Counsel because the General Counsel (Anthony Mondello) considered them to be excessively personal.

Congress has appropriated hundreds of millions of dollars every year since 1964 to encourage the employment of the disadvantaged, but the Commission has failed to establish a reporting system to ensure that the disadvantaged—and only the disadvantaged—are benefited. Examination of sample records showed that a large number of employed trainees had been graduated from high school, some had attended college, many were employed at the time of application, and some were from families in which other family members were employed.

Some agencies are more successful than others in finding qualified minority-group members for the higher grade levels and this variation places on the Commission the burden of showing why, considering its regulatory function, it has not successfully moved lagging agencies. The slow progress and poor results of the EEO program in the Department of Defense, as shown in Table 9, compared to the

TABLE 9

Full-time Black Employment in Department of Defense and All Other Federal Agencies

(as of May 31, 1972) (from the CSC Report on Minorities)

		Total Full Time	Total Black	% Black
GS 1–4	DOD	139,222	19,150	13.8
	All	166,618	47,104	28.4
GS 5–8	DOD	178,638	17,596	9.9
	All	215,128	41,451	19.2
GS 9–11	DOD	149,706	6,807	4.5
	All	169,330	12,014	7.1
GS 12–13	DOD	101,003	2,511	2.5
	All	128,260	4,820	3.8
GS 14–15	DOD	22,369	257	1.1
	All	54,697	1,603	2.9
GS 16–18	DOD	979	6	0.6
	All	4,804	128	2.7
Total DOD		591,917	46,327	7.8
All Other		738,837	107,120	14.5

rest of the federal establishment, and compared to the Department of Labor (Table 10), is a dramatic example of this difference.

TABLE 10

Full-time Black Employment in Departments of Defense and Labor

(as of May 31, 1972) (from the May 1972 CSC Report)

		Total Full Time	Total Black	% Black
GS 1–4	DOD	139,222	19,150	13.8
	DOL	1,599	913	57.1
GS 5–8	DOD	178,638	17,596	9.9
	DOL	3,547	1,442	40.7
GS 9–11	DOD	149,706	6,807	4.5
	DOL	1,965	466	23.7
GS 12–13	DOD	101,003	2,511	2.5
	DOL	3,636	426	11.7
GS 14–15	DOD	22,369	257	1.1
	DOL	1,762	169	9.6
GS 16–18	DOD	979	6	0.6
	DOL	135	8	5.9
Total	DOD	541,917	46,327	7.8
	DOL	12,644	3,424	27.1

Table 11 shows the wide disparities among regions in EEO performance and compares the percentage of blacks in the regional population with the percentage of black employees at different grades. Although the Commission has recognized the obvious relevance of general population statistics and the principle of evaluation on the basis of comparison with the surrounding recruiting area's minority representation[11] (Leonard Cronin, Boston regional director, explained that his apparently poor internal EEO record is the result of a low percentage of blacks in New England—3.3 percent), Irving Kator feels that "skills composition of minorities" is a more significant variable.[12] Even if one assumes it to be a

TABLE 11

Federal Agency Employment of Blacks by Region

(November 30, 1971)

Region	Percentage of Blacks in Population of Region*	Percentage of Black Employees	Percentage of Black Federal Employees at Each GS Grade Grouping					
			1–4	5–8	9–11	12–13	14–15	16–18
Atlanta	19.5	6.7	15.2	6.5	3.4	1.2	0.9	1.6
Boston	3.3	3.5	6.1	4.0	2.0	1.5	2.2	2.1
Chicago	6.6	15.4	29.0	19.5	8.1	4.4	2.6	0.8
Dallas	15.0	5.2	10.7	5.6	2.7	1.3	0.6	—
Denver	1.5	2.4	4.6	2.9	1.2	0.9	0.9	1.2
New York	11.6†	13.1	2.6	16.9	6.7	3.6	3.0	4.1
Philadelphia	11.7‡	15.2	28.5	17.3	7.6	3.6	2.5	2.6
Seattle	1.7	2.3	4.4	1.2	0.9	1.2	1.5	4.7
San Francisco	6.7	8.3	15.3	11.3	4.0	2.0	1.3	1.0
St. Louis	4.8	9.8	19.3	10.3	5.9	2.3	2.0	1.6
Central Office Area (Washington, D.C.)		21.4	49.4	32.9	13.7	5.5	2.8	2.1

* These percentages were based on the 1970 census figures found in the 1973 *World Almanac.*

†Percentage of blacks in population is only an approximation, since the New York Region includes New York, New Jersey, and Virgin Islands, and neither black nor nonblack population of Virgin Islands was considered in computing the percentage of blacks in the New York Region.

‡Percentage of blacks in population is only an approximation. The Philadelphia Region includes Delaware, Maryland. Pennsylvania, and West Virginia, but excludes those counties and cities in Maryland and Virginia which are part of the Washington, D.C., Standard Metropolitan Statistical Area. Both the black and nonblack populations of the *entire* states of Maryland and Virginia were considered in computing the percentage of blacks in the Pennsylvania Region.

meaningful, knowable quantity or quality, the "skills composition of minorities" in different areas have not been compiled or analyzed by the Commission—and it is doubtful that they could be. And, for all the all-important upper-middle and upper grades, multiple regional or even nationwide recruiting areas surely should be the source of minority-group candidates as part of an affirmative-action program.

It is unlikely that variations in the "skills compositions" among minority-group members in different regions of the country could explain disparities in minority employment as well as would a history book on the American South, or a sociology book on race relations in major northern American cities. The Civil Service Commission has been assigned the task of eliminating regional disparities, but the Civil Service Commission is not doing its job very well.

There is an interesting corollary to Kator's "skills-composition" theory that eliminates it as a possible explanation of regional disparities in minority employment. Where private discrimination is greater, the number of blacks available for public employment may reasonably be expected to be greater than would otherwise be expected. For example, if the private job market in middle-level and high-level positions in the Atlanta region is unfavorable for blacks, the "skills composition" of blacks available for federal recruitment in that region may be even higher than in some other regions.

The Commission's attitude toward testing and qualification greatly affects whether minority group members will ever enter the federal service. In September 1971, the Urban Institute, an independent, nonprofit research organization in Washington, D.C., published a scholarly study entitled *The Validity and Discriminatory Impact of the Federal Entrance Examination* that concluded, after analyzing the pass-fail rates of black and white students from a sample group of 100 colleges that:

> After examination of the available information concerning the validity of the FSEE [Federal Service Entrance Examination] and the comparative passing rates of black and white students from matched schools, the conclusion that *the use of the FSEE is unfairly discriminatory to many black applicants* seems unavoidable. It is unfortunate that this test has been used extensively for so many years with apparent inadequate validation. *Pending strong evidence of its validity,* the operational use of the FSEE for screening applicants to Federal Service should be suspended.
>
> Of the sample studied, 8.6% of the black students passed the FSEE compared to 42.1% of the white students.[13]

4

The Appellate Lemon

Making a mid-level bureaucrat accountable is like landing a man on the moon.

JOHN GARDNER

For redress of the abuses described in the last two chapters, employees must look to the Civil Service Commission, which regulates employee appeals of adverse actions, and the EEO discrimination complaint system. Table 12 shows how the appeals system functions.

Regular Appeals

An employee against whom adverse action is taken may request a hearing by his agency. The decision of the agency appeals examiner is only a recommendation to the agency, which need not be followed. Management need only state reasons for not following the examiner's recommendation. (An appeals examiner must, to be successful, persuade management to accept his findings, which makes him a negotiator with fact-finding powers. His opinion may do much to delineate the issues. He may be inclined to understate his case in order to convince the deciding management official of the reasonableness of his recommendation.)

The Commission's reforms regarding the ineffectiveness of appeals hearings, has been, until recently, anemic. In 1970 the Commission's Bureau of Policy and Standards recom-

Table 12 The Appeals Process

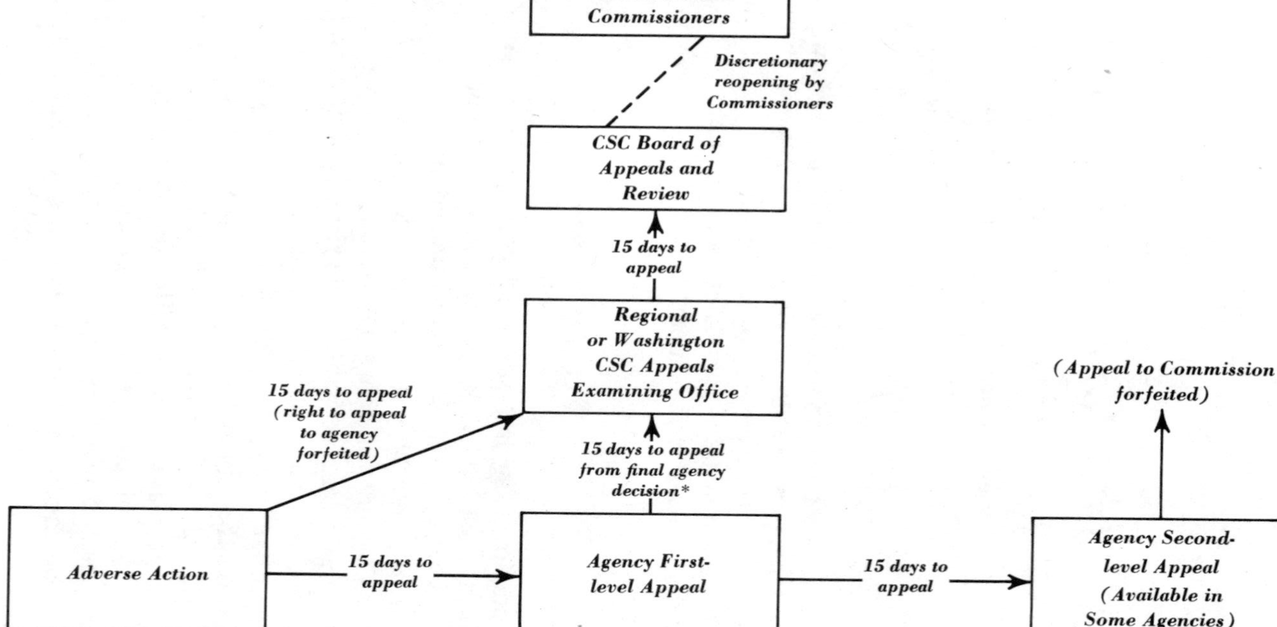

*Employee may elect to appeal directly to Commission if no agency decision within 60 days.

mended that the authorized management official must accept the recommendations of the agency appeals examiner unless he found them (1) clearly erroneous, (2) contrary to law, (3) unsupported by the evidence, or (4) beyond his authority to carry out. The suggestions could hardly have been described as revolutionary, but they were rejected. The commissioners, in a meeting attended by the executive staff, deleted the proposed changes as being too restrictive of the agencies. There was concern that a recommendation would "fly in the face of agency policy."

An employee who is the recipient of any adverse action may waive a hearing by his agency and go directly to an appeals examining office of the Commission. If he chooses to go to the Commission, he may no longer appeal through his agency. If the agency hearing finds against him, he may appeal to the Commission's Appeals Examining Office, where another hearing may be held. He may also have the case removed to the Commission if his agency has not reached a decision within sixty days. (A few agencies have their own second-level appeals system and if an employee elects to appeal again within his agency, he loses any right to appeal to the Commission.) After an employee has received a hearing before the Appeals Examining Office of the Commission, he may appeal an adverse decision to the Commission's Board of Appeals and Review. Ultimately, he may appeal to the courts.

Let us see how this system works for the appellant.

In fiscal year 1970, the agencies received 4,618 adverse-action appeals. Of these, 836 (or approximately 18 percent) were rejected by the agency or canceled by the agency or the employee.[1] The agency upheld the initial decision of its supervisor in 77 percent of the 2,626 appeals which the agencies decided at the first level of agency appeal. Six percent were reversed on procedural errors. All 6 percent of these cases could have been reinstated. In 12 percent of the cases the action was modified. Only 125 (about 3 percent) of the decisions of agency management were reversed on the merits out of the initial 4,618 adverse actions appealed.

In fiscal year 1971 agencies received or had on hand 7,808 adverse actions. Of these, 913 (or approximately 13 percent) were rejected by the agency or canceled by the agency or by the employee. The agency upheld the initial action in about 80 percent of the 2,594 appeals which agencies decided at the first level. Approximately 6 percent (196 cases) were reversed on procedural errors. In approximately 12 percent of the cases the action was modified. In only about 3 percent (115) of the cases was the decision of the agency reversed on its merits. One-third of the employees in adverse action hearings were not represented by another employee, a union representative, or legal counsel.

In fiscal year 1972 agencies (not including the U.S. Postal Service) received or had on hand 3,451 adverse actions. Of these, 110 (approximately 3 percent) were rejected by the agency or canceled by the agency or the employee. In about 80 percent (828) of the 1,033 appeals which were decided at the first level, the agency upheld the initial action of its supervisors. Approximately 12 percent, 126, were reversed on procedural grounds. In about 4 percent (40) of the cases the decision was modified. In only about 4 percent (39) of the cases was the decision of the agency reversed on the merits. In one-third of the cases the employee was not represented.

In fiscal year 1970, 678 employees appealed adverse first-level decisions in the five agencies that have their own second level of appeal. The first-level agency decision was reversed in 97, or about 14 percent, of all actions appealed. In fiscal year 1971, 879 employees appealed adverse first-level decisions in the five agencies having their own second level of appeal. The first-level agency decision was reversed in 64, or about 7 percent, of all actions appealed. In fiscal year 1972, 70 employees appealed adverse first-level decisions in four agencies (U.S. Postal Service not included) having their own second level of appeal. The first-level agency decision was reversed in 16, or about 23 percent, of all actions appealed.

In fiscal year 1970, 1971, and 1972, the Commission con-considered respectively 703, 923, and 1,242 appeals made directly to the appeals offices of the Commission. Commission hearings upheld the adverse action in 488, 703, and 998 (69, 76, and 80 percent) direct appeals; 22, 18, and 11 percent were reversed on procedural errors; and 9, 5, and 9 percent of the adverse actions were reversed on the merits.

In fiscal years 1970, 1971, and 1972, the Commission considered respectively 403, 588, and 738 appeals after an agency first-level decision. The Commission upheld 320, 468, and 602 (79, 80, and 82 percent) agency decisions, reversed 41, 61, and 61 (10, 10, and 8 percent) on procedural errors, and reversed the agency on the merits in 42, 59, and 75 (11, 10, and 10 percent) of the cases.

Of the 605, 699, and 982 cases that were decided by the BAR in 1970, 1971, and 1972, the Commission's appeals office decision for the agency was upheld in 92, 89, and 90 percent of the cases. (The BAR did not differentiate between procedural grounds and merit in the cases reversed in favor of the appellant.)

When the agency appealed the Commission's Appeals Examining Office decisions, the BAR reversed 37, 48, and 46 percent of the decisions favoring the employee.[2]

EEO Discrimination Complaints

A rigorously fair complaint system is one of the most effective "affirmative-action" programs that the Commission could establish. The adjudication of individual cases can deter discrimination by agency management if they know that an employee will have a good chance of winning an appeal, and that disciplinary action will be taken against discriminatory supervisors.

In 1970, over 12,000 federal employees contacted agency

EEO counselors about bringing discrimination complaints. The commission's EEO discrimination complaint system shown in Table 13, is somewhat newer than its appeals process, but, as young as it is, it already shows signs of becoming as flawed and useless as the appeals process on which it is modeled, and which it reflects.

In exploring the ills of the appellate system, it is helpful to look, at the same time, at what is wrong with the Commission's handling of EEO discrimination complaints.

An employee must first have his complaint considered by an EEO counselor within his agency, who may attempt an "informal resolution" of the problem prior to the filing of a formal complaint. If the complainant remains dissatisfied with the informal resolution (if any), he may file a written complaint with an EEO officer of his agency.

The agency's director of EEO must then assign, for the "prompt" investigation of the complaint, a person who "shall occupy a position in the agency which is not, directly or indirectly, under the jurisdiction of the head of that part of the agency in which the complaint arose." After the complainant has reviewed an investigative file compiled by the agency, the agency again provides an opportunity for adjustment of the complaint on an informal basis.

If a satisfactory adjustment is not arrived at, the complainant may appeal to the Civil Service Commission, who will appoint a hearing examiner who must be an employee of another agency (usually a Commission EEO appeals examiner). The hearing is recorded and transcribed verbatim. The appeals examiner must then transmit (1) the complaint file (including the record of the hearing); (2) the appeals examiner's analysis of the matter which gave rise to the complaint and the general environment out of which the complaint arose; and (3) the recommended decision of the appeals examiner on the merits of the complaint, including recommended remedial action, where appropriate, to the head of the agency or his designee, who then makes the decision of the agency. (Recommendations of disciplinary

Table 13 Discrimination Complaint Process

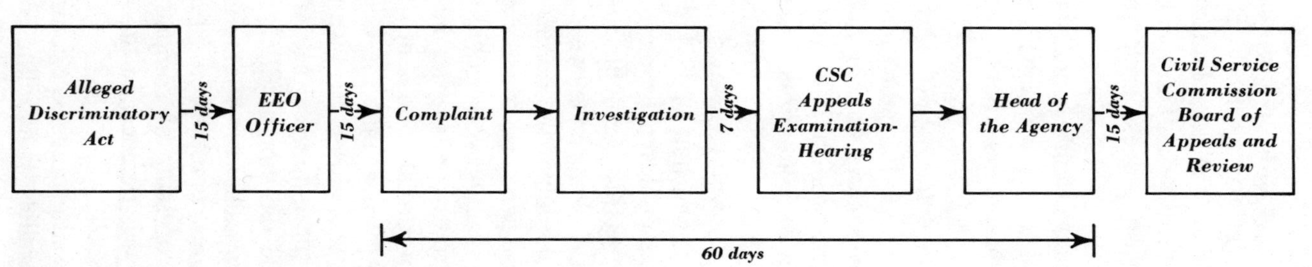

Exclusive of hearing time. An informal 60-day limit has been placed on hearings.

action, if any, against supervisors or officials are included in separate memoranda sent to the agency head.) If he is dissatisfied with the agency decision, the complainant may then appeal to the Commission's Board of Appeals and Review. At all stages of the complaint process, the employee has the right to representation.

The similarity between the Commission's appeals system and its process for the handling of EEO complaints is apparent. And the lot of EEO complainants is similar as well, as shown in Table 14.

Internally the Commission follows the pattern of the rest of the government in its handling of discrimination complaints and contacts with EEO counselors. One formal complaint was filed within the Commission in 1970 and three were filed in 1971. Contacts with counselors, however, greatly decreased, from seventy-two in 1970 to twenty-one (nineteen made by Commission employees, two by job applicants) in 1971. During the second half of 1970 and all of 1971, fifty-two employees contacted a counselor within the Commission. Twenty-one of the fifty-two contacts failed to result in an informal resolution of the employees' problems, but only the four formal complaints mentioned above were filed with the Commission. Therefore, for that period of a year and a half, seventeen employees contacted a Commission counselor but failed to receive an informal resolution and also failed to file a formal complaint.

Of the four formal complaints filed against the Commission for 1970–71, one complaint was closed because it was not filed in a timely manner by the employee. Mr. Clinton Smith, the Commission's internal director of EEO, claims that the complaint was filed six months after the incident at issue.[3] Two of the four complaints were rejected because "they did not fall within the processing of complaints of discrimination." One complaint was decided on the merits against the employee.

The Commission's handling of discrimination complaints appealed from other agencies parallels its handling of inter-

TABLE 14

EEO Appeals to the Board of Appeals and Review

	1968	1969	1970	1971
A. STATUS OF APPEALS				
1. On hand, beginning of period	38	66	83	77
2. Received during period	273	353	362	418
Total	311	419	445	495
3. Appeals closed during period	245	336	368	355
4. Remaining, end of period	66	83	77	140
B. DISPOSITION OF APPEALS				
1. Decision on discrimination				
a. Corrective action by agency or CSC	63	66	103	63
b. Discrimination not found	126	214	175	177
Total	189	280	278	240
2. Other decisions				
a. Affirmed agency decision not to accept complaint	22	20	24	54
b. Remanded, BAR to agency	20	27	4	20
c. Cancelled by BAR or appellant	4	7	28	32
d. Rejected by BAR	0	0	25	4
e. Affirmed agency decision to cancel complaint	5	1	9	5
f. Commissioners declined to reopen	5	1	0	. . .
Total	56	56	90	115
C. TYPE OF DISCRIMINATION ALLEGED				
1. Race/Color	192	238	285	257
2. Religion	21	20	15	27
3. National Origin	32	46	29	24
4. Sex	0*	32	36	42
5. Not Identified	0	0	1	1
6. Other	0	0	2	4
Total	245	336	368	355

* The first appeals on discrimination based on sex were received in fiscal year 1969.

nal complaints. The reason for the low percentage of discrimination findings, suggest Commission officials, is that most valid complaints are withdrawn because "corrective action" is offered.[4] But evidence suggests that corrective action may not be all that corrective, since a considerable number of appeals to the Commission and to the BAR are against actions that are unsatisfactory because, presumably, they do not correct the alleged abuse.

On September 14, 1971, the U.S. Commission on Civil Rights stated: "During 1971, the Commission's Board of Appeals and Review issued decisions on the issue of discrimination in 240 cases. It affirmed agency corrective action or discrimination in over 26 percent of the cases decided in which discrimination was an issue. . . ." These statistics are misleading, however, in that they lump together 57 BAR decisions *against* complainants with 6 BAR decisions *in their favor.* The fifty-seven decisions were affirmations of "corrective action" taken by the agencies that were considered unsatisfactory by the complainant and appealed to the BAR on the basis of their inadequacy. The BAR actually upheld the employee *not* in 63 cases out of 240 (26 percent), but in only 6 cases out of the 240 (2.5 percent).[5]

The adequacy of "corrective actions" allegedly taken after a finding of discrimination in 1970 and the first half of 1971 from the complainant's point of view is questionable. "Priority consideration for next promotion," for example, can hardly be satisfactory to those who felt they had been discriminatorily denied those promotions in the first place. "Training opportunity received" may, in some cases, be a euphemism for the agency's contention that lack of promotion was not discriminatory but a result of the employee's insufficient qualifications. "Agency improved personnel practices," the largest category of "corrective actions," are by the Commission's own admission, corrective actions that do not benefit the complainant directly.[6] Yet another category is "Adverse action reduced and/or rescinded." A complainant who claims that adverse action of any sort against him is discriminatory may find a mere reduction in severity inappropriately termed corrective.

Information given by Irving Kator on October 20, 1971, to the Senate Subcommittee on Labor offers several other examples of what the Commission calls "corrective action" (Table 15). None of the above "recommendations" of "corrective action" is inherently favorable to the complainant, and some are clearly less than what the complainant asked for.

TABLE 15
Agency "Corrective Actions"

Agency to reconsider two-day suspension	1 case
Supervisory training for supervisors	2 cases
Alleged discriminatory officials to take special training	1 case
Give career counseling to complainant	1 case
Renew offer to complainant of temporary 120-day promotion	1 case

In 1970, only 1,025 (8 percent) of 12,063 agency employees who were counseled filed formal complaints with the Commission. In the first nine months of 1971, counselors were contacted 10,628 times but only 989 formal complaints were filed. The Commission believes these figures demonstrate the success of the counseling program, because the number of formal complaints has dropped. A total of 3,615 (34 percent) employment problems were "informally resolved" at the counseling stage.

What casts doubt on the efficacy of the program is that 6,024 (57 percent) were not reported to have received either an "informal resolution" of their problem or to have filed a formal complaint. What happened to these 6,024 employees (a small number of whom may have been job applicants)?

Irving Kator answered:

> The counseling system was not intended to guarantee that every employee who comes in would have corrective action taken. [Mr. Kator is fond of referring to "informal resolution" as "corrective action," even though they are not strictly

> the same.] Counselors let people come to understand what their problems are, that they did not get promoted because they did not meet certain specified qualifications, and so forth. We don't know whether the man is satisfied or not. If he is not, he can file a complaint. I'm not surprised by the 57 percent who go away without filing a complaint.

Yet his answer still does not reveal what happened to the 57 percent. That they may have been told why they were not promoted—an explanation actually considered under Commission practice to be an "informal resolution"—ignores the possibility that counselors may turn away employees by misinforming or discouraging them. The lack of standards by which to judge "informal resolution" makes the unexplained fate of six thousand employee contacts even more significant. An "informal resolution" may be merely a counselor saying he did not think the employee had a valid grievance. It was unclear from the Commission's records how many "informal resolutions" were satisfactory to the employees involved.

When Kator was asked to distinguish between "informal resolutions" in which something less than "corrective action" was offered to the aggrieved employee and "informal resolutions" in which "corrective action" was taken, he wrote:

> Inasmuch as EEO counseling is programmed to be informal, EEO counselors are not required to maintain any records other than certain basic ones needed to enable agencies to fulfill the reporting requirements outlined in Appendix C to Chapter 713 of the Federal Personnel Manual. Counselors do not report on their counseling of any individual unless the counsellee files a formal complaint of discrimination. For this reason, it is not known in how many counseling contacts there was an informal resolution without "corrective action," nor what types of "corrective action" were taken at the counseling stage. . . . Figures are not available on disciplinary action arising from a counseling session and there is no breakdown of corrective actions taken as a result of counseling.

In other words, what, if anything, was actually done for the 3,615 employees counseled in the first nine months of 1971 whom the agencies' counselors and the Commission allege received an "informal resolution" is as much a mystery to the Commission (and therefore to Congress and the public) as what eventually happened to the mysterious 6,024 who did not even receive the bureaucratic notation of an "informal resolution".[7]

Perhaps even if a complainant received no personal relief, he and others might benefit from the disciplining of supervisors guilty of discriminatory conduct. The deterrent effect might go far to assure adequate "affirmative action." In 1970 disciplinary action was taken in fifteen cases as follows:

Five supervisors issued letter of warning.
Five supervisors orally admonished.
Letters of reprimand issued to three supervisors in one case.
One discriminatory supervisor suspended.
One foreman barred from supervisory duties.
One supervisor reprimanded and reassigned to nonsupervisory work.
One supervisor facing disciplinary action retired.

During the first half of 1971, disciplinary action was taken in fourteen cases as follows:

Two supervisors orally reprimanded.
Two supervisors in one case issued letters of warning.
One supervisor cautioned regarding informal disciplining of employees.
Two activity officials in one case orally admonished.
One activity official admonished.
Three discriminatory officials issued letters of reprimand.
One military chief of staff relieved of position, given supervisory training.

Two supervisors received "appropriate disciplinary action" [in two cases not further described].

It is hard to see how most of these penalties can be considered "disciplinary action," since no apparent financial, promotional, or positional losses seem to have been suffered by the "disciplined" supervisors.

Commission officials offer several explanations for the low percentage of supervisors disciplined. First, they claim that the source and/or cause of discrimination is often "systemic"—institutional or historical—and discriminatory situations of this complexity and ambiguity cannot ordinarily be attributed to individual actions.

The Commission neither recommends nor suggests disciplinary action if the supervisor is not found to be directly responsible for discrimination, and this narrow view is the main reason for so small a percentage of disciplinary actions. But if direct accountability entails knowledge and intent; or knowledge and gross negligence, accountability through acquiescence entails knowledge and negligence through inaction, because of a duty to know and a failure to discover and eradicate practices over which one has power and authority.

Second, Commission officials are concerned that, if disciplinary action becomes common, supervisors may become too passive in their dealings with minority-group or female employees. As Irving Kator says, "If managers start 'going tiptoe'—that might be a problem."[8] This rests on the unconvincing and unsupported assumption that sensitivity to and accountability for EEO complaints result in passive management; on the contrary, *present* management is *passive* regarding an ineffective complaint processing system.

Third, Hampton, Rosen, and Kator were distressed about the possibility that the careers of managers or supervisors would be permanently ruined if a permanent record of the finding were maintained in their Official Personnel Folder. Similar solicitude has not been shown for careers ruined because of the injustices of the Commission's complaint system.

Fourth, if disciplinary actions become more prevalent, Commission officials fear a loss of agency cooperation and the concealment of evidence. Such fears hardly take into account the difficulties in hiding information from the Commission if it were willing to use its power.

Furthermore, the brand of "cooperation" the Commission is getting presently from the agencies is no bargain—as the long delays in complaint processing, to point to just one example, show.

Irving Kator said in a speech at an EEO conference in November 1970:

> It is not necessary to find a culprit in order to find discrimination. There will be few cases in which direct evidence of discrimination will be shown; most discrimination will be found by circumstantial evidence. Employment patterns are of significance in determining if there is discrimination and oftentimes there is no one person who can properly be charged with discrimination . . . but where a culprit is found, disciplinary action should follow. If it does not, the complaint system loses its credibility.

When Mr. Kator and his supervisors discuss disciplinary action or accountability for "systemic" discrimination, they assume that it is only reasonable or helpful to discipline a supervisor who is *directly responsible* or directly accountable for the discrimination. They fail to consider other forms of accountability, such as the possibilities of disciplining supervisors who are accountable *through acquiescence* to discriminatory practices, or supervisors or officials who can be held accountable *by virtue of their positions* for discriminatory practices, because of the affirmative duties inherent in their position of authority.

Better reporting and closer study of counseling activities are essential, for they will almost surely show that employees are being discouraged from filing complaints. James A.

Scott, assistant director of the EEO office, said at an EEO conference in November 1970:

> Even with a present governmentwide cadre of over seven thousand EEO counselors, there are still some weak spots in this phase of the program. Some employees do not know that this EEO counseling service is available to them. Many counselors, particularly those who are infrequently called upon to perform in their EEO roles, receive no follow-up or refresher training. EEO counselors often have no private place in which to interview aggrieved employees. Some ineffective counselors have been allowed to remain in their posts.

On February 23, 1971, the National Alliance of Postal and Federal Employees sent out a questionnaire to all EEO counselors in the Post Office and to some counselors in other agencies as well. Dr. Charles Thomas, head of EEO in the Post Office, directed EEO counselors not to respond to the questionnaire, yet many did. Among their comments were the following:

> The EEO program is an appeasement action allowing itself to be a house organ.
>
> A beautiful paper program.
>
> Full-time counselors with true investigative authority and proper training are needed.
>
> EEO is a token symbol, window dressing, and the EEO counselor a "flak-catcher" for management.
>
> I face personnel roadblocks—my supervisor is the personnel office.
>
> I am not doing a good job. I have since December 1970 been subjected to discrimination, harassment, and denied work in my area.
>
> No line supervisors should be counselors. The hands of counselors are tied by "Uncle Toms." "Doc" Thomas has ordered all counselors not to make replies [to the Alliance's questionnaire]. No cooperation from management—if you call for help, they reply that you are too militant.

I have been refused permission to view personnel records by chief personnel officer.

I have received a directive that we are not to give a personal statement [to the Alliance questionnaire]. I am sometimes harassed.

Counselors may be concerned with future promotional opportunities.

I'm not given enough space and facilities; not given a proper conference room.

The counselor is on his own for information.

Design Defects

The failings of the appeal program should come as no surprise to the Commission. Numerous internal studies of the Board of Appeals and Review and of the appeals process have been conducted and have pointed out these failings.[9]

Historically, appeals and review have been considered a part of the personnel administration function of the Commission. No attempt was made to review an action for more than procedural compliance until 1930, when the Commission created a Board of Appeals and Review. The BAR, however, was not seen as an independent adjudicatory body, but as an extension of the personnel office. The decisions of the Commission were considered advisory and subject to overrule by the agency director until the Veterans' Preference Act of 1944 was amended in 1948.

The perspective of the Commission's appeals system as part of its client-oriented personnel functions persists. Before a conference of appeals examiners in June 1969, Nicholas Oganavic, then executive director, said, "The appeals program is not an extension of an arm of Congress; nor is it a regulatory agency. The Commission is the central personnel agency of the President of the United States. . . . The Commission's appeals examiners are not hearing officers or hearing examiners, they are appeals examiners."[10]

Most of the activities of the Commission concern the provision of services to the management of federal agencies—executive manpower, training, testing, investigations, evaluations (inspections). The pervasiveness of this service approach seems, unfortunately, to extend to the appeals program.[11] The service approach focusing upon agency participation has extended to the EEO program.[12]

The training and career patterns of hearings examiners help to ensure that they will carry to their jobs a management perspective. Most examiners have spent time as investigators of employee suitability for the Bureau of Personnel Investigations, a job that stresses the view of agency as client.[13] In the case of examiners who hear discrimination complaints, a proper ethnic balance has not been achieved. Of eleven EEO examiners allotted to regional offices, eight do not belong to a minority group; one examiner is an Oriental; none is female. Examiners seem closely identified with management. In one agency installation with three counselors, one was dating someone in top management and a second was the director's secretary's brother. An obvious reason for employee suspicion is that an agency's EEO counselors are almost always appointed by management[14] and are often of so high a grade that employees feel uncomfortable about approaching them.[15]

All examiners are under the supervision and control of regional directors, and the problem of going against the bias of one's superior comes into question. In the regional offices of the Commission, appeals examiners are responsible to the regional director. The regional director is an operating official whose primary commitment is to the smooth functioning of all the Commission's programs, rather than solely to the appeals program. Concern for the Commission's good relationship with an agency and for the regional director's ability to cope with agency pressure may affect his outlook. Thus, appeals are influenced by the regional director, and in some areas they are even decided by him.

The participation of the regional director in the adjudication of cases varies. In the Philadelphia region, the regional director does not make an initial decision, but the appeals office does not have authority to issue a decision with which the regional director disagrees. In the Dallas region the regional director only reviews decisions of the appeals office. In the Boston region, however, the regional director not only reviews decisions but he also makes the decision itself when the examiner is "on the fence." This process means that some questions will be decided by persons who have had no contact with the presentation of evidence, who have had no opportunity to judge the demeanor of the witnesses, who may not have even examined the case materials. Indeed, policy positions that affect an appeal may already have been decided before a case reaches a Commission hearing or the Board of Appeals and Review. Both the hearing and the process are then pro forma.

Statutory Neglect: When Regulating, Relinquish

The atrophy of the Commission's regulatory powers is nowhere better shown then in its regulation of agency hearing examiners.

The Administrative Procedures Act of 1946 was intended to give agencies broad judicial and legislative functions. Crucial in preventing abuses was the independence of hearing examiners, and every attempt was made to ensure this independence. The Commission was responsible for selecting qualified examiners and an examiner was to "be removed by the agency in which he is employed only for good cause established and determined by the Civil Service Commission on the record after opportunity for hearing."

Congress realized that subtle pressures which might undermine the independence of examiners should also be prohibited by providing that examiners would rotate to different agencies, and that examiners would not perform duties inconsistent with their duties and responsibilities as hearing examiners. The Commission was given a specific statutory mandate to protect the independence of hearing examiners, with special regulatory authority to fulfill these responsibilities—that is, authority to "investigate, require reports by agencies, issue reports, including an annual report to Congress, prescribe regulation, appoint advisory committees as necessary, recommend legislation, subpoena witnesses and records, and pay witness fees."

In 1961, the Commission established its Office of Hearing Examiners, responsible for planning, operating, and directing a nationwide program for their employment and compensation. In 1963, the Commission adopted changes in the program, including higher examination standards and provisions for keeping eligible lists up to date. Yet, from the beginning of this program, the Commission has been criticized for its ineptitude and vacillation.

The Administrative Procedures Act provided for the protection of examiners from capricious removal by agencies, by requiring a formal hearing with confrontation and cross-examination of witnesses.[16] The Commission chose to interpret this as a hearing that should be conducted by itself, and this interpretation has done much to cause a prevalent abuse—agency circumvention of the formal hearing requirement, as, for example in procedures for a medical disability retirement, in which the initial decision of the Commission is reached before a hearing is held. The hearing received by an employee was an "oral hearing" and not a formal hearing under the Administrative Procedures Act.[17]

The Commission has circumvented another provision of the Act. According to Charles Dullea, head of the Office of Hearing Examiners, it has issued no cease-and-desist order requiring a regulatory agency to stop assigning duties inconsistent with the responsibilities of hearing examiners, nor has it put a stop to the failure to assign cases in rotation. The Office of Hearing Examiners does require that the agencies send the job sheets of hearing examiners for review. However, the agencies are not required to furnish regular periodic reports and there are no special inspections or reviews.

Support services for hearing examiners leave much to be desired. In a hearing before the Subcommittee on Administrative Practice and Procedure of the Senate Committee on the Judiciary, John T. Miller, Jr., representing the American Bar Association, said:

> The Civil Service Commission already has broad responsibilities for training government employees, and it would be a natural one, you would think, to handle this problem [continuing legal education]. But I suggest that there is a fundamental incapability on the part of the Civil Service Commission in this area. . . . There are about six hundred hearing examiners in the federal government. This year they had two sessions for these gentlemen. Forty-five hearing examiners attended—these experiences have led us to conclude that the Civil Service Commission's efforts have been so slight when compared to the magnitude of the need that it appears obvious that a resolution to the problem must be found elsewhere.

Bearing the Burden

Once the appellant or complainant reaches the hearing arena, he has just begun to fight, and his weapons, compared with those of the agency, are slight. His lack of discovery or subpoena powers can hamper his ability to gather information essential to his case. In an EEO complaint the "leads" an investigator, an employee of the accused agency, fails to perceive, fails to follow up, or follows up inadequately may make the difference between success and failure for the appellant.

So long as the full burden of proof is placed upon the appellant and the assurance of impartial, aggressive investigators or examiners is lacking, adequate discovery procedures are not merely desirable, but essential.

Commission officials cite a regulation to show that no appellant or complainant has been harmed by the lack of subpoena power:

> The agency shall make its employees available as witnesses at a hearing on a complaint when requested to do so by the appeals examiner and *it is administratively practicable to comply with the request.* When it is not administratively practicable to comply with the request for a witness, the agency shall provide an explanation to the appeals examiner. If the explanation is inadequate, the appeals examiner shall so advise the agency and request it to make the employee available as a witness at the hearing. If the explanation is adequate, the appeals examiner shall . . . make arrangements to secure testimony through a written interrogatory. [emphasis added]

The inadequacies are obvious: no cross-examination of a hostile witness; no opportunity to pursue helpful, unclear, or surprising testimony; the possibility of a witness's artful preparation of answers; and the loss of the hearing examiner's chance to see a witness's attitude and demeanor. Placing the burden of proof on the appellant or complainant is particularly onerous, given the agency's full access to information. Further, the wide use of discretion allows an agency to structure its adverse action in such a way that it may obscure the real issues.

In determining whether an agency has properly disciplined an employee, there is no question more basic than whether or not the agency has proved its case. Yet the agency must sustain no precise burden of proof. Appeals staff members commented: "There is no more definite guide than each individual examiner's understanding." "My test is that they [the agencies] must convince me." "The action has to be reasonable." "There is no definition because there are no strict rules of evidence, but the appeals examiners use their best judgment."

In discrimination complaints, common sense is more just in its understanding of discrimination than is the Commission. Most people would think that if a supervisor treated Chicanos differently from the way in which he treated Caucasians, he should be considered discriminatory unless he could give sufficient reason. If the reason given were something nebulous like "lack of initiative," most people would still think the supervisor discriminatory unless he were able to point to actual situations in which Chicanos clearly showed "lack of initiative," compared to other employees. But the Commission's version is that the employee must show that the supervisor had a *motivation* to discriminate. The minority-group member, rather than the supervisor, is required to explain the supervisor's deviation from the norm.

It is quite correct for the Commission to require that the employee alleging discrimination show *something* has happened, but after such prima facie evidence, the supervisor or the agency should provide a convincing explanation for the unusual behavior. Placing the burden on the complainant to prove that dissimilar treatment is *clearly* discriminatory treatment results in the present system where "discrimination is difficult to prove."

The agency should rarely find the burden of proof as onerous since its managers and supervisors have access to personnel information to justify their actions. In many areas of the law, the party with the information necessary to prove a point is assigned the burden of presenting that evidence.

The situation for probationary employees is even worse. Those who file a complaint alleging a discriminatory dismissal do not receive a review of the substantive reasons for their separation.[18] The BAR at present cannot presume discrimination if the reasons for separation are found to be insufficient, because the BAR refuses even to examine the reasons for separation. "Discrimination is difficult to prove" when evidence that a probationer's dismissal was caused by discrimination is inadmissible.

The Civil Rights Commission's report on the Federal Civil Service Rights Reinforcement Effort in September 1970 stated: "Free legal aid should be provided on request to all lower-grade employees who require it. In this connection, CSC should take the lead in establishing a governmentwide pool of attorneys who are prepared to volunteer their services in discrimination complaint cases or adverse actions involving minority-group employees."

The Commission has not followed this sound recommendation. When Irving Kator was asked how many employees were represented in complaint processing at each stage, he replied, "We made a rough study when the issue came up with the U.S. Civil Rights Commission. We have not compiled statistics on this problem. Provisions for representation are under consideration now. The problem is not lack of representation, but the quality of representation, which could be better in some cases."

Kator provided the following information showing complainants' representation at EEO hearings between January and July 1971; no information on representation during

TABLE 16
Representation at Hearings

Total Decisions Reviewed	117
Civil Rights Organization Representative	5 or 4.3%
Private Attorney	26 or 22.2%
Union Representatives	40 or 34.2%
Other Individual	30 or 25.6%
No Representative	16 or 13.6%

investigation and appeal, or on how many of the complainants who did not request a hearing had representation, was provided (Table 16).

Because representation is necessary to protect the complainant's fundamental interests, the 13.6 percent rate of nonrepresentation at an EEO hearing seems too high. The high percentage for "private attorney" (22.2 percent) indicates that problems of quality of representation may be severe.

Quality Uncontrol

John Hardesty, a member of the BAR, "doesn't think anyone has defined 'such cause as will promote the efficiency of the service' or ever will." One of the most serious failures of the Commission rests in its inability to develop standards by which to judge the actions of employees, causing judgments in its appeals system to be made on an ad hoc basis. The definition of aberrant behavior is left in the hands of the agency, which is unlikely to include in the definition such behavior as failure to enforce the laws, failure to pass along pertinent information, or failure of management officials to fulfill their personal responsibilities.

Commission officials argue that the complexity of the civil service and the fact that the aims of the federal agencies vary greatly prevent the development or application of uniform standards. They also counsel caution about doing anything that may interfere with agency performance. The very complexity and diversity of the civil service indicates the need for standards because the Commission's reliance on agency interpretation of unacceptable conduct, combined with increased complexity, may soon become abdication. The Commission has failed to participate meaningfully in the development of uniform agency codes of penalties that would bring some order.

The BAR says that it does not regard its previous decisions as precedents, primarily because no two cases are identical and because differences in federal agencies prevent any meaningful use of precedent—a very questionable assumption.[19]

In practice, some appeals examiners use their previous decisions, as well as decisions of the BAR, as precedent and accept from employee representatives the citation of previous decisions. But without the guidance provided by a clearly defined burden of proof or by a creative use of prior decisions, examiners must rely more upon attitude, experience, and the vagaries of the moment in deciding any particular case.[20]

Some determinations based on procedure are made by two members of the BAR. On cases determined on the merits, many of the decisions are made by only three of the Board members. Because members of the BAR rarely write the decisions (almost all BAR opinions are written by appeals examiners), one questions the review that cases may be receiving.

The format of BAR decisions does little to aid in the formation of standards. It consists of an introduction, a section entitled "analysis and findings," and a brief section entitled "decision." Legal decisions are generally written in one of three ways: the first states only the conclusion; the second recites the facts and states a conclusion; the third discusses the facts by relating them to the issues involved, indicating their relevance to those issues and to the conclusions. A decision that gives only a conclusion provides no insight into the policies underlying it; it is as much an edict as a decision.

BAR decisions tend to fall into categories one or two. Frequently they are little more than the conclusory language, "we find the removal to be for such cause as to promote the efficiency of the service." While some decisions list the facts of the case and its appellate history followed by the opinion of the Board, nowhere are the facts related to the decision, the issues clearly delineated, the options discussed and dismissed, or the policy choices clarified. Dissenting votes are not recorded nor are dissenting opinions provided; the chairman alone signs decisions for the Board.[21]

The lack of published EEO complaint decisions that include the facts of each particular case, reasoned, articulated conclusions from those facts, and comparisons to the facts and conclusions in previous cases makes it impossible for a complainant to assess his claim in light of prior successful or unsuccessful claims and to argue on the basis of similar prior decisions. Published dissenting opinions might also be useful to the Commission in determining whether or not to reopen a case.

The BAR and the Commission have resisted wider publication on the grounds that such publication would violate the employee's right of privacy, but the Commission may be more concerned with the privacy of the agencies. William Berzak, chairman of the BAR, stated that an agency might not like publication if a large number of its cases were reversed in a short period of time.

Indeed, the importance the Commission attaches to its own and agency privacy is illustrated in the case of Ernest Fitzgerald, who, when he *requested* an open hearing, was refused on the grounds that an open hearing would violate his right of privacy. After being denied an open hearing, Mr. Fitzgerald took his case to a U.S. District Court which ordered that due process required that Mr. Fitzgerald be granted an open hearing. This decision was sustained on appeal and the Commission was ordered to hold an open hearing. (The Commission is never at a loss for reasons for closed hearings. When pressed about the desirability of an open hearing, Berzak responded, "You must keep in mind the small size of our hearing rooms.")

Recalling Transcripts

Although the Commission now provides for verbatim transcripts of both Commission and agency hearings, one questions their usefulness. Some examples will indicate the grounds for such skepticism. The issue in one hearing was whether or not the employee's resignation was voluntary. When counsel asked her if she felt that she had resigned voluntarily, she replied, "Absolutely not!" The verbatim transcript, however, indicated that she had responded, "Absolutely!"

In another case a portion of clearly remembered testimony could not be found in the verbatim transcript of the appeals hearing. The employee and her attorney, who was handling the appeal of the case to the courts, sought the original stenographic tapes first from the Department of Justice, which was representing the Commission. An assistant attorney general responded, "Please be advised that the Civil Service Commission merely has a certified copy of the transcript. It is suggested that you contact the Hoover Reporting Company which must have retained the tape made during the . . . hearing." The letter indicated that a carbon copy of the letter had been sent to the General Counsel's office of the Commission.

The Hoover Reporting Company attorney responded: "With regard to the stenographic tape in the above hearing, we wish to advise you that we have nothing in our files pertaining to this hearing. As required in all confidential hearings before the Civil Service Commission, the stenographic tape of the proceedings and all copies of the transcript prepared therefrom—the original and two carbon copies—were forwarded to the Civil Service Commission."

Understandably perturbed, the attorney asked the court to locate the stenographic tape. The Justice Department responded immediately for the Commission, stating the "Office of General Counsel, Civil Service Commission . . . had unsuccessfully searched for the tape in the General

Counsel's files, but, upon receipt of the Hoover Reporting letter, he found the tape in the Executive files, which are maintained separately from those files maintained by the Office of General Counsel." The Justice Department then informed the attorney that the tapes could be examined in the General Counsel's office.

The employee, the attorney, and a trained stenotypist examined the transcription tapes, but did not find the recalled cross-examination. They found discrepancies, however, in the tapes. Pad 1, in which the cross-examination would have occurred, was on new white paper and Pad 2 was on older, yellow paper. Pad 1 had no editing marks by the reporter, while Pad 2 was carefully edited.

It is not possible to be sure that there was tampering with the transcription and with the transcribed notes. But the lack of procedures sufficient to ensure the integrity of transcriptions, the difficulty in obtaining the transcribed notes, and the discrepancies that were found do give the appearance of subterfuge. Other regulatory agencies, such as the Federal Trade Commission, leave the original tapes in the hands of the reporting company in case there is any question about the accuracy of the transcript. Some reporting companies will not allow their reporters to attest to transcription notes that have been taken out of their hands.

The case has other disturbing aspects. If it were the procedure in all cases for transcriptions and tapes to be returned to the Commission, why was the General Counsel's office unaware of this policy? If the office were aware of the policy, why was not a thorough search made for the transcription tapes when first requested, since the office would know they must be somewhere in the Commission?

Without Recourse

A failure to protect employees from reprisal for their use of the appeals system or the EEO complaint system does much to reduce the usefulness of existing procedures. If employees cannot be protected from reprisal, they are less likely to expose corruption and wrongdoing or to refuse to participate in illegal acts.

A study by Les Aspin, congressman from Wisconsin, of what happened to individuals reinstated by private industry after they had challenged their dismissals on the grounds of discrimination before the National Labor Relations Board suggests what a Commission study of federal employment might discover. Many workers refused reinstatement, most frequently for fear of company retaliation. The study found that three-quarters of those actually reinstated had left the company within two years. Their story is not much different from those who refused reinstatement in the first place. The most frequent reason given for leaving the company was "bad company treatment." "Bad company treatment" usually involved a specific complaint: "They were always on my back," or, "I always got the worst jobs," though sometimes the complaints were general: "It was really awful," or, "I hope I never have to go through that again."

In a 1970 report Dr. David Rosenbloom, professor of political science at the University of Vermont and an American Society for Public Administration fellow who studied the Commission's EEO program stated, "Perhaps the most important limitation on the [EEO] complaint system is that it cannot completely protect an individual from future mistreatment, and consequently many are reluctant to make use of it."[22] (Employees who are called as witnesses in the appeal of adverse-action cases or who utilize the appeals process also question the efficacy of Commission attempts to guard against reprisal.)

During interviews in the summer of 1971 Irving Kator was asked how the Commission guards against reprisal by agency officials—when a complaint is filed, or when a witness testifies against agency management, or when, in the agency's estimation, an investigator investigates too diligently, or when a representative employed by the agency advocates a complainant's case too zealously—he said that he did not think that reprisal was a "significant problem." In those rare cases in which, he admitted, it might exist, he insisted that the complainant need only file another separate discrimination complaint alleging that reprisal had occurred.

"Reprisal is a new issue," Kator explained. "That's why it should be handled separately, since it would just obfuscate the issues if handled with the original complaint." But since complaints take so long to process, how can the employee receive the Commission's immediate attention concerning his plight, which is very likely ongoing? Kator replied, "If an employee alleges reprisal during his complaint, we contact the agency [by letter] and ask them to make a report—sometimes we will send the Bureau of Personnel Management in."

Kator could not remember any cases in which he had instructed BPME to inspect an agency because of an allegation of reprisal, nor could he remember if any officials were disciplined because of BPME action on a reprisal charge, nor did he know of any efforts to make known to employees or complainants throughout the federal service that formal means are open to them to bring a charge of reprisal.

When Kator was asked about the possibility that the *threat* or *fear* of reprisal might prevent many employees from filing any complaint at all, he replied: "There is no question that anyone thinks twice about filing a complaint. You would, I would, just as everyone thinks twice about going to court [on any matter]. There are always action and counteractions possible. If you can get rid of it, fine. I don't know how to get at it." (Kator showed his recognition of reprisal, however, when he said on June 14, 1971, in mimeographed instructions outlining discrimination complaint investigation: "Because of the new procedures fear of reprisal has lessened, and there is less reluctance to file a complaint.")

Commission officials like to emphasize that the number of reprisal allegations is small. But reprisal, like blackmail, is by its nature difficult to detect, since its victim often fears the perils of trying to expose his tormentor more than he does suffering the reprisal. The fact that more than six thousand employees went to EEO counselors in the first nine months of 1971, but did not file a complaint and did not receive an alleged "informal resolution," however defined, is extremely suggestive of widespread fear of reprisal.

The case of Dr. Samuel Schienberg illustrates how the discretionary power an agency has over an employee and his work may be great enough to make even a successful exercise of appellate rights meaningless.

Dr. Schienberg, a distinguished scientist, was a leader and principal geneticist of the Pioneering Blood Antigen Research Laboratory of the U.S. Department of Agriculture. Dr. Schienberg's experiments—representing a research effort of nearly thirteen years—required the use of pigeons and chickens that had taken years of breeding to produce. In the fall of 1969 and the spring of 1970, Dr. Schienberg was ordered to move his birds into an incompleted building; there were no water pipes for washing the cages, drinking, and flushing fecal wastes. The floor was not sloped so that it could be washed properly. The building lacked proper heating and air-conditioning units for temperature-sensitive birds (indeed, the heating unit in one room was a hazard to humans).

On March 9, 1970, Dr. Schienberg concluded an agreement with Dr. G. W. Irving, administrator of the Agricultural Research Service, providing that air-conditioning units would be installed, that year-end funds would be used to complete the building satisfactorily, and the birds would be moved into each section as it was completed. During the summer many of the changes were made and Dr. Schienberg moved many of the birds into the building.

On March 16, 1970, D. E. J. Warwick, then assistant director of the Animal Science Division, ordered Dr. Schienberg to move all the birds in. Dr. Schienberg continued to move animals into the building, but would not move all of them immediately. He expressed his conviction that the facilities still were hardly satisfactory. On June 1 he was dismissed for insubordination.

Dr. Schienberg appealed the adverse action to the Commission. After the hearing had been completed but before a decision had been reached, the Agricultural Research Service destroyed 450 pigeons and 250 chickens—all but six of the experimental animals. Dr. Schienberg was neither notified nor given an opportunity to purchase the birds.

Dr. R. E. Hodgson, director of the Animal Science Division, when asked if the birds' destruction were not a flagrant violation of Dr. Schienberg's rights, replied that one could not assume that Dr. Schienberg would win or that, were he to win, he would be returned to the same position. The birds were destroyed, according to Dr. Hodgson, because of the cost of maintaining them, yet he did not know the cost of maintaining the birds, nor did he appear to have considered the research value of the animals to the government, were Dr. Schienberg's experiments to be completed.

Employees, employee representatives, and even an occasional Commission official feel that the potential for reprisal exists even beyond the imaginations of insecure workers. It is difficult for an employee to prove reprisal during the appeals process, since many of his witnesses are still employed by the government and in fear of reprisals on themselves. Yet reprisal in many forms is very much alive in the Civil Service and, in a climate of wide discretion and little Commission control, it flourishes.

Recent Changes

Since this report was issued, several changes have taken place in the appeals and EEO discrimination complaint systems of the Civil Service Commission. Soon after *Behind the Promises* was issued in June 1972, the Commission announced changes in the regulations concerning the EEO complaint system, including new procedures to allow a complainant to raise the issue of harassment in conjunction with his original complaint.

The Spoiled System, issued at the same time, recommended a number of changes in the Commission and agency appeals system. (A list of these recommendations and the Commission's response to them is contained in Appendix I.) Among them were (1) the publication of BAR and appeals office decisions, (2) provision for open hearings, (3) the organizational independence of the BAR and Appeals Examining Office, (4) the elimination of agency appeals, (5) provision for a hearing prior to an employee's removal from any agency position, and (6) Appeals Examining Offices and the BAR be given authority to modify penalties.

On December 15, 1972, the Administrative Conference of the United States recommended, after study, changes in the appeals process. (These recommendations are contained in Appendix B.) Among the Conference recommendations were (1) with some exceptions, an employee should have the opportunity to have a prompt evidentiary hearing before a proposed adverse action becomes effective, (2) except in rare cases, an employee should be able to elect to hold an open hearing, (3) Commission regulations should make clear that the employing agency has the burden of supplying the evidence and the burden of persuasion, (4) the Commission's appellate authority should be clarified, (5) hearing officers should not provide advice to parties nor participate in ex parte communications with other Commission officials, and (6) that an independent agency to adjudicate appeals was not necessary if changes were made in the Commission's system. A number of the Administrative Conference recommendations were similar to recommendations made by our two reports.

On March 30, 1973, after hearings had been conducted on our reports by the House Post Office and Civil Service Committee and after the completion of an internal Commission study, the Civil Service Commission issued proposed changes in the adverse-action and appeals systems. (A copy of these proposed changes is included in Appendix B.) The proposed Commission changes adopt many of the recommendations made in our report and by the Administrative Conference of the United States. For example, the Commission recommended that all appeals be made to the Commission, and that changes be made to ensure the organizational independence of the appeals functions. However, the Commission rejected the recommendation that an evidentiary hearing be held prior to the termination of an employee.

On February 5, 1974, the General Accounting Office released a report to Congress, *Design and Administration of the Adverse Action and Appeals Systems Need to Be Improved* (a digest of which is contained in Appendix B). The GAO study reviewed the findings of previous studies of the appeals process including those made by Professor Guttman, (an American University law professor who, in 1970 as a consultant to the Commission, evaluated its appeals program), the Administrative Conference of the United States, and the Nader Report. Many of the GAO findings and conclusions were similar to those contained in our report: e.g., excessive time required for appeal at the agency level; most employees not granted hearings until after penalties imposed; lack of authority by the BAR or regional appellate offices to mitigate agency penalties. The GAO report supported *The Spoiled System's* description of structural faults in the Commission's appeals process. The FAO report concluded: the lack of separate and distinct organization within the Commission of each of the activities [personnel guidance to agencies and supervision of the appeals process] creates doubt as to its objectivity and independence in administering the appeals system."

The GAO recommendations were similar to those of the

Nader Report and the Administrative Conference of the United States. Among these recommendations were that regional appeals examiners report directly to the BAR; regional examiners and the Appeals Examining Office be empowered to make decisions independently of the regional director and executive director; the Board and not the Bureau of Policies and Standards establish Commission appellate policy and the Board be responsible solely to the Commissioners. In addition, the GAO recommended that the Commission should act on its proposal to eliminate agency appeals systems as soon as possible.

Since our report was issued, a number of changes have been made in the appeals process, most of which are salutary and consistent with the recommendations of our report. Many of the Commission's proposed changes will become effective in the fall of 1974: agency hearing systems will be abolished and a new structure established to protect the independence of the Commission's appeals process. Among the changes reported to be made by the Civil Service Commission are: better monitoring of appeals statistics by the Appeals Program Management Office; clearer definition of the role of the appeals examiner; and circulation of significant appeals statistics.

Regardless of the implementation of these well-advised changes in the appeals process, the importance of an independent agency capable of securing the accountability of federal employees remains crucial as an external method of ensuring the evaluation of employee performance. The means of providing for such accountability will be discussed in chapter 8.

5

Waiting For Godot

> Injustice anywhere is a threat to justice everywhere.
>
> MARTIN LUTHER KING

If the results are not always salutary, the administrative process should at least produce expeditious decisions at minimum cost to the employee.

Of the 228 adverse-action cases (removals, suspension, demotions) on hand in the Board of Appeals and Review on July 27, 1971, 24 cases were over a year old. As of October 27, 1973, the BAR had 351 adverse-action appeals on hand, of which 183 were over one year old, and 45 of the cases received between June 9 and August 4, 1973, were still pending. The BAR was at least three or four months behind in processing cases.

The tolerance of this backlog is inconsistent with the short fifteen-day limit for filing an appeal imposed on the employee. While some extensions may be given to employees, Commission regulations allow dismissal of an appeal for failure to prosecute; no similar penalty is available to discourage agency delay. Since agencies rejected perhaps as many as 836 appeals for untimeliness in 1970, 100 in 1971, 110 in 1972, and 66 in 1973, it appears that time requirements are rigidly enforced against the employee.

Delays are costly to the individual employee, since he must exhaust his administrative remedies before appealing to the courts, and in most cases an employee is separated before he receives a hearing. During the period in which his appeal is pending, the employee may be without a job and income. Other employment may be difficult to obtain while the action is pending and opportunities for advancement are lost.

Delays in the appellate process are also costly for the government. In 1971, Commission cases lost in court (18 percent of those appealed) cost the taxpayers $610,000 in back pay, a figure that does not include the service credit for retirement, leave pay, or the possible cost of providing a job position for the restored employee.

Commission response to the backlog of cases has developed slowly. The BAR budget for 1971 was based on staffing plans for the previous year's 2,100 cases, but the BAR was faced with 4,000 cases. Only a $5,000 increase for the BAR was sought for fiscal year 1972. In fiscal year 1973, $930,650 was expended by the BAR, which represents a 34 percent increase over 1972. For fiscal year 1974 an 11 percent increase in the BAR budget was sought over 1973.

The Commission's handling of EEO complaints is no more expeditious than its handling of ordinary appeals. Delay can extend for months or years, and even then an employee may find no relief. Consider the case of Hoover Rowel.[1] In 1959 Hoover Rowel and seven other black employees of the Grounds Maintenance and Landscaping Unit at the National Institutes of Health (NIH) filed a written complaint charging that they had been denied promotions because of their race. No action was taken. In April 1964, Rowel sought aid from the Civil Rights Committee of the American Federation of Government Employees (AFGE), which filed an official complaint with the EEO office of the Department of Health, Education and Welfare (HEW). An investigator contacted the complainants, who repeated their charges, but no acknowledgement of the complaint was received. When the AFGE representative called the office, she was told, to her surprise, that the complaint had been withdrawn.

After determining that the complaint had not, in fact, been withdrawn, the AFGE representative again contacted the EEO officer—only to be informed that the file had been "misplaced." A new complaint was filed on May 7, 1965, and on May 14 HEW formally assigned an investigator.

When questioned about delay in the case, the NIH employee investigating the case said that he was "not interested" in the requirements of the executive order for rapid processing. (The investigator also explained that he had "such good relations with his Negro employees that they voluntarily stayed away from his annual employees' barbecue because they knew it would cause him embarrassment with his neighbors if Negroes were seen as guests in his back yard.")

While waiting, Mr. Rowel did receive some agency action in June 1966—a suspension for insubordination. (The hearing committee that later exonerated Rowel commented on discrepancies in the testimony of witnesses for the supervisor.)

In October 1966, the AFGE representative requested the assistance of the American Civil Liberties Union and an amended discrimination complaint was filed on January 31, 1967. In June 1967, the deputy EEO officer of the Department of HEW in which the National Institutes of Health are located, issued a decision sustaining a number of the complaint's allegations.

On June 30, 1967, the ACLU attorney requested a hearing, which was finally held on February 14, February 28, and March 13, 1968. A decision was to be rendered by September 25. During the hearing, additional evidence of discrimination was introduced: one white man with low seniority had been promoted over Rowel; he was a functional illiterate and Rowel had to read the daily instructions to him before he could issue orders.

On December 10, 1968, a decision was issued that supported the findings but suggested no disciplinary action against the supervisors, who were found guilty of discrimination, and provided no back pay or remedial promotion to the complainant.

An appeal was then taken to the BAR. Briefs were filed in January 1969. Not until September did the BAR hand down a decision—affirmed, but requested relief denied. The case was referred to the Bureau of Personnel Management Evaluation to ascertain whether disciplinary action against the supervisors should be taken. The investigation found that none was warranted.

After ten years Rowel was forced to take his case to the U.S. Court of Claims to obtain an adequate remedy. The court required that an individual administrative determination would be required as to whether a particular individual would have been entitled to a promotion. The case has yet to be finally resolved.

The effects of delay in the EEO complaint system are manifold. Until October 1971, when the U.S. Court of Claims ruled that employees and job applicants denied promotions or jobs because of racial discrimination were entitled to the pay they would have received had they been promoted or hired, the financial loss of complainants because of processing delays was considerable. If the financial loss is now less severe, the complainant still is very often left in the unenviable position of working under the supervisor or officials against whom he has filed a complaint, and thus is easily subjected to blatant or subtle intimidation or reprisal. He frequently has difficulty in deciding whether or not to stay in the federal service. Since the complainant understandably may develop increasingly negative attitudes toward the "justice" provided by an agency with which he is already on strained terms, his job morale is lowered.

Delays do general harm to the federal EEO program. Complainants, their representatives, their friends, and fellow employees may become disillusioned with their agency's and the Commission's commitment to the EEO program, not only in the complaint area, but in other program areas.

The willingness of aggrieved employees to use the complaint system may significantly decrease, and agencies may deliberately use delays to encourage a recalcitrant employee to withdraw his complaint.

Supervisors guilty of discriminatory acts who remain undisciplined may commit other discriminatory acts and opportunities for reprisal or intimidation are increased. Other supervisors and officials may be encouraged to continue discriminatory attitudes. Management or personnel policies that contributed to or caused a complaint may remain unimproved and top management may be encouraged in its attempts to circumvent or even openly flout Commission regulations or guidelines in other EEO programs.

The significant impact that a rigorous complaint system could have in the implementation of affirmative action programs is largely lost, and the importance of discrimination complaints comes to be undervalued by personnel managers of the federal agencies. Commission officials themselves admit that overdue complaints place a severe strain on the credibility of their complaint program.[2]

Discovering the true extent or nature of delay in the processing of discrimination complaints requires a tortuous statistical analysis, since the Commission's EEO office does not compile information breaking the processing time of complaints into categories that reflect the nature of their final disposition.[3]

Since information on the ages of pending cases was unavailable, we must look at a breakdown of the ages of closed cases.[4] The first source of delay is found at the agency level.

Of the 838 EEO discrimination cases closed by agencies during 1970 and reviewed by the Commission:[5]

412 (49.2%) were closed after less than six months of processing;

309 (36.9%) were closed after more than six months, but less than a year of processing;

87 (10.4%) were closed after more than a year, but less than eighteen months of processing;

23 (2.7%) were closed after more than eighteen months, but less than two years of processing;

7 (0.8%) were closed after more than two years of processing.

During the first half of 1971, agencies reported dispositions on 460 complaints of discrimination. Of these:

257 (55.9%) were closed after less than six months of processing;

135 (29.3%) were closed after more than six months, but less than a year of processing;

41 (8.9%) were closed after more than a year, but less than eighteen months of processing;

12 (2.6%) were closed after more than eighteen months, but less than two years of processing;

15 (3.3%) were closed after more than two years of processing.

An examination of more recent EEO statistics shows that the situation has not appreciably changed.

Of the 1,308 EEO discrimination cases closed by agencies during 1972 and reviewed by the Commission:

728 (55.6%) were closed after less than six months of processing;

397 (30.3%) were closed after more than six months, but less than a year of processing;

118 (9.0%) were closed after more than a year, but less than eighteen months of processing;

18 (1.4%) were closed after more than eighteen months, but less than two years of processing;

47 (3.6%) were closed after more than two years of processing.

During fiscal year 1973, agencies reported dispositions on 1,915 complaints of discrimination. Of these:

1,084	(56.6%)	were closed after less than six months of processing;
647	(33.7%)	were closed after more than six months, but less than a year of processing;
144	(7.5%)	were closed after more than a year, but less than eighteen months of processing;
31	(1.6%)	were closed after more than eighteen months, but less than two years of processing;
9	(0.5%)	were closed after more than two years of processing.

Commission regulations explicitly state that a complaint is overdue when a decision has not been rendered within sixty days, "exclusive of time spent in the processing of the complaint by the appeals examiner." Irving Kator established an informal deadline of sixty days for the Commission-appointed EEO appeals examiner to complete his work. Therefore, the maximum length of processing time within the agency for a complaint with a hearing should be four months, were the Commission's regulations and guidelines adhered to. But Kator felt that an additional sixty days leeway is necessary to provide for unforeseen administrative bottlenecks, delays by complainants, and difficulties in investigation—"contingencies that might arise."

Even given Kator's personal assessment that six months (sixty days regulatory plus sixty days for "contingencies" plus sixty days hearing time) should be the longest that any complaint should take, still 50.8 percent of the complaint dispositions "reviewed" in 1970 had taken more than six months to process. Moreover, in 1970, of the 426 complaints reported closed after six months, at least 310 did not include any hearing time, and therefore were at least four months over the sixty-day limit, and at least 172 of the 203 complaints reported closed after six months in the first half of 1971 were similarly overdue.

Many of the Commission's problems with agency failure to comply with regulations were neatly solved by the Commission when it abolished regulations establishing the sixty-day limit. The Commission now considers complaints to be overdue after 180 days, but the record of delay has not improved.[6]

Of the complaint dispositions reviewed in 1972, 44.5 percent had taken more than six months to process. In 1973 43.5 percent of the complaint dispositions reviewed had taken more than six months to process. Moreover, in 1972, of the 1,308 discrimination complaint cases reported closed for the fiscal year, 993 (76 percent) included no hearing time; and in 1973, 1,459 (76.2 percent) of the 1,915 discrimination cases reported closed included no hearing time.

During the period that the Commission followed a loosely enforced sixty-day deadline, the records of several agencies left much to be desired. An examination of Tables 17, 18 and 19 shows that the abolition of the sixty-day deadline did not improve the records of these agencies and may be a factor that has led to an even less rapid handling of cases.

Although hundreds of discrimination complaints are old when eventually closed, the figures do not show an even more disquieting fact: almost all of the discrimination complaints that were decided on the merits had taken more than six months to process.[7]

Delays are not caused by agency inaction alone. The Commission's Board of Appeals and Review, although it refused to accept twenty-nine complaints in 1970 and 1971 because complainants appealed past a fifteen-day deadline, has never required an agency to relinquish to the BAR itself an overdue complaint.[8] Its heavy backlog of cases in processing appeals contributes to the delay as well. Almost all cases were requiring more than three months, and many were requiring more than four months. (One case had been pending five or six months.) The BAR is not at present even able to read the complaint file and render a decision within the sixty-day limit. It sometimes remands the complaint file back to the agency for further investigation, which may have been what happened to the one case closed that was received in the period from June 27 to July 24, 1971.

TABLE 17
Complaints Pending More than 60 Days
(as of September 23,1971)

Agency	Number of Complaints in Process	
	60–119 days	More than 120 days
Defense Supply Agency	1	2
Department of Agriculture	5	10
Department of the Air Force	9	10
Department of the Army	16	30
Department of Health, Education and Welfare	11	41
Department of the Interior	0	7
Department of the Navy	25	28
Department of the Treasury	3	12
General Services Administration	1	9
U.S. Postal Service	23	88
Veterans Administration	8	6

(as of November 30, 1973)

Agency	Number of Complaints in Process		
	60–119 days	120 to 180 days	More than 180 days
Defense Supply Agency	3	30	16
Department of Agriculture	18	12	7
Department of the Air Force	16	61	25
Department of the Army	25	96	76
Department of Health, Education, and Welfare	18	154	123
Department of the Interior	8	13	11
Department of the Navy	54	71	39
Department of the Treasury	12	16	4
General Services Administration	6	23	17
U.S. Postal Service	151	367	197
Veterans Administration	70	27	6

TABLE 18
Cases Pending in the "Big Six" Agencies
As of June 30, 1971

Agency	Total number of cases pending	Total number of cases over 60 days old
Department of the Air Force	45	20 (44%)
Department of the Army	78	52 (67%)
Department of Health, Education and Welfare	62	56 (90%)
Department of the Navy	89	42 (47%)
U.S. Postal Service	188	114 (61%)
Veterans Administration	30	9 (30%)
Total	492	293 (59%)

As of November 30, 1973

Agency	Total number of cases pending	Total number of cases over 60 days old
Department of the Air Force	108	77 (71%)
Department of the Army	156	121 (78%)
Department of Health, Education and Welfare	188	172 (92%)
Department of the Navy	182	125 (68%)
U.S. Postal Service	623	518 (83%)
Veterans Administration	132	97 (74%)
Total	1,389	1,110 (80%)

In order to illustrate why the BAR remanded cases to the agencies, Chairman Berzak provided the following information for the period from April 15, 1973, to October 27, 1973. Of seventeen cases remanded to the agencies for further processing,

> five were remanded where the agency found the complaint not to be within the purview of the regulation;

Table 19 Cases Pending in All Agencies (as of November 30, 1973)

Agency	*Total*	*Under 60 days*	*60–90*	*91–120*	*121–150*	*151–180*	*181–210*	*211–240*	*241–270*	*271–300*	*301–330*	*331–365*	*1–1½ years*	*1½–2*	*2–3*	*3–4*	*Over 4*
Agriculture	47	17	9	9	2	3	1	1	1	....	1	....	2	....	1	....	....
Air Force	108	31	8	8	11	25	16	4	3	....	2	....	....	....	....	....	....
Army	156	35	14	11	11	9	11	6	8	13	7	10	21	....	....	....	....
DSA	44	11	3	....	10	4	3	2	3	1	....	2	5	....	....	....	....
GSA	32	3	2	4	2	4	2	4	3	1	3	2	2	....	....	....	....
HEW	188*	16	7	11	12	19	6	10	16	21	16	6	39	3	2	4	....
Interior	35	14	3	5	1	1	2	2	2	1	1	....	3	....	....	....	....
Navy	182	57	22	32	13	19	10	9	4	7	2	1	6	....	....	....	....
Treasury	37	9	6	6	8	4	1	....	....	....	1	....	2	....	....	....	....
USPS	623	105	81	70	75	95	60	52	36	16	9	4	19	1	....	....	....
VA	132	35	15	55	15	6	3	3	....	....	....	....	....	....	....	....	....

** There has been a substantial decline of outstanding cases as of December 14, 1973.*

three were remanded where the agency modified or rejected the complaints examiner's recommendations without specifying any reason for the modification or the rejection;

three were remanded where the agency made no attempt at informal adjustment of the complaint;

two were remanded where the agency found the complaint to be untimely;

two were remanded where the agency closed the cases because of the complainant's failure to proceed with the complaint;

two were remanded for a hearing.

These delays are particularly distressing when one considers the long prior delay probably suffered by the complainants. Commission officials contend that it is the complainants who are often at fault,[9] but an internal flash report on EEO hearing as of April 3, 1971, suggests the real causes of delay in at least the eleven of seventy-nine hearings on hand that had been with EEO examiners for more than sixty days.

Out of the eleven overdue hearings, two were delayed entirely because of action or inaction by the agency, one was delayed entirely because of inaction by the Commission, three were delayed by the agency and the complainant, one was delayed by the Commission and the complainant, and only one complaint was delayed solely by the complainant. (In that one complaint, the complainant was ready to proceed but his representative postponed the hearing and later withdrew.)

In two of the five cases in which the complainant was implicated in the delay, he had postponed the hearing because of lack of representation. These cases had earlier been subject to delay not caused by the complainant. In two other cases, the complainant's representative and not the complainant postponed the hearing. In both these cases the complainant's representative then withdrew, thereby suggesting that the postponement was not sought by the complainant. In the fifth case, the complainant and the agency jointly delayed the hearing (previously delayed by the agency for two months) because of failure of representatives of both complainant and agency to show up.

Since problems with representation are most likely to cause delay only in the hearing process and almost all other complaint processing is exclusively the burden of the agency, it would appear that the agency's ability to delay far outweighs the complainant's.[10] (An analogous report of November 1973 shows similar results—these two reports are reproduced in Appendix D.)

Out of the fifty overdue cases for the four-week period ending November 24, 1973, twelve were due to complainant delay; eight were due to a combination of agency and complainant delay; and thirty were due to agency delay alone. Overdue cases for this period represented 30.1 percent of the workload of 166 cases, as compared with 19.4 percent during the corresponding period one year before.

Of the twelve cases overdue because of complainant delay, difficulties pertaining to complainant representation accounted for seven cases. The remaining five cases concerned difficulties in obtaining witnesses; and in one such case, it was due to agency failure to notify the witnesses.

Of the eight cases due to a combination of agency and complainant delay, the primary causes were either the hearing examiner's being on leave or preoccupied with some other "top priority" investigation or problems relating to complainant's representation and witnesses.

Of the thirty cases delayed because of agency action, causes such as leaves of hearing examiners, backlogs, lack of a sufficient number of representatives in the agency to handle its EEO hearings, conflicts with other EEO hearings, and rewritings of drafts of decisions accounted for most of cases pending over sixty days.

Delay remains a serious problem in the EEO complaint program. Also serious is the inability of the Commission to provide statistical breakdowns on time consumed in investigation, in predecision review, and in administrative handling and transit despite Commission regulations requiring the reporting of such information by federal agencies.

James Frazier disagreed in August 1971 with the Commission's official emphasis on complainant cause of delay when he stated: "I don't think that it is usually the case that the complainant will delay. . . . It's the decision-making process of all of this—people letting things stay on their desk too long. . . . Agencies sit on them. . . . If people made it a priority issue rather than backburnered it, time [limits] could be met. Also, not enough manpower is devoted to it. It never is—no, sometimes it is—a priority issue." Unfortunately Jim Frazier's statement to the study group could have been spoken today.

While waiting for the Commission to move, federal employees may make use of a new law, the Equal Employment Opportunity Act of 1972, which established that federal and state employees be provided the same rights regarding discrimination as employees of private industry.

The law provides some judicial relief for those employees who have suffered consistent agency delay in the processing of complaints. Federal employees must still take their discrimination complaints to the agencies. If the agency or the Civil Service Commission has not taken final action within 180 days of the filing of the complaint, however, the employee may commence a civil action in a U.S. District Court.

An Equal Employment Opportunity Coordinating Council has been established by the Act, whose mandate includes responsibility for developing and implementing agreements, policies, and practices designed to maximize effort, promote efficiency, and eliminate conflict, competition, duplication, and inconsistency among the EEO operations, functions, and jurisdictions of federal agencies. Such a council should find much to do.

Potentially, the most significant effect of the Act may be to begin to apply the standards of Title 7 of the Civil Rights Act to federal employment. Under the standards established for tests in private industry, it is doubtful that the Federal Service Entrance Examination could, for example, survive a court challenge. The Civil Service Commission and other federal agencies will now find their policies and practices subject to attack in court.

The Act, by providing a civil remedy for employees, may relieve some of the problems of reprisal since an employee can now seek a federal court injunction prohibiting the agency from harassing him for filing a discrimination complaint.

One Washington civil rights attorney said that federal equal employment opportunity will become a "most fertile ground for litigation." Back-pay liability under class-action provisions may run to millions of dollars.

Rather than being moved slowly by lengthy and costly litigation, the Commission should begin now to evaluate the programs of every agency and to develop a plan to eliminate discrimination. Because the act may well mean that all judicial interpretations applying to private industry will now apply to the federal government, the Commission should begin to modify federal employment practices to meet those standards. As a first step the Commission should confer and establish liaison with the Equal Employment Opportunity Commission to apply EEOC guidelines to the federal government.

The administrative process, in terms of high quality and speed of resolution, should make court actions less necessary. By creatively using the powers which it presently holds and by adopting its program to EEOC guidelines, the Commission can do much to create an efficient and efficacious administrative remedy.

If the administrative process is to function adequately, employees must be represented adequately. The use of private and government attorneys to represent complaints should be encouraged, and the Commission should welcome proposals that provide such representation.

Not only with discrimination complaints but with rules and regulations dealing with all EEO programs, public access and participation is essential. Although present regulations allow interested private groups to file complaints and receive responses, employees', citizens', women's, and minority-group organizations do not have the access to information that is provided to the agencies through the Interagency Advisory Group (IAG). All plenary sessions of the IAG and all IAG committee meetings should be open to the public and complete transcripts of proceedings published. Members of the public and interested outside groups should be allowed participatory access in discussions of EEO policy (and other personnel policies) at IAG meetings and should be given a right to testify. This "advocacy gap" alone does much to ensure that Commission regulations are not as exacting or Commission enforcement policies as rigorous as they would be if citizen groups were able to participate fully.

Open IAG meetings are just one small, progressive step toward making the Civil Service Commission truly accountable and its actions reviewable so that Congress, interested private groups, and the President can evaluate with confidence how well the Commission is accomplishing its various missions.

This book cannot convey adequately the courage and frustration of thousands of federal employees and the organizations that represent them. Groups representing blacks, Chicanos, and women have struggled for years, often without publicity or notice. It is time now that their voices be heard. The Commission and the public have an unredeemed obligation to these groups to give them the access and the coverage they deserve.

Congress has a special responsibility to oversee the Commission's programs. It can, for example, have an immediate impact on policies concerning the collection and reporting of statistics. The Labor Committees of the House and the Senate should particularly examine the responses and statistics of the Commission and the reporting systems that gave rise to them. Additional and more specific changes in the Equal Employment Opportunity Act of 1972 may seem advisable.

Any member of Congress can request that the General Accounting Office undertake a study (as it did on the employment of disadvantaged persons within the federal government) of any area of the Commission's stewardship of the federal Equal Employment Opportunity program. If the Commission does not write a new script, it may well find one written for it.

6

The Bargaining Game

The bureaucracy is defective in imagination and somewhat wanting in sympathy.

SENATOR PAUL DOUGLAS

Federal inspectors hold some of America's most thankless and difficult jobs. Standing for long hours in the heat, noise, and odor of a processing plant, meat and poultry inspectors help to protect the consumer from contaminated products. Mine inspectors, construction inspectors, and ICC inspectors are often exposed to hazardous or unpleasant conditions. Combined with the physical hardships is industry pressure encouraging inspectors to compromise their responsibilities.

The Civil Service Commission's inspectors seem more ordinary. Often nattily attired, armed with the Federal Personnel Manual, Commission inspectors face less strenuous conditions. Drinking coffee and chatting with agency officials about personnel management, classification groups, and organizational guidelines, sensory deprivation seems their greatest occupational hazard. Yet these bland guardians of bureaucracy may be the most important of all federal inspectors, for they affect the performance of every federal agency and department.

The Bureau of Personnel Management Evaluation (formerly the Bureau of Inspections)[1] is responsible for examining the overall performance of an agency or department, its management and personnel techniques, its administration of Commission programs (EEO, appellate, federal safety, incentive awards, merit promotion, labor-management relations), and its performance in exercising delegated authority in such personnel areas as classification of employees.

To this end, the Bureau conducts, for a federal department or agency, a nationwide review, consisting of inspection of its national headquarters and of a limited number of regional, or field, installations.[2]

Questionnaires are sent to supervisors and employees; interviews are held with managers, personnel officers, supervisors, employees, and union representatives; the personnel records of the agency are examined. At each field installation, a "closeout" meeting in which all information is gone over is held between installation officials and Commission inspectors. Written reports are then prepared on each installation and, from these reports and on the inspection of the headquarters office, a final report is written summarizing the findings.

In some instances, after a nationwide review has been completed, follow-up inspections of selected installations may be conducted to determine compliance with recommendations.

In addition to these nationwide inspections, the Bureau also conducts special investigations in response to congressional inquiries, adverse publicity, or employee complaints, or to review the performance of specific Commission programs, such as labor-management relations and the Federal Women's Program.

The New/Old Game

If the decentralization to which the Commission is more and more committed is to be controlled, the only hope rests with a strong inspection system, yet the Commission has begun to decentralize the inspection function itself. On October 9, 1969, with the advice of the Commission, President Nixon issued a memorandum to the heads of all executive departments and agencies requiring that officials establish inspection programs within their organizations.[3]

The genesis of these recent changes shows the prominent role of federal agencies in forming Commission policy. Many of the ideas leading to the new direction of the inspection program were developed at a May 1968 Personnel Directors' Conference, called by the Commission, and then elaborated on by a committee of the Interagency Advisory Group (IAG 266), in which fifteen agencies were asked to participate in October 1969.

Commission officials see the new approach to inspection as an examination of the total management picture—a recognition that personnel management is affected by the decisions of managers as well as the decisions of personnel officers. By teaching agencies how to inspect themselves, the Commission hopes to increase the effectiveness of inspections. Eventually the Commission will perform only a quality-control function, assessing the effectiveness of agency self-inspection, helping the agencies establish their programs, and freeing manpower for better oversight. The new Commission approach assumes, however, that its interest and those of agency officials in sound agency management are identical. But when one considers that the Commission is supposed to represent the interests of employees and the interests of the public, one questions whether they are indeed the same.

Fair treatment of employees may frequently be consistent with "sound management." Yet in some instances sound management may seem to be disciplining employees who threaten to expose agency failures, or maintaining the status quo through the judicious use of incentive awards and rigged promotions, or preserving the system even if it means continuing discrimination. To officials of the Department of Agriculture it may be "sound management" to reduce industry pressure by transferring aggressive meat and poultry inspectors. To some officials, it may be sound management not to apply regulations against themselves.

The Commission believes that its greatest impact is through consultation and persuasion, and that a policeman's role is to be avoided. Although it consistently has defined regulation quite narrowly, exercising control only in those areas where it has the power to withdraw delegated authority, the Commission still has been reluctant to regulate with strength. Its apparent desire is to become a management consulting firm, and to rid itself entirely of regulatory activities.

The danger of the new direction is that it would reduce substantially the effectiveness of Commission inspections, and, if inspections are ineffective, there will be little if any control over agency policies. Just how the Commission's effectiveness can be reduced can be seen in already existing agreements with the armed services.[4]

Since 1962, the Civil Service Commission has had inspection agreements with the Army, the Air Force, and the Navy regarding those civilian employees who are covered by civil service regulations. Plans for scheduling inspections are made with the cooperation of the service, as are the content and coverage of the inspection. Generally, the Commission must "limit its inspection of installations" between nationwide inspections. The Commission is not to inspect for a period of one year, for example, an installation inspected by the army or air force. Thus, by self-inspection of a troublesome installation, Commission scrutiny can be avoided. The navy agreement limits Commission inspections if the navy "plans" to inspect an installation within six months, and states further that if the Commission inspection discloses serious negative findings, a regional director of the Commission may ask the navy to provide a follow-up survey before taking remedial action.[5]

In judging the objectivity of armed services self-evaluations, the Commission might want to review systematically installations that the armed service has recently evaluated, and yet it is precisely this practice which is limited by the inspection agreements.

While the Commission has asked the armed services to agree to observe certain criteria in conducting personnel investigations, the repeated violation of these standards indicates a lack of effective oversight. No periodic reviews are conducted by the Division of Adjudication and Appraisal of the Bureau of Personnel Investigations, and no periodic reports are required from the armed services.

The risks of accommodation inherent in the Commission's philosophy of inspection and in the organization of the Bureau of Personnel Management Evaluation becomes clear after examining how inspections are conducted, beginning with the way in which an inspection is planned.

The most complicated planning goes into a nationwide inspection, which covers an agency's headquarters as well as a number of its field installations. Planning determines the scope of the inspection, the installations to be inspected, and the program areas to be given particular emphasis. The nature and character of the nationwide inspection is largely predetermined through the planning process.

Preparation of the plan begins in the central office of the Commission, which contacts its bureaus for suggestions of areas and problems to be covered.[6] Only occasionally does it appear that these internal contacts within the Commission are coordinated. In some areas, an operating bureau and, in fact, the leadership of the Commission may have interests that directly conflict with the needs of a thorough inspection. (In examining EEO, for example, the Commission is concerned with its own image, since it administers the program.)[7] The Commission also consults with the agency to be inspected.

In many instances, agency requests for coverage of a program at specific installations may be the sincere recognition of problems; in other instances, these requests may be an attempt to misdirect Commission inspections. The ability of the agencies to define the issues through day-by-day contacts with the Commission and through specific contacts in the planning of inspections limits the direction and scope of Commission inspections. Little contact for the purpose of planning is made with minority groups, the Congress, the General Accounting Office, or the public. Contact routinely occurs with the Office of Management and Budget, "to determine the extent and nature of coverage which each are interested in." Because of its control of the appropriations process, the OMB serves as the President's enforcement agency and helps ensure that inspections conform to the administration's needs of the moment.

After a proposed nationwide inspection plan is drafted by the central office, the plan is sent for comment and possible revision to regional offices of the Commission whose employees do previsitation and on-site planning with the field installation of the agency.

The constant bargaining process that exists between the Commission and the agencies can limit even the selection of installations by the regional office. One regional office had planned to look at one installation, whereupon the agency complained to the survey director in Washington, who directed that another be substituted.

Thus the organizational structure of the Bureau of Personnel Management increases the risks that the effects of inspections will be vitiated. Survey directors, who have broad responsibilities for planning inspections and drafting the final inspection reports and recommendations, and inspectors are assigned permanently to the same agencies. This close association reinforces tendencies and encourages cronyism in the same way that service too long and too friendly at the same plant has caused misbehavior and accommodation by some meat and poultry inspectors.[8]

The danger of this system is well illustrated by an inspection conducted at the Philadelphia Naval Shipyard by the Philadelphia Regional Office of the Commission in 1969. Of 111 removal actions, the Commission examined only two. When questioned, the inspector in the Philadelphia Regional Office replied that he did not inspect some of the areas because he knew the personnel men at the shipyard and knew that they ran a good installation.

Inspection begins with notice to the installation that an inspection is planned. Although some Bureau employees and, at one time, Commissioner Andolsek believed that the Commission should visit installations unannounced, the "catch them with their pants down" philosophy is not favored. Gilbert Schulkind, director of the Bureau at the time of the study, said that these tactics set the wrong tone and that, while an agency might be able to hide one or two particularly egregious files, even with advance notice it would be unable to conceal much from experienced inspectors. He feels that advance notice helps by allowing the agency to gather and provide statistics, thus reducing the time which the inspection team must spend at the installation.

Agencies are required to notify employees where and how to contact the inspection team. (In some agencies, management seems to have been less than diligent. During one inspection the inspection team found a large number of undelivered employee notices.) But the Bureau's attitude is quite relaxed—"word gets out," said Schulkind.

Even when employees do receive notice it may be difficult for them to meet with Commission inspectors. Employees may be required to sign up for Commission interviews at an installation's personnel office, stating why they want to meet with Commission inspectors, or Commission inspectors may be assigned offices next to the installation's personnel office, or agency personnel may answer the phone and take messages for the inspectors.[9]

Failing to Respond

To help determine opinions and feelings, the Commission sends anonymous questionnaires to randomly selected employees. It has discontinued sending questionnaires to supervisors as well.[10]

According to Eckhart J. Muessig, director of program evaluation of the Bureau, these questionnaries are the real indicators of the attitudes of employees; frequently a common grievance indicates trends to be examined. Agency heads, he pointed out, would find it difficult to express such opinions for their employees.

Recently the Commission adopted a new employee questionnaire that can be computer-coded. Several questions contained in the old questionnaires have been deleted, among them questions concerning treatment of women and racial minorities.[11]

The average time allowed by a Commission inspector to review each eleven-page questionnaire is five minutes. Alvin Norcross, deputy director of the Bureau, indicated that questionnaires were not heavily relied upon and that other methods, such as interviews with union representatives and with employees, were a better way for an inspector to get a feeling for trends.

Commission inspectors interview management personnel, personnel specialists, supervisory personnel, employee representatives, and employees (either chosen by the agency or because they have asked for appointments). The interviews are limited to uncovering trends, since Commission inspectors are unable to provide any individual relief for employees. (Nathan Wolkomir, President of the National Federation of Federal Employees, feels that many employees are not aware of this fact and that Commission inspectors offer false hope.)

Many union officials are cynical about the fruitfulness of interviews with employee representatives as a tool in the

Commission's evaluation of labor-management relations. Hardly surprising; at a series of inspection conferences the Commission's policy toward labor-management relations in inspections was stated:

> In our inspections we must avoid becoming a third party in possible disputes or problems between management and the union. We must tread the line carefully, for example, between (1) determining whether management is carrying out its responsibilities under the Executive Order and under its agreement with the union, and (2) being "used" by the union in its cause against management when there are avenues provided in the system which the union should use.

Employee interviews last three-quarters of an hour on the average. (The time may be less, since the time reports on which these figures are based frequently include group interviews, in which several employees are seen during an interview.) Interviews with management officials, personnel staff, and supervisors are more extensive: supervisory employees received an average of 72 minutes per interview; management officials received an average of 139 minutes per interview.[12]

Part of each inspection is devoted to the examination and evaluation of personnel actions, including appointments, transfers, reassignments, promotions, suspensions, reductions in force, retirements, performance ratings, and removals and separations. This review is accomplished primarily by analyzing personnel folders. Since the Commission may not visit an installation for a number of years and perhaps may never have visited it, it is important that enough cases in each category of personnel action be evaluated in order to understand the performance of the agency and that these cases receive a thorough examination. Yet in some inspections, the Commission inspectors were devoting only four to ten minutes apiece to review only a few personnel actions. When examples of cursory inspection were raised with Bureau officials, it was explained that the

Bureau could always get patterns through other means. If the Bureau were indeed looking for systematic problems, it surely would be worth scrutinizing why violations were being found. It appears, however, that the Bureau's cursory review is continued when patterns of violations are discovered.[13]

The Bureau limits its review of personnel actions to those taken within a year prior to the inspection. Since many installations have not been inspected for several years, and perhaps may never have been inspected, the one-year limitation, particularly in cases where violations are found, prevents the Bureau from developing long-term trends. Personnel folders concerning adverse actions, removals, and separations* are removed thirty days after the completion of the action to a storage facility in St. Louis, Missouri. The Commission does not contact former employees as a part of its review. The Bureau feels that this is acceptable since the cases may have had a review before the BAR.[14] Yet the BAR is neither able nor willing to analyze the cases to evaluate the functioning of an agency's appeals system. Nor is it charged with doing so. An employee concerned with the performance of the appeals system is told by the BAR that the Bureau must evaluate the system. The employee is then told by the Bureau that it examines so few dismissal actions because employees have the opportunity to take their cases to the BAR.

If an inspection team finds violations in a personnel action or in a classification action, it does not inform the affected employee or former employee. (Schulkind explained this policy by noting that many violations—presumably in the classification area—were not in the employee's favor, and that in those cases favorable to the employee the agency must "adjust" the problem. But since the employee is not

*Adverse action, removal, and separation have different meanings. An adverse action may be a removal, but it may also be a suspension for a period of more than thirty days. A separation may occur because of a disability or other causes, yet not be a removal.

informed, even if adequate follow-up is possible, the standard by which a satisfactory "adjustment" is judged is provided by the agency and the Commission.)

In sum, the review of personnel actions has become a pro forma process.

Inspectors' attitudes are crucially important—a sloppy or timid review will produce a sloppy or timid report. Yet internal Commission guidelines to inspectors stipulate: "The on site action phase is that period of time when the inspection team is a *guest of the agency* being inspected. It is that period when each inspector, as the *Commission's representative,* is *on display* and *subject to scrutiny by officials and employees of the agency.* As the Commission's representative, each inspector's conduct should be above reproach and should reflect favorably upon the inspector and the Commission. [emphasis added]

This directive is illustrative of pervasive attitudes that affect the inspector. His ideal attitude becomes clearer when one considers another injunction of the Commission: "As controversial matters appear, efforts should be made to resolve them prior to the closeout."

In some instances, agency personnel and Commission inspectors have even divided the areas to be reviewed. And one Commission inspector said, "We don't follow each other around." Agency inspectors occasionally have reviewed personnel actions. Turning areas of the inspection over to agency representatives not only means that the agency is judging itself by its own standards, but it means also that in the final Commission report, the agency will be reading its own recommendations. The Commission does not convince the agency; the Commission is convinced, on the basis of agency-collected data, that agency recommendations are sound. The proper roles of the agency and the Commission are nearly reversed.

Before an inspection team leaves an installation, it conducts a closeout session with agency officials to inform them of the findings and to discuss recommendations. Under the "new" direction of the Commission, inspectors are encouraged to motivate changes in personnel policies by having the agency respond on the spot to Commission recommendations.

The head of the agency or the director of the installation, however, decides who attends the closeout; employees and union representatives do not attend. Thus, if the managers and personnel officials agree with Commission recommendations, the Commission is quite correct in assuming these recommendations will be implemented. And as long as the suggestions do not threaten positions, endanger favored practice, or violate personal or institutional predilections, the Commission may be successful. The Commission is left with cooperation because it has excluded controversy or meaningful change.

The work product of the Bureau is the inspection report, a record of the findings of the inspection team, and presumably a useful tool to "motivate" changes in agency policy. But reports ordinarily are not released until seven months after installation inspections have been completed. (It is not unusual for reports to be released after a year, and some reports have been delayed for two years.) Delay reduces the impact of a report.[15]

This delay has been attributed to the complexity and detail required in report drafting—as one Bureau official expressed it, "We're not assembly line workers; we are building a Rolls Royce." But surely some of the delay may be the result of the review process. Bureau staff, survey directors, the Bureau director, and the Commission executive staff all play a part in the review. And perhaps this review costs more than time. Extensive consultation between the team leader and the survey director ensures that the draft report reaches the survey director pretty much as he wants it. Reports and recommendations may be altered, according to inspectors, principally in (1) the sequence in which the information is presented; (2) the tone of the report (the Commission is sensitive to an accusatory tone and tries to use dispassionate language); (3) grammar; (4) format—or ensuring that certain items stand out.

Regions have been encouraged to send draft copies of inspection reports to the agency for comment. Considering the Commission's philosophy of cooperation, a failure of the agency to agree with a finding may confront the inspector with an embarrassing choice.

Commission directives state: "As a result of agency review [of the inspection report], specific critical findings and recommendations can be moderated in the report by including the agency commitments or stated plans for taking action. In this way, the report details a record of action to improve personnel management, rather than a record of inadequacies."

Particularly damaging information is carefully evaluated in the central office of the Commission. Commission instructions state:

> Comments are sometimes submitted as attachments to Form 784 (transmittal of Inspection Report) which the regional office may want to keep in house . . . for example, because the information may have been divulged under restricting conditions and is not intended for discussion between the Bureau and agency headquarters. Accordingly, to avoid *possible embarassment to a regional office or injury to agency/CSC relationship,* each submittal as an attachment to form 784 should be clearly labeled in capital letters, "NOT TO BE DISCUSSED WITH AGENCY HEADQUARTERS" or "FOR DISCUSSION WITH AGENCY HEADQUARTERS."[16] [emphasis added]

Gilbert Schulkind was asked if the procedures outlined for the BPME memo meant that the public must rely on the assurances of the Commission that the findings are adequately resolved and that politics do not intervene. "Yes," he responded, "that's right."

The Never-shown Hand

One obstacle to a thorough evaluation of the Bureau's performance is the Commission's refusal to allow the public to examine its work product—the inspection reports.[17] Without such examination evaluation of the Commission's work is difficult.

In some instances there may be a particularly compelling ethical obligation to publicize inspection findings. If an inspection should find that the enforcement of a health and safety law, such as the Coal Mine Health and Safety Act, was impeded by negligent or improper use of personnel, there should be a duty to bring these matters to the attention of the public and of Congress.

The publication of inspection reports could increase the Commission's ability to gather information. As practices were publicized, more employees and managers would contact the Commission. Publication could provide an effective means of causing problems to surface.

Because of the need for public accountability and review of this important function, the author filed in August 1972 suit in federal court under the Freedom of Information Act. On August 20, 1973 the U.S. Court of Appeals for the District of Columbia, in establishing new guidelines for such cases, ordered the Civil Service Commission to present a detailed justification of its refusal to provide the information. Ronald Plesser, the attorney in the case, called the decision "one of the two or three most important decisions interpreting the Freedom of Information Act." The petition of the government for Supreme Court review of the case was denied. The case is now pending in the District Court awaiting Commission justification of its refusal.

The Commission report issued to the FTC in 1965 found that personnel management was not making a full contribution to the agency mission; the Nader Report examining the Federal Trade Commission, released in 1969, found employees wandering through the halls not understanding what they were to do. The Commission report suggested changes in workload partly because managers had expressed the fear of running out of work, and it suggested that "surplus" project attorneys, used for planning, be reclassified downward or retrained because they did not perform trial work; the Nader Report found great deficiencies in planning, and documented the fact that many trial attorneys were handling small cases of little benefit to consumers.

Had the Commission published its report, the finding would have been subject to scrutiny and criticism. Publication would have shown, for example, that some findings were based on inadequate investigation. (Commission inspectors found no evidence of discrimination in the treatment of employees despite a long-standing situation in the Bureau of Deceptive Practices stenographic pool that had, for years, been causing a turnover of qualified black women, who left for better job opportunities.)

The possibility that the Commission is protecting itself from scrutiny is suggested by a warning found on the first page of inspection reports: "Agencies may not release Commission evaluation reports or excerpts from reports to the public. Any question regarding the propriety of the release of information in this report should be discussed with the Central Office of the Commission." So the agencies, whose sensitivities and reputations the Commission wishes to protect, cannot themselves make the report public.

Any citizen may see action plans,[18] eagerly distributed by Commission officials. Evaluations of the results, however, are unavailable under any circumstances.

Examination of excerpts from the Commission's inspection reports of EEO programs in the Federal Maritime Commission and in the Department of Labor suggests why the Commission so zealously guards its reports.

The report on the Federal Maritime Commission included the following findings:

Agency's commitment to the spirit and intent of the Executive Order is inhibited by the absence of a well-coordinated leadership.

Lack of coordination of EEO leadership detracts from the effectiveness of EEO efforts and contributes to lack of understanding of program intent and objectives among supervisors and employees.

Director of EEO has not kept up with recent changes in EEO area.

Counselors are trained and aware of their responsibilities but have little contact with EEO officials.

Director of EEO relies too heavily on personnel office for program leadership.

Women's coordinator not aware of program intent and objectives.

No effort made to establish contacts with minority community and schools to create awareness of agency's manpower needs.

The recommendations of the report in response to the above findings were somewhat pale:

Assure that EEO counselors, women's coordinator, and director of EEO work together to assess the status of the program and evaluate its goals and objectives.

Assure that women's coordinator is brought into program and made aware of her responsibilities and commitments under the action plan.

Establish contacts with minority community and schools to ensure manpower input from such areas at all levels.

No mention is made of any enforcement or follow-up plans by the Commission. No date is set by which time BPME will expect compliance with any of its recommendations. No reference is made to any previous evaluation reports (if any) for assessing compliance with previous recommendations. No proposal is made, in spite of the lack of leadership found, for a power of review and veto over future employment and promotion actions until the Maritime Commission has improved its program.

The Maritime Commission EEO report also included another finding: "Upward mobility efforts have been ill-planned due to a lack of a formal job structure and training program. . . ." To remedy this problem the report recommends to management that its future efforts in Upward Mobility be "accomplished within a framework of advancement opportunity for all employees—with special reference to EEO Action Plan Item 3A—full utilization of present skills." Once again, there is no mention of any BPME plans of enforcement or follow-up on this recommendation.

The EEO section of the evaluation report on the Department of Labor reveals some interesting facts about that department's action-plan program:[19]

> Certain key managers and supervisors have not seen any significant personal role for them to play in the Department's EEO efforts, particularly in field offices. In our judgment *this situation has been aggravated by a general absence of action plans throughout the Department.* [emphasis added]
>
> Initial efforts by headquarters operating Administrations and Offices to develop an action plan were generally weak in three vital areas. The plans were not sufficiently specific in stating: (1) what would be done; (2) who would do it; and (3) when it would be done.
>
> Absence of an overall Departmental EEO action plan weakened the Department's efforts to give leadership. We understand the Department has now developed such a plan. [Does this mean that perhaps the evaluators did not even see the plan since they only "understand" that one exists?]

Some field offices have few minority members in professional jobs. The following material comes from a Department of Labor inspection report:

> In the New York Region, Wage and Hour Division, five out of eighty-six investigators were minority members.

In the Boston Region, Wage and Hour Division, one out of fifty-four investigators was a minority member.

In the Birmingham Region, Wage and Hour Division, one out ninety-nine investigators was a minority member.

In those instances, a contributing factor has been crash recruiting, which made effective use of minority candidate sources more difficult.

Although the Department has made substantial progress in the employment of women, with women holding a wide variety of professional jobs at all grade levels, there are still opportunities to make further progress.

Of the headquarters employees responding to questionnaires, 19 percent indicated a belief that women receive fewer employment opportunities. This belief was repeated by a number of women employees we interviewed, who pointed out that the department's record on employment of women appears to be weak in certain offices, occupations, or in some instances in the higher grades or in supervisory jobs.

Certain statistics tend to support the feelings of these employees:

While women received 331 of 576 promotions in Manpower Administration in 1969, they received 3 out of 43 promotions to supervisory positions.

In Wage and Hour Division in 1970, women received 49 of 337 promotions made by the time of our headquarters review, and 1 of 7 promotions to supervisory positions.

In the most numerous occupational group (Investigators) in Wage and Hour Division, women held 62 out of 1,105 positions.

The Department of Labor's EEO evaluation report ended with the following ten recommendations:

1. The Department should concentrate its efforts on identifying and responding to remaining problem areas in its attempts to provide equal employment opportunity for minority members and women.

2. A particular effort should be made to recruit minority

members for personnel specialist and other administrative jobs.

3. To secure more positive response, supervisors and managers need to be clearly informed that theirs is an active rather than a passive role in efforts to equalize employment opportunity.

4. The Department should analyze the supply of minority students available in its primary professional occupations (e.g., economist), and take steps calculated to help increase the supply where needs exceed the existing supply.

5. Negro recruiters should be used for recruiting at Negro colleges.

6. The "Project Insight" awareness training should be thoroughly evaluated before offering it on a wider basis.

7. The Department should develop for itself, and should assist its Administrations and Offices in developing, an EEO action plan which is specific in terms of (a) what will be done, (b) who is responsible for doing it, and (c) when each item will be done.

8. The Department should insist on comprehensive feedback on EEO problems and activities from field to headquarters so that responsive program direction can be given, and so that top management can be adequately informed.

9. Lists of EEO counselors and outside EEO contacts should be updated and republished, and this should be done periodically to keep them current.

10. The Department should revitalize its efforts to employ the handicapped by giving strong central leadership and by closely reviewing the efforts made by its administration and Offices.

As with the Maritime Commission report, there is no indication of action on the part of the BPME.

What happens to the recommendations—the action plan drafted for the agency? For one thing, the agency reports its own progress in writing or in "informal" agency contracts that may consist of a phone call or a visit by an inspection officer. The Commission sometimes follows up inspections through actual on-site reinspections to determine compliance with Commission requirements, but the Federal Personnel Manual enjoins Commission inspectors from making such reviews to consider whether or not the agency is planning some type of follow-up review of its own.

In some regional offices follow-up reviews are conducted by agencies that have an established internal evaluation program. If the new direction of Commission inspections is successful, most agencies will have this capacity.

Inadequate follow-up can nullify an adequate inspection report, and follow-up has sometimes been disappointing. When the findings of the Regional Office were submitted to the Chicago Payments Center of the Social Security Administration in June 1971, the Commission told the agency that inspectors would follow up with a visit to the center within six months. As of the end of February 1972, the Commission's pledge of "We shall return" had not been redeemed.

In some instances, the Commission has not adequately followed up serious regulatory violations indicating systematic problems. During an inspection of the Philadelphia Payment Center of the Social Security Administration in January 1971, union representatives reported nineteen promotional actions not in conformance with the merit promotion plan. In all but one, inspectors concurred,[20] and in examining twenty-three additional promotions the Commission found three to be improper. In March 1971, the Commission submitted its findings, requirements, and recommendations to the Philadelphia Payment Center. The Commission stressed that serious violations of regulations had occurred, requiring not only corrective action in individual cases but also solution of more pervasive management and personnel problems; it was concerned particularly that employee faith in the merit promotion program could be seriously shaken.

The response of the payments center would hardly have

restored that faith. The center said that it was seeking advice and assured the Commission that things would change. They later informed the Commission that corrective action had been taken, but noted that in their own reexamination of promotion rosters, it appeared that many wrongfully promoted employees would have qualified for promotion anyway. On the basis that similar actions would no longer be taken, the Commission decided to let the wrongful promotion actions stand. No verification was required; no follow-up on-site inspection was conducted.[21]

Even these minimal follow-up reviews are being replaced by Planned Assistance Visits (PAVs) that stress informal contact and a consultative role for the Commission. Short visits during which the inspectors need ask little more than "How are things going?" can be counted as a PAV.

Special inquiries—on-site inspections of the performance of specific installations in implementing public policy programs—have given way to special studies, conducted about four times a year, in which a particular program such as EEO is examined in a number of agencies. A letter to all personnel directors from Bernard Rosen, referring to a special study of the merit promotion system, indicates the Commission's attitude: "The Commission is not evaluating the merit promotion program at any agency or agency installation; rather we are attempting to capture a nationwide overview of progress toward the goals of quality staffing and employee equity in this important aspect of federal personnel management."

The Bureau's performance in inspections creates for the Commission a self-fulfilling prophecy. Its inspection policies and practices restrict its access to adverse information about the performance of the federal service. By so structuring its access, by limiting information, and by ignoring the contradictory facts that do emerge, the Commission reinforces its assessment of a smoothly functioning federal service, thus justifying its management orientation and cooperative approach. The failures of the Bureau of Inspections deprive the Commission of the objective details and balance it so badly needs.

7

Merit and The System

> Behind my arrest and today's interrogation, there is a great organization at work. . . . And the significance of the great organization, gentlemen? It consists in this, that innocent persons are accused of guilt and senseless proceedings are put in motion against them, mostly without effect, it is true, as in my own case.
>
> FRANZ KAFKA, *The Trial*

When Dwight D. Eisenhower became President after twenty years of Democratic administration, a number of jobs deemed to be of a confidential or policy-determining nature were exempted from the testing and qualification requirements of the Civil Service's merit system. Nearly twenty pages of the Code of Federal Regulations list these Schedule C exempt jobs.[1] This listing is known around Washington as the "plum book."

In 1971 1,445 positions were listed in Schedule C and 553 more positions were listed as noncareer executive assignments, representing .0618 of 1 percent of the total federal employment. The 553 noncareer assignment positions, however, represent about 11 percent of the 4,855 jobs at GS-16, -17, and -18. (A new proposal of the Nixon administration, called the Federal Executive Service plan, would fill up to 25 percent at GS-16 and above with noncareer employees.)[2]

Political consideration in hiring is tolerated because each party realizes that it may one day be the party returning to power, but permissible limits tend to expand.

The nature of testing and qualification requirements for higher grades enables political or personal influence to be effective, for at many high-level positions, there are no written examinations. Rather, examinations amount to questionnaires listing education and experience. Points are given for different types of experience and a qualification score is established.

While standards are used in determining how particular experience must be scored, the agency may draft flexible qualifications. It may ask for selective certification or name certification. Selective certification is based upon the agency assertion that the position requires particular experience. Thus it is possible to tailor a job to fit the individual. (Said one personnel officer, "Let me work on the SF 171 [the position qualifications form] and let me advise the applicant on completing the SF 51 [personal history form] and I can qualify an orangutan for any job.")

Name certification means that in the view of the agency the position requires the unique talents of only one person. Although name selection is rarely used, it most often figures in cases of political pressure. At times, name requests are quite prevalent. In 1969, for example, over 60 percent of those appointed competitively to technical and professional positions in the Office of the Director of the Manpower Administration of the Department of Labor were certified by name requests. When requested names were temporarily unavailable in some instances, better-qualified candidates were passed over until the desired candidate could be reached.

Although politics brings unqualified persons distinguished only for their party loyalty into the civil service, a far more dangerous practice is the requirement of political orthodoxy for a qualified applicant, for to test political orthodoxy is merely to adapt the spoils system to the increasing complexity of governmental operations.

Harry Flemming, while personnel adviser to President

Nixon, indicated that the hallmark of the administration's appointment policy was concern about political loyalty,[3] but, "We're politically sophisticated, balanced, of course, by the search for competence." Whether such an emphasis can be confined to high-level political appointees is questionable.

In December 1970, Flemming advised on hiring consultants (theoretically hired for their expertise), "All persons you intend to employ in consultant capacities must be first submitted to this office for clearance. This clearance must be accompanied by a written justification for his being hired."

Political influence has remained a potent source of interference with the career service because the apparent safeguards against abuse are wholly inadequate. Reassignments, reorganizations, and other management techniques can be as effective as outright denial of employment on the basis of political affiliation.

The Indentured Bureaucracy

The Secretary of Agriculture leaves to become a vice-president of Ralston-Purina, one of America's large corporate farmers; the new Secretary of Agriculture comes from the Board of Ralston-Purina. Interstate Commerce commissioners leave to become employees of transportation conglomerates and vice versa. Regular exchanges of personnel occur not only among high-level employees, but among middle-level (GS 13-15) employees as well. The employee of Housing and Urban Development responsible for the regulation of interstate land sales leaves his position to join a large interstate land sale company.

In 1971, there were 1,101 former military officers, with the rank of major or lieutenant commander or above, and former civilian employees who were GS-13 and above, working for defense contractors, and 232 former employees of or consultants to defense contractors were working for the Department of Defense at salaries equal to or above the minimum GS-13 salary.[4]

The corporate-governmental interchange of personnel exists in every agency in which government substantially affects the interests of corporate giants. So pervasive has this interchange of personnel become, that an extension of it has been institutionalized. By Executive Order 11451, President Johnson established the President's Commission on Personnel Interchange, one of the stated objectives of which is to foster a better understanding, relationship, and cooperative action between business and government, by exchanging high-talented/high-potential executives for one- to two-year periods. Its $162,000 budget for 1972 is part of the appropriation to the Civil Service Commission's office. In 1970, nineteen industry executives joined the government while twelve government employees joined industry. In 1971, twenty-four corporate executives assumed government posts while eight federal employees joined corporations. The government pays the salaries of the corporate executives working for it and corporations pay the salaries of the federal employees working for them. Since more corporate executives have moved to temporary government posts than have federal employees moved to corporate posts, the federal government, in addition to the $162,000 paid for operating expenses, has paid about $460,000 in additional salaries.[5]

Despite the recommendation of the President's Advisory Panel on Personnel Interchange that the Commission "should take steps to ensure that the opportunity to participate in this program be open to business organizations of varying sizes and locations throughout the country," the list of corporate participants in the program reads like the Fortune 500.[6]

The President's Advisory Panel also stressed: "It is particularly important that the benefits of this program be made available to promising young men and women from minority groups. If applications of promising executives from minority groups are not received through normal applications process, then special efforts should be made by the Commission to recruit them. Access to this program must be open to every kind of business and every segment of our population."

According to Neil A. Stein, deputy director of the President's Commission on Personnel Interchange, in 1970 there were two black participants in the program, one from government and one from industry, and no female participants.

The President's Advisory Panel examined the potential effect of several conflict-of-interest statutes on the program and reported, "The Panel is convinced that the program can avoid potential conflicts of interest by careful and sensitive assignment process and that it will in no way prejudice the opportunities of the many able young men and women who are building a career within the civil service." Several pages of the Panel's report discussed how corporate executives could maintain their stock-option plans while working for the government.

Placements of participants are worth noting. (For a list of participants and their assignments see Appendix F). An engineering manager of Humble Oil and Refining Company is placed as a petroleum engineer in the Environmental Protection Agency; a senior staff supply analyst of Humble is placed as a staff assistant, office of Assistant Secretary for International Affairs in the U.S. Treasury Department; and a strategic systems project officer of the Department of the Navy is placed as a planning manager of the Westinghouse Electric Corporation.

The benefits to industry are clear, as is the increased encroachment of private interest on government. An employee need not even represent his company in a hearing after he returns in order to be extremely valuable. He may merely provide information about current operations of the agency in which he is working. His knowledge of the agency and the contacts made while there will themselves be valuable. If he is in an advisory role, his perspectives concerning large corporations, consumer protection, or the feasibility of regulations will have made his service worthwhile. In actuality, the government is providing a number of large corporations with valuable experience.

While interchanges of corporate and governmental personnel take place and while a conscious politicization of the civil service occurs, the civil service system focuses upon the loyalty and security of future employees. America's astronauts are perhaps the most famous citizens investigated by the U.S. Civil Service Commission. As one Commission official commented, "It's not just by chance they are all-American boys or their wives are good looking. We run a background investigation on each man and on his wife. You don't want a guy up there as a hero whose wife is calling him a bum." However, the Commission's investigative program extends far beyond a concern for the stability or public relations value of spacemen.

Few functions of the Civil Service Commission have created more public concern and elicited more criticism than its investigations of the loyalty and suitability for employment of federal employees that are conducted by the Bureau of Personnel Investigation.

Although the Commission's investigative function dates from the 1883 Civil Service Act, it did not become heavily involved in loyalty and security matters until 1942, when it issued War Service Regulations that provided for the denial of examination or appointment on the sole basis of questionable loyalty. President Truman's March 1947 Loyalty Order established the Loyalty Review Board and responsibility for appeals taken from agency actions concerning the loyalty of employees. Hearings held before the Loyalty Review Board in the Civil Service Commission were not open, and charged employees were denied the right to confront and cross-examine witnesses.

In April 1953, President Eisenhower issued Executive Order 10450 (Security Order), which made the appointment of all new civil servants subject to investigation and established the standards by which federal employees could be removed on the basis of suitability.

> (a) Dismissal from employment for delinquency or misconduct; (b) Criminal, infamous, dishonest, immoral, or notoriously disgraceful conduct; (c) Intentional false statements or deception or fraud in examination or appointment; (d) Refusal to submit testimony as required by S5.3 of this chapter; (e) Habitual use of intoxicating beverages to excess; (f) Reasonable doubt as to the loyalty of the person involved to the Government of the United States; or (g) Any legal or other disqualification which makes the individual unfit for service.

These standards are broadly drawn and subject to interpretation, initially by the Commission, which has been particularly rigorous in its application of the standard concerning immoral conduct. Unmarried women have been dismissed from the federal service for having spent a single weekend with a male acquaintance, and the Commission's concern with private sexual conduct has been particularly intense when homosexuality is involved.[7]

The type of investigation performed depends on the nature of the position for which the employee is applying. Investigations may be made in the area of loyalty, suitability, and security, and positions requiring security clearance are classified critical sensitive, noncritical sensitive, and nonsensitive.[8]

The Commission generally conducts suitability investigations in the competitive service, and the employing agencies conduct them in the excepted service.[9] The most common investigation is the National Agency Checks and Inquiry, made as a matter of course on applicants for employment, and, when requested, on present employees. (Government records are checked and, when needed, written inquiries are made about the individual's loyalty, character, associations, experience, and arrest record by contacting former employers, colleges attended, law enforcement agencies and references supplied by the applicant.[10]

If the National Agency Check shows adverse information, the Bureau investigates further to obtain details and if reasonable doubt about loyalty develops through further derogatory information, the case is referred to the FBI.

If the Commission decides that the individual is not suitable, it will recommend against hiring, or require that the agency remove the employee. Rights of notification and appeal are provided.[11] If the Commission okays the individual, the file is referred to the agency, which may then make a separate determination.

Full field investigations are mandatory for all critical sensitive positions and may be requested by the agency for noncritical sensitive positions.[12] They may also be made as part of the preappointment selection process.

A full field investigation covers the background ties of an individual, with emphasis on the last fifteen years and concentration especially on the last five, and includes (1) a National Agency Check; (2) personal interviews with present and former employers, supervisors, fellow workers, and references; (3) a check of police, credit (when practical and justified), and other pertinent records as, for example, FBI field office and military service records. Coverage varies depending upon the needs of a particular agency.

The commission also conducts "Administration of the Merit System" investigations concerned with the suitability or fitness of individuals with criminal records, bad employment records, fraudulent statements, or alleged fraud or collusion in examinations.

For top executive, administrative, procurement, and personnel positions and for high-level professional, scientific, and technical jobs that involve substantial administrative responsibility, the Commission conducts qualifications investigations. According to the Commission, these investigations provide necessary information on previous job performance that cannot adequately be determined by written tests or appraisals of experience statements.

The Bureau of Personnel Investigations is one of the most client-oriented bureaus of the Commission, probably because its investigative services are paid for by the agencies at a rate of $650 for each full field investigation.[13]

"We're working for another agency," one investigator said. Even the Bureau's checking up on its own investigators is designed primarily to ensure that agencies receive what they pay for. As the Chief of the Division of Reimbursable Investigations said, "Our customers are accepting what the investigator says about the witnesses' testimony. . . . We are policing the investigator to see that he does not do a sloppy job."

Looking at full field investigations as a service provided to the agency at as low a cost as possible creates tension between economy and the protection of those investigated. Decisions about how many people to interview or how thoroughly to review derogatory information are made within a system that stresses economical service to a client. The investigator's daily report forms ask only for a time accounting on each activity.

The Division of Adjudication and Appraisal within the Bureau of Personnel Investigation has the responsibility for appraising the operation of the internal-security programs of federal agencies. Despite the requirement that all programs be appraised, the resources devoted to the appraisal function are small and safeguards are few. Thus abuses proliferate. A senate report found:

An eighteen-year-old college sophomore who applied for a summer job as a secretary in a federal department was asked questions about the boy she was dating that included: Did he abuse you? Did he do anything unnatural with you? You didn't get pregnant, did you? There's kissing, petting and intercourse, and after that did he force you to do anything to him, or did he do anything to you? (Senate Report #92-873, May 15, 1970, p. 21.)

The *Congressional Record* of June 13, 1968, reported that an applicant for a position as an operating engineer in the General Services Administration was questioned extensively not about his loyalty to the United States, but about his sexual habits and practices. Invasion of privacy is not limited to job applicants. Supervisors in the Department of Health, Education and Welfare were told to report employees who took part in moratorium or antiwar demonstrations.

The Making of the Commission Investigator (and His Judgments)

Kimbell Johnson, director of the Bureau of Personnel Investigations, until 1973, was proud of his staff, which was well trained and highly qualified and notably low in female or minority-group members. In February 1971, three of the eighty-nine investigators above GS-10 were black, one a GS-13. (Johnson feels the Bureau's poor showing in EEO is not from a lack of effort. According to him, qualified blacks are in such demand that it is difficult to hire or retain them. A further possibility was suggested by an investigator who noted that blacks face resentment in black areas and discrimination in white residential areas. Women, Johnson explains, are underrepresented because investigation is not appropriate work for a woman.)

He described the typical investigator as a generalist with high verbal abilities who scored at the top of the Federal Service Entrance Examinations.[14] Each applicant has been subjected to an intensive investigation and interview before a panel of three men—one from the Bureau, one from the personnel office, and one from another Commission bureau.

The Bureau's training program for investigators begins with a week of orientation in Washington and is followed by about a week in the field with an experienced investigator. The trainee is then given selected interviews to conduct, and after two weeks the experienced investigator determines whether or not the trainee is able to begin independent investigations. For two months every final investigative report of the trainee is reviewed; after six months, 10 percent of his final reports are reviewed.

Complaints against investigators can be filed by agencies or by the public, but although Mr. Johnson reported that any complaint is investigated within twenty-four hours, there is no record of how many complaints are received or of any disciplinary action. The few described by Johnson involved complaints about fabricated reports and false time reports. Johnson did tell of one investigator receiving a written reprimand for asking an improper question.

Once a year each investigator's performance is reviewed—a supervisor reinterviews some persons interviewed by the investigator. More than one case is usually reviewed since, as a supervisor said, "Everyone can have a bad day. If you hit one unfavorable comment you give him a break."

The investigator, whose opinion has a strong effect on the decision of a case, has wide discretion. Since he is limited in time and resources,[15] some selection of sources is necessary. He decides when a witness is competent and who should be interviewed. He must also decide when not to interview and when he has interviewed enough people.

When comments are based upon prejudice or bigotry, the investigator is to let the testimony speak for itself: with overt statements, such as, "She is immoral like all Wasps," the investigator need only record the statement verbatim. But, when the statement is less explicit, as when a middle-class white describes a lower-class white by saying "He associates with a pretty rough bunch of people," the investigator must recognize the possible prejudice and pursue the question.

Was a young white woman in a small Southern city a hussy inviting blacks and whites to attend a loud pot-smoking party as her older neighbors portrayed her, or might she just have had a few friends in for a quiet evening of television? The investigator must not only decide whether to pursue the matter with additional questions, he must also determine whether or not to get the other side of the story. Should he check with the local police to see if complaints were received? Does he interview the officers who answered the call? A simple decision to let the matter rest would be justified: the story appears reasonable, no overt discriminatory statements were made, and the story was corroborated by other neighbors.[16] Yet such a decision could leave an unfair picture of the individual.

Rather than serving as a portable tape recorder who is "just interested in the facts, ma'am," the investigator is bombarded by opinion and confronted continually with questions requiring the exercise of discretion—a discretion complicated by racial, ethnic, age, and class differences. The near absence of female and minority-group investigators means that the bureau is deprived of investigators especially sensitive to these groups.

The discretion of the investigator is influenced by his background and training and by the perspectives and priorities of the Bureau. If the information uncovered is reasonable and corroborated, the duty to the agency will be met. The investigator's discretion is exercised against a background that stresses efficiency and reasonable cost. What would be the response of the agencies and of the Bureau to an investigator who consistently extended his investigation for a day or two to check derogatory information?

The Commission's instructional material on avoiding unwarranted invasions of privacy is vague. One instruction prohibits inquiries about race, religion, or political affiliation and then lists several exceptions including "directly relates to security fitness or subversive activities." To many investigators exactly what political affiliation or political expressions relate to subversive activities are unclear. Does membership in the Peace and Freedom party justify inquiry?

If an investigator feels that a credit bureau check is appropriate, does he record only the credit information, or does he also record information on religious affiliation and housekeeping habits that many credit bureaus maintain? Commission directives admonish the investigator searching credit bureau files to

> be alert to obtain all information pertinent to the investigation. This may include information regarding such matters as employment, unemployment, reputation, marital status, residence, and paying habits. Some credit bureaus maintain clipping services and any noteworthy publicity is recorded by them. Some check police and civil court records regularly and include pertinent information in the subject's credit record. In some cases applications for credit and financial statements prepared by the subject are available through credit bureaus. These bureaus often have information available resulting from investigations they have made of applicants for credit or for other reasons.

Commission procedures also allow the use of confidential informants, whose names cannot be divulged to the subject. The most outrageous charges may be made by a person never known to the subject and to whom the subject never has a right to respond. How does the investigator determine the soundness of confidential informants?[17]

Commission instructions also invite investigators to look to private groups and private citizens for information, including the files of groups who may have particular ideological predilections. The type and number of such organizations to which an investigator may turn is left vague and undefined.

Ritchey P. Williams, chief of the Bureau of Reimbursable Investigations, claims that constant review of full field investigations puts a check on improper questioning. He indicated that it is possible to tell, for example, if leading questions have been asked by examining a witness' testimony. A response such as "Yes, as far as I know J. J. had no child out of wedlock," would indicate that a leading question had been asked. He neglected to add that an investigator can easily hide leading questions by recording the conversation as if the information had been volunteered.

To see what can happen, we append a report on President Nixon as it might have been written by the Civil Service Commission. Sections inapplicable to the report, such as search of police records, have been omitted.

REPORT ON RICHARD MILHOUS NIXON

Record searches and review of the public record indicated subject's involvement with the COMMUNIST PARTY OF THE UNITED STATES.[18] Specifically, despite subject's reputation as an anti-Communist, subject was intimately involved with Communist leaders in the early 1950s, once being photographed on property belonging to Whittaker Chambers, an individual identified as associated with the Communist Party by the House Un-American Activities Committee.[19] In 1950 subject visited the Soviet Union where he was engaged in private conversations with ranking Red officials.[20] In 1969 and 1970 subject sent associates to confer with Communist leaders of North Vietnam. Subject has visited Communist Rumania, Red China, and the Soviet Union, meeting with top Communist leaders. According to public records, subject was accused in 1972 by Robert Welch, founder of the John Birch Society, of being part of a Communist conspiracy. In the same year, the Young Americans for Freedom charged subject with leftist influence.

During a visit of subject to South America in 1958 anti-American riots broke out. In 1970 subject crossed state lines and spoke in San Jose, California. After his speech a rock-throwing disturbance occurred.

Despite application, subject was not hired as an agent for the Federal Bureau of Investigation. Subject's parents were members of a religious sect, segments of which have reportedly advocated the violation of federal laws.[21]

It is reported that in 1960 subject appeared before a large audience with a noticeable growth of beard. Subject had reportedly used openly such profanity as "F--- the ABA."[22] During law school and while in the Navy, subject is reported to have been involved in gambling.[23]

In 1952 subject's immediate supervisor is reported to have considered dropping subject due to personal financial involvement. Only last-minute pleas saved subject's job. In 1961 subject left his job after failing to obtain a promotion. In 1962 subject was refused another position in the same field. Subject has frequently changed jobs. Subject applied twice for his present position before being accepted. In his present position subject has been reported leaving his office to go bowling. Subject has reportedly used the office phone to make long-distance telephone calls inquiring about football games.

Subject's selection and management of subordinates has been questioned and subject reportedly has little contact with subordinates concerning matters of great sensitivity. Subject has placed hidden microphones in his office.

While holding the position of vice-president of a large enterprise, subject is reported to have bought his wife no more than a cloth coat and only warm woolen mittens as a Christmas gift for his two children.[24]

The Commission performs, in actuality, a central distribution role in an information and intelligence network that spreads throughout the government and into the Congress. But questions have been raised about the reliability of its sources.

The files of the House Internal Security Committee contain 740,000 file cards. In an August 13, 1971, interview,

Marty Michaelson, a staff aide to Congressman Robert Drinan, who is a member of the Committee, described the nature of the card files: "The value of the files as investigative leads is doubtful. They contain a mass of clippings which primarily serve to establish guilt by association."

Local police whose records are tapped by the Commission often monitor activities of those involved in the legitimate exercise of political rights. In New Jersey, for example, local police maintained a file on citizens involved in the antiwar movement. In Washington, D.C., police photographed for their files teachers peacefully demonstrating at city hall against a reduction in personnel and conditions in the schools.

The Bureau maintains three types of files. The Security Investigations file, which has been centralized in Washington since 1948, is used to furnish "leads" and possible sources of information regarding loyalty matters. The file contains approximately 2,500,000 index cards containing information relating to Communist and other subversive activities. According to the Commission this information has been developed from published hearings of congressional committees, public investigative bodies, reports of investigations, publications of subversive activities, and various other newspapers and periodicals. Kimbell Johnson refers to the file as a type of newspaper morgue. Among the periodicals clipped are *Ramparts, Progressive Labor,* the *New York Times,* and the *Congressional Record.* See Appendix E for a list provided by the Bureau.

The Security Investigations Index file consists of approximately 10,000,000 records showing the date of initiation and the location of personnel investigations in the federal service since 1939. According to the Commission, "It is a fruitful source of referral of cases to [the] FBI for full field loyalty investigation."

The Bureau also retains investigative reports of all full field investigations.[25] According to Kimbell Johnson, about

25,000 investigations are added each year to the approximately 1,000,000 in hand.

If the validity of the information is questionable, so is its use. Before an employee is removed from the federal service on suitability grounds, he must be confronted with information and given an opportunity to respond,[26] but considering the lack of specificity of many charges, the lack of a formalized hearing procedure, and the inability to confront and cross-examine accusers, this requirement of confrontation is a rather less effective protection than the Bureau believes it to be. And when the question is not whether the act was committed, but whether it constitutes immoral conduct, the confrontation requirement is no protection at all.

Unlike a removal, no reason is necessary when an agency decides not to appoint an individual or when it decides that a position is not going to be filled. In both removal or decision not to hire, the agency is able, in effect, to use the Commission's information without being monitored by the Commission.

Chairman Hampton has insisted that "the Commission and other executive agencies [do not] maintain a blacklist which names individuals rated unfit for appointment on the basis of unevaluated items of information clipped from newspapers or drawn from other sources." The use of such file information prior to selection of employees, however, means that selection can be made on the basis of political predilections. According to a statement in the *Congressional Record* of February 3, 1970 by Senator Sam Ervin, the Department of Health, Education and Welfare used its computerized files to blacklist scientists.

Hampton claims that "files of a similar nature are used frequently by business to determine a credit rating," but if the report of a credit-reporting agency is used as the basis of denying private industry employment, a citizen, under the Fair Credit Reporting Act, has a right to be informed and a right to have explained to him the information in his file to ensure that it is accurate and current. Applicants for federal jobs and civil servants do not have this protection.

Investigative programs are intended basically to be predictive systems and they should be analyzed according to their cost and benefits. With no empirical data to evaluate their predictive value, their benefits are difficult to judge.

Their monetary costs are somewhat easier to establish. The estimated cost of the Commission's own investigative program for 1971 was $3,733,900, not including the $1,647,000 paid by the agencies to the Commission on a reimbursable basis, the costs of several departments which perform investigative functions delegated by the Commission, or the cost of the agencies' own internal-security programs and investigations.

There are, however, other costs, The people who are excluded from employment on the basis of faulty information or of faulty standards are one cost. And as the government comes to employ more and more people, potential exclusion of employees because of involvement in "controversial" activities has an increasingly chilling effect upon the expression of dissent.

8

Toward A New Civil Service

> We will revere and obey the law and do our best to incite a like respect and reverence in others; we will strive unceasingly to quicken the public's sense of civic duty; and thus in all these ways, we may transmit this city, greater, better, and more beautiful than it was transmitted to us.
>
> THE ATHENIAN PLEDGE

The Civil Service Act of 1883 held out the promise of ending the spoils system, but by concerning itself only with the selection of qualified persons, it failed to recognize the impact of other aspects of the system. Present civil service policies are a patchwork of laws, rules, and regulations developed since 1883.

Although the responsibility for the failure to incline the individual employee to perform his duty is not entirely attributable to the Commission, it must bear a significant portion. It has adopted for itself a role concerned with detail and mired in procedure. When mounting red tape forced it to abandon much of that role, it forsook any responsibility for the type of behavior exhibited by employees within the civil service. Moved by inertia and expediency, it came to identify with the agencies it was to regulate by adopting a consultative and passive role. In carrying out this role it has concentrated on technique rather than change. With no vision of its own, it has adopted the vision of others.

In many ways the civil service and the Civil Service Commission have been a unique experiment in the control of large organizations—an experiment which appears to have failed. Large organizations have developed the ability to manipulate and desensitize individuals and to separate them from meaningful participation in political and economic decisions, leaving the dictates of the organization as the sole determinants of behavior. Although the Commission cannot accomplish a change in the federal environment by itself, it is in a unique position to begin to grapple with the problems of institutional lawlessness. The Commission's handling of the appeals function indicates its unfortunate failure to seek this role.

If the Commission can be faulted for not climbing the mountain, it can also be censured for not staying on the plain. The Commission's own internal operations and its response to political encroachments upon the civil service and the rights of employees have prevented it from being effective even within the increasingly narrow scope it has defined for itself. It is fair to say that unless there are changes in the Commission's perspectives and vision, its behavior will continue to contribute to the perpetuation of a new spoils system.

Some critics call for the abolition of the Civil Service Commission, but it would be far better for citizens to call for the creation of a true Civil Service Commission instead. A restructured and revitalized Commission, capable of creating a new environment in the federal service, is possible, and the recommendations made throughout this report show how the Commission can improve its programs. The pressures of Congress, citizens, employees, and public-interest groups can do much, but the Commission first must be responsive to external suggestions.[1]

To begin with, adjudication of employee appeals should be removed from the Commission and placed in a separate agency. When the Commission first developed the Board of Appeals and Review, it envisioned an independent adjudicatory body, but that independence has not come to pass. The Commission remains closely tied to the executive and principally performs a service function for other governmental agencies. The Commission lacks both the independence and the will to serve as an adjudicatory body that often must come into conflict with the management of executive agencies.

The purpose of an adjudicatory agency would be not only to protect employees but to protect the public as well. As an adjudicatory body and as an agency with the power to issue regulations, it could properly be called "The Employee Rights and Accountability Board." One of the first tasks of the Board would be to attempt to define, on a case-by-case basis, acceptable employee behavior more precisely.

The Board would address the problems of accountability in large organizations. Since public officials can arrogantly ignore the laws they undertook with their oaths of office to enforce, meaningful accountability must come from outside. Under the aegis of this Board, civil service employees would be punished for failure to enforce the law. Precedents are available.[2]

Existing statutes provide not only for removal of officials who fail to enforce the law, but for fining officials who perform their public duties improperly. For example, a Washington state statute provides for fines of $200 to $1,000 for each illegal exemption granted by a property-tax assessor. The Board would be authorized to receive and act upon citizen complaints in recognition that citizens intended to be protected by legislation should have the means to ensure that such protection is real.

In effect, the Board's concern would be with the complex problem of controlling the discretion of administrators in the enforcement of legislation. When an employee is given a duty to act under statute (or accepts with his job an internal delegation of authority to carry out a portion of that duty), no discretion is involved. Officials of the Department of Interior who failed to ensure adequate mine inspections, failed to perform the duties assigned to them by Congress. When duties are more broadly stated, however, such as the responsibility of establishing reasonable standards, discretion begins to be involved, although officials are always under an obligation to act and to act reasonably.

A public servant may be given the discretion to act or not to act, and he may choose to act but do so in a negligent or improper manner, as in the Food and Drug Administration's failure to release the names of five models of potentially hazardous toys until December 22, 1972 when most of the Christmas shopping season had passed; or an official given discretion to act or not may refuse to act even though the facts compel a reasonable person to action. Discretion is not intended as license. Congress has both the authority and responsibility to establish a system that controls administrative discretion.

The principal sanction available to Congress is its appropriation power. The power of the purse, however, is not always an effective tool in changing administrative behavior, since reductions in appropriations can rarely be tied to the behavior of specific individuals.

But an Employee Rights and Accountability Board could ensure that an official's failure to fulfill his duty to the public could affect his personal well-being, had it available the varied sanctions of the civil service—reprimands, letters of warning, suspensions, and removals. To these might be added fines and behaviorial sanctions, such as additional training, or a visit to the mines or factories in which safety standards are to be applied or a week spent at a children's hospital to see the victims of burns from unsafe fabrics.[3] As the Board gained experience, a set of highly differentiated sanctions could be developed in controlling official behavior.

The first requisite of the Employee Rights and Accountability Board would be independence. To this end it would not be subject to review by the Office of Management and Budget. Periodic and detailed review of its performance by Congress would accompany lengthy terms for its Commissioners.

Employees as well as citizens would be given access to the complaint process. Employees are in a particularly advantageous position to provide information about incompetence or dishonesty occurring in the administration of public programs.

In a system where ethical whistle-blowers were protected, buck passing, in both directions, could come to an end. Thus, the meaningful imposition of personal responsibility would change the structure itself to give the administrator better access to information, and an administrator would have a positive incentive to seek out discouraging reports of program deficiencies. Such a change in structure would possibly be as great a benefit as the change in the type of individual that might be attracted to such a reinvigorated public service.

The Board should also have the power to conduct inspections of the personnel programs in federal agencies. Inspections would assure compliance with regulations and would also provide another source of complaints.

The Board would not be an ombudsman. It would not resolve individual problems of citizens confronting the bureaucracy. It would be concerned principally with the development and application of sanctions to change the perspectives and behavior of federal officials. The Board would in fact be a completion of fulfillment of the concept of a Civil Service Commission. It would not be a radical departure from the present theory of the civil service but simply update practices to respond to the development and spoilage of the regulatory state.

Why would the Board not follow the same path trod by the Civil Service Commission? How would the Board be immune from the counter-regulatory process? The answer is that the Board would provide no services for federal agencies, which would prevent the development of a client relationship. Nor would it be a functionary of the executive branch.

Service-oriented programs could be left in a revitalized Civil Service Commission, which could then serve as a true management consulting firm, reducing the need of federal agencies to rely heavily upon outside consultants.

The Board would simplify removal procedures by abolishing agency hearings on adverse actions and providing a single hearing before an examiner representing the Board. The Board would review decisions of appeals examiners, with employees having a right of appeal to a circuit court of appeals. Such simplified procedures would not only protect employees, but would also decrease delay and encourage an adjudication of cases on the merits.

The present system loses many talented employees who are repelled by its arbitrariness and impersonality. Rather than dissuading a potential employee, a new civil service would attract and keep the competent and the dedicated, who would see that they would be subject to discipline objectively applied, based on standards rationally related to public performance.

Citizens who are the victims of bureaucratic lawlessness should not wait for congressional action to restructure the civil service; rather they should make use of the legal tools presently available.

No significant body of law exists on the imposition of personal responsibility upon administrators. Obstacles to such responsibility seem to be developing. The doctrine of immunity from personal liability has been extended to lower-grade employees; the applications against individual employees of the Federal Tort Claims Act are limited; prosecutorial discretion of law enforcement officers is close to absolute.

Much of the common law dealing with the application

of sanctions against officials developed before extensive congressional delegation of power formed the basis of much administrative action. The law has relied upon the traditional remedies of mandamus and injunction, rather than seeking to fix personal responsibility as a means of affecting the behavior of administrators in the exercise of delegated power.

Mandamus and injunction have traditionally been available to compel or prevent only specifically prescribed or proscribed acts, concerning which goverment officials had no discretion.* While these remedies have been valuable in compelling official action, the limited category of actions to which they have been applicable has reduced their effectiveness.

A court order telling an official that he had not performed his duty can be a blow to prestige and to power. However, no penalty is imposed upon the individual. An administrator can refuse to fulfill even the clearest obligation of his office and face nothing more than the possibility that he may be required to act. Considering the limitations on the use of mandamus and injunction and the cost and length of citizen suits, even this possibility is remote.

However, there is a legal theory which offers some hope for citizens who attempt to impose personal responsibility on employees for their derelictions. This theory does nothing other than provide meaning to the often repeated slogan, "A Public Office Is a Public Trust." The New Jersey Supreme Court has stated the legal justification for the concept:

> The members of the board of chosen freeholders and of the bridge commission are public officers holding positions

*In the 1972 Consumer Safety Act, the Senate Commerce Committee had included a provision extending the traditional mandamus remedy to discretionary actions of an official in the agency to be established under the legislation. The provision was deleted from the Committee's final recommendations and was not included in the law. However the action of the Commerce Committee is an example of legislation providing citizens with new tools to control administrative behavior.

> of public trust. They stand in a fiduciary relationship to the people whom they have been elected or appointed to serve. ...As fiduciaries and the trustees of the public wealth they are under an inescapable obligation to serve the public with the highest fidelity. In discharging the duties of their office they are required to display such intelligence and skill as they are capable of, to be diligent and conscientious, to exercise their discretion not arbitrarily but reasonably, and above all to display good faith, honesty, and integrity.[4]

The fiduciary concept can apply to many categories of official behavior. For example, "that a public office is a public trust" is a realization of the relationship between the administration of public health and safety laws and citizens intended to be protected. The fiduciary stands in a relationship of trust and reliance and is under a special obligation—to act for the benefit of another. The fiduciary relationship was developed in the law to protect those who must deposit faith in another. The relationship is so zealously protected by the courts because without it commercial intercourse and activity requiring trust would be hindered. The relationship attaches because one of the parties cannot protect his or her own interests and must deliver the responsibility for part of his or her well-being into the hands of another.

Health and safety statutes normally contain, as part of the congressional findings, a statement that the laws are needed to protect the public and that the laws are passed for that purpose. The citizen is intended to be directly affected and by statute the responsibility for his well-being is placed in the hands of agency officials. There is also an active solicitation of trust emanating from the government. In pamphlets, speeches, and testimony, government officials are constantly assuring citizens that government agencies are protecting them from a number of hazards.

The official assumes the fiduciary relationship with the assumption of his office; he undertakes an obligation to act for the benefit of another. The laws and statutes he swears to uphold as a condition of his employment contain the health and safety laws which delegate to him the responsibility to act for the benefit of the citizens he is to protect. The statute and his oath of office and conditions of employment provide this element in the relationship. The relationship that he assumes is certainly as important as the doctor-patient relationship.

The official who is charged by law with the obligation of enforcing, implementing, or administering the law is the fiduciary. If he delegates all or part of this authority he cannot escape his obligation as a fiduciary. However, by assuming the delegation of authority, other employees are also under the obligation to act for the benefit of others, assuming for themselves the duties of fiduciaries. In cases of nonenforcement of the law, at least the original official would be guilty of a breach, although not necessarily all officials who have delegated responsibilities. An official could escape by showing he had acted properly to enforce the law.

The fiduciary concept evolved in private commerce, which stressed economic interests and financial interest. In areas of health and safety, the government has power to deal with matters that have no counterpart in the private sector.

In order to sue the government, citizens must be recognized by the courts to stand in a relationship with the government which gives them an interest in the matter they wish to litigate. Recent federal court cases granting citizens standing to sue have liberalized the relationship required.[5] By analogy, these cases indicate that the courts recognize the basic elements of a fiduciary relationship between citizens and public employees.

Whether a particular type of relationship were a fiduciary one would depend in part upon policy. The policies given in suits by government against its employees under a fiduciary theory are the need to have the government operate efficiently, the necessity of maintaining the trust and faith of citizens in their government, and the desire to maintain and improve the quality of government service. These policies are also present with a health and safety statute.

Public employees standing in a fiduciary relationship to the public would be less likely to be manipulated by concentrated private power. Much of the influence-peddling and cronyism, inimical to democratic processes, would be eliminated. In addition, a failure to enforce the laws will not only have a long-range effect on citizen confidence in government but also an immediate effect in injuries and death that could have been prevented or in lost income or lost opportunities.

Once this fiduciary duty was found to exist, breaches of it might be determined in a number of different ways. The statute itself could be examined to determine whether or not the official has carried out any specific statutory mandates. Examination might be made of official actions and regulations to see whether or not a diligent and good faith effort was made to enforce the law. Delay might be examined to determine whether or not the law was strictly enforced. What would constitute a breach of fiduciary duty would vary from case to case. The intensity of the fiduciary relationships may vary. A more intense relationship would require a less severe act to constitute a breach. Factors which might be considered in determining the intensity of the relationship are the strength of congressional findings concerning the seriousness of the health and safety hazards, the scope of the authority delegated by Congress to remedy the evil, the resources available to enforce the statute, and the time which the statute had been in operation.

The fiduciary principle was developed in common-law litigation on a case-by-case basis. The strength of the common law is its emphasis upon the establishment of principles through decisions in case after case. The fiduciary principle emerged from this process as a tested means of controlling behavior within a necessary relationship of trust. The application of this fiduciary principle through specific cases would allow the courts to adapt the principle to the facts of individual cases. Both consistency and flexibility are assured. The most appropriate common-law remedy for breach of fiduciary duty would be remittitur of salary. This remedy is preferable for several reasons. It would not be a personal recovery by the citizen but a remittitur to the government and the citizen's way of protecting the fiduciary relationship. It would be a self-calibrated remedy. Assuming some relationship between wage and responsibility, the sanction would expand as authority expanded.

Remittitur of salary can be apportioned according to the amount of time involved in a breach of duty and the number of duties attached to a position that are mishandled or neglected. Apportionment need not be made if the violation of duty was such an integral part of the responsibilities of the office that it fairly could be said that the official was not entitled to any compensation.

Alan Morrison, the Director of Public Citizen Litigation, has recently used this theory in seeking the remittitur of 5 percent of the salaries of the Commissioners of the Civil Aeronautics Board for failure to perform their public duties. The case is now before the District of Columbia Court of Appeals.

Precedent exists for applying fiduciary principles to government employees in suits which hold that government employees owe a fiduciary duty to the government.[6] These suits are often referred to as "recapture suits." The standards of conduct that the courts have applied in these cases were derived from public policy, commercial law, and the standards of conduct enumerated in criminal conflict-of-interest statutes and the codes of employee conduct. The bulk of these standards rest directly or indirectly upon common-law fiduciary principles. Under these suits, the government need not prove actual damage. The breach of relationship itself is sufficient to give rise to a remedy.

The fiduciary concept is a flexible one that represents a well-developed body of law in which the courts have experience dealing with exercises of discretion. Armed with such a legal theory and a farsighted and imaginative judiciary, the citizen has a hope of making of "A public office is a public trust" more than a hollow phrase.

The fiduciary concept is also fertile ground for legislative action. In fact, in Committee Print Two, Section 113 of the Consumer Safety Act was based upon such a fiduciary principle. That section of the act read:

> 113(a) Employee as Fiduciary. Any person in the Agency who administers, enforces, or implements any portion of this Act is a fiduciary to any individual who might be personally injured or killed by any consumer product which presents an unreasonable risk of injury and, as a fiduciary, is obligated to prevent such injury or death by prohibiting the exposure of individuals to consumer products presenting unreasonable risk of injury or death.

The section provided a civil action for breach of fiduciary duty:

> If the court finds that any person or persons in the Agency have breached their fiduciary duty by any act or omission or by any series of acts or omissions the section provides that the court (1) shall order performance or cessation of performance, as appropriate; (2) may temporarily suspend any person or persons without pay from the Agency for a period not exceeding three months; (3) may remove an individual or individuals from the Agency; or (4) may take any other appropriate action against any person or persons in the Agency who have breached the fiduciary relationship.

That section would have enabled the court to deal with administrative dereliction in a context other than traditional mandamus. The section also would have provided the courts with a number of flexible remedies to affect the behavior of civil servants. An item of highest priority for citizens and consumer groups should be the inclusion of a similar provision in other statutes.

As a result of strong protests from the Nixon administration, this section was dropped from the Consumer Safety Act. According to Joseph Young in his *Washington Evening Star* column, "The Federal Spotlight," Chairman Hampton believed the provision would cause chaos in the government's career merit system. Chairman Hampton believed that the merit system could collapse if employees were denied the due process they received under adverse-action safeguards. Chairman Hampton might want to review those safeguards and the performance of the bar discussed earlier. Not without reason, employees might find the safeguards offered by a review in U.S. District Court superior to those offered by the BAR. Certainly consumers and citizens would be better protected by such a review.

In addition to administrative remedies, litigation, and new legislative approaches, citizens can undertake other projects. From every federal agency and local office of such agency, citizen groups should press for an annual statement of priorities. What does the agency consider to be its most important programs? Does the agency have the resources to carry out its programs? Has the agency's experience over the past year changed its evaluation of the programs or policies it should be pursuing?

Each year, every employee in the federal government is given a performance rating. Citizen groups could provide an evaluation of key agency officials. How well has the official run his local operation? How receptive to citizen groups has he been? What types of activities has he focused on? Has he been involved in activities that might constitute a conflict of interest? These evaluations might be sent to agency headquarters for consideration in an official's evaluation, or they might be publicized to give the public some indication of his performance.

Any relevant information may be sent to the Clearinghouse on Professional Responsibility (P.O. Box 486, Washington, D.C. 20005). The Clearinghouse was established to encourage citizen and employee responsibility and is directed by Peter J. Petkas. Only Mr. Petkas and Ralph Nader have access to the box. With the approval of the correspondent, the information is either referred to the agencies and other public interest groups, with a request for action, or is filed for future reference. Information that is not routine can and has formed the basis of immediate action whether by Mr. Petkas, by another staff member, or by Mr. Nader.

Complaints to agencies about employee performance, particularly concerning high-level officials, are often futile. The filing of citizen complaints, however, is not always a futile act—against some employees such complaints may be useful. Complaints should include a concise statement of facts, the nature of the complaint, and the desired action. When a significant agency program is affected by official dereliction, citizen complaints establish a record of agency knowledge of the situation. Copies should also be sent to the agency officials in charge of the program, the head of the agency, congressional committees and legislators who review the agency's operations, to other public interest groups, and to the press.

A review of state constitutions and state laws might reveal to citizen groups accountability provisions applicable to state administrative officials. Strategies similar to those employed at the federal level may also prove fruitful at the state and local levels.

Citizens should also realize that the protection of dedicated federal employees is particularly important. Inspectors, the consumer's cops on the beat, are particularly deserving of support and protection when their attempts to protect the public lead to retaliation or reprisal. Citizen groups can also provide potential employees with some understanding of the conditions they will face in an agency. When citizens find organized groups of employees attempting to improve the quality of public service, liaison and cooperation with such groups should be undertaken. A new coalition of those affected by bureaucratic lawlessness, both within and outside government, can do much to make the bureaucracy responsive to the legitimate interests of both groups.

Nor are employees without recourse. Not only through unions, but also through professional and scientific associations dedicated to protecting their members who adhere to professional ethics, employees can begin to change the performance of federal agencies. As individuals, employees should be alert to the nature of the system in which they serve and should understand the nature of responses they may face if a legitimate attempt to improve agency performance is begun.

Congress, citizens, and federal employees must begin to examine the assumptions and the results of the government's present personnel system. Only by so doing can these groups overcome the institutional lethargy that has enveloped this important area and begin the long and difficult task of creating a new civil service.

Appendix A

Recommendations for Changes in Adverse-Action and Appeals Systems

Personnel Recommendations

Recommendation 1: William Berzak, chairman of the Board of Appeals and Review, should be removed as chairman. The mismanagement of the Board, the lack of information, and the subterfuge in which Mr. Berzak indulged indicate that he should be replaced. The new chairman should be chosen from outside of the Commission and ideally would not have served as an agency personnel official.

Recommendation 2: The three members who are of retirement age of the remaining six members of the Board of Appeals and Review, excluding Mr. Berzak, may retire. As they leave, these members should be replaced from outside the Commission. The Commission has begun this process. Mr. Virgilio Roel and Mr. Cameron Smith from the Department of Housing and Urban Development and the Department of Agriculture have been added to the Board. The other members appointed should not be associated with the federal personnel establishment. Perhaps an outstanding member of the defense bar which handles civil service cases or a civil liberties attorney would be appropriate selections. As a minimum requirement, members of the Board of Appeals and Review should be attorneys.

Recommendation 3: The Commission should provide a new career pattern for BAR employees, for employees of the Appeals Examining Office, and for regional appeals examiners to reduce the development of attitudes similar to those of the operating agencies. It might be appropriate to begin a study of possible alternative careers with the plan proposed by Professor Egon Guttman in his report to the Commission.

Recommendation 4: The Commission should improve the training of appeals examiners and BAR examiners. For appeals examiners, a training manual and examiner's handbook should be prepared. As part of their training, examiners should be exposed on some formal basis, perhaps through seminars or discussion groups, to the attitudes of employee groups, employee unions, to civil liberties organizations (such as the American Civil Liberties Union), to minority-group organizations, to consumer organizations, and to public groups such as the National Civil Service League. Such training would also include a clearly stated concept of the burden of proof.

Recommendations Concerning Openness and Access to Information

Recommendation 5: In order to evaluate the appeals program, the BAR must maintain a number of statistics which it indicated were not available. Among these are: (1) the number of cases remanded for procedural errors which are reinstituted by the agency, and statistics on the disposition of such reinstituted actions; (2) statistics concerning the reasons for cancellation of appeals at each stage of the appeals process; (3) separation of categories between actions sustaining and actions overruling the agency action maintained from the initial appeal to the final decision by the BAR; (4) a determination of the percentage of cases appealed by the agencies to the BAR on procedural grounds and on the merits; (5) the nature of corrective action taken by the agency in adverse-action cases before a determination is made by the BAR; (6) the length of time each case has been pending in the agency, in the appeals offices, and in the BAR; (7) processing time for RIF appeals; and (8) a determination of the cases initially appealed which were canceled by employees and by agencies.

Recommendation 6: The BAR should assign within its own office full-time responsibility for the development and maintenance of a case index file, as suggested by Judge Washington.

Recommendation 7: The Commission should undertake a thorough and comprehensive study of the subsequent history of successful appellants, EEO complainants, and reinstated employees. Included in such a study should be a systematic review of coercion, reprisal, or retaliation which might have been taken against appellate witnesses or against agency employees.

Recommendation 8: The Commission should publish in some convenient form available to the public all BAR and Appeals Office decisions.

Recommendation 9: Even if the constitutional requirement of due process may require open hearings, the Commission should open its hearings to the public as an independent decision of its own.

Recommendation 10: Provision should be made for recording dissenting votes and publishing dissenting opinions in BAR decisions.

Recommendations Concerning Procedure

Recommendation 11: The Commission, except where an employee poses a significant physical threat to himself, fellow employees, or to the public, should provide for a hearing before adverse action is taken. Such a suggestion was made by Judge Washington and in the Pellerzi plan submitted to the Commission by a former General Counsel of the Commission. The Pellerzi report suggested: "Except in very special circumstances, no employee will be adversely affected until after the opportunity for a hearing and a decision by the agency head or his designee."

Recommendation 12: Transcription tapes of all Commission hearings should remain in the hands of an independent third party who may certify their accuracy.

Recommendation 13: The Commission should seek the power to subpoena witnesses in personnel hearings. The witnesses needed in an employee's defense may no longer be employees of the agency or agency employees reluctant to testify for a number of reasons.

Recommendation 14: The Commission should establish an expert advisory council consisting of independent professionals to aid in the determination of complex scientific or technical questions which might arise in an appeal.

Recommendation 15: The Board of Appeals and Review should

clarify its procedures. Among the actions which should be taken by the BAR are: (1) the development of a policy against which the granting of stays to an agency that were reversed at the first appeal level can be evaluated. Such stays should be granted only in unusual circumstances; (2) the Commission should grant to the BAR the authority to reduce the penalties in adverse-action cases; (3) the BAR should establish as its standard of review a review on the record. It should not act to substitute its judgment for the decision made by an Appeals Examining Office. The BAR should not leave the appellate record open. Provision could be made for the inclusion of new evidence by a specific remand for a hearing.

Recommendation 16: The Appeals Examining Office and the BAR should expand the review of personnel actions when an allegation of coercion, reprisal, or retaliation is made concerning the action itself or in connection with any witnesses or potential witnesses. Reprisal against a witness who had appeared should be considered within appellate scrutiny.

Recommendations Concerning Regulation Changes

Recommendation 17: The Commission should allow some review on the merits of the dismissals of probationary employees. This would reduce the absolute discretion which an agency exercises and might do much to reduce the numerous probationary appeals made on the basis of discrimination.

Recommendation 18: In reassignments and transfers, the Commission should consider whether the action has been taken in an attempt to circumvent the employee's appellate rights. If the employee establishes a prima facie case that such circumvention is occurring, the agency should have the burden of showing that this is not the motivation of the action.

Recommendation 19: The Commission should more clearly delineate the misuse and violation of personnel regulations for which agency officials will be disciplined and seek to make these regulations meaningful by their application.

Recommendations Concerning Structural Changes in the Appeals Systems

Recommendation 20: The BAR should report directly to the Commissioners.

Recommendation 21: The Appeals Examining Office should report directly to the BAR and be administratively responsible to the BAR.

Recommendation 22: The appeals examiners in each region should be empowered to make independent decisions without the concurrence of the regional director and should report directly to the BAR and be administratively responsible to the BAR.

Recommendations Concerning Agency and Commission Hearings

Recommendation 23: Employee appeals should be made directly to the Commission. There should be no agency hearings. The agency has an opportunity to review its actions through its supervisory personnel and through the personnel office. Only one hearing should be provided and that hearing should be provided by the Commission. This would simplify the appeals process and reduce the time and cost for both the agency and the employee. Since this recommendation would require increases in the number of appeals examiners and in the budget of the Commission, Recommendations 24, 25, and 26 suggest more immediate actions which can be taken.

Recommendation 24: No agency second-level appellate system should be approved by the Commission. Professor Guttman suggests that such second-level agency appeals which limit appeal rights to the Civil Service Commission are violations of the Veterans Preference Act.

Recommendation 25: Hearings at the Civil Service Commission after an agency hearing should be expanded in scope to allow a redetermination of matters decided in the agency hearing. The purpose of the agency hearing is to allow the agency to remedy its own mistakes. If this remedy has not occurred, the primary hearing should be the Commission hearing and the conduct and scope of the Commission's hearing should mirror this principal importance.

Recommendation 26: The agency head or his designee should be bound by the decision of the agency hearing unless it is contrary to law.

Recommendation 27: The Commission should exercise leadership and bring its hearings and agency hearings and appeals examiners under the Administrative Procedures Act. The courts are expanding the concept of due process in these hearings, gradually imposing upon them the requirements of the Administrative Procedures Act. Many Commission reforms have had the same impact. The Commission should assume leadership in this area and voluntarily apply APA requirements to its hearings.

Recommendations Which Have Been Accepted by the Commission

Recommendation 28: The Commission agreed to distribute novel and significant appeals decisions internally to regional appeals offices and the Appeals Examining Office.

Recommendation 29: The Commission agreed to review EEO complaint procedures to assure followthrough in cases where discrimination was found.

Appendix B

Reports on Adverse Actions and the Appeals Process

Recommendation [72-8] Adverse Actions Against Federal Employees Administrative Conference of the United States Adopted December 15, 1972

A critical part of the mission of the Administrative Conference is to study the processes of government to assure the full protection of the rights of private citizens, including the rights of federal employees. At the same time, the Conference is equally concerned about assisting government agencies to devise and implement efficient administrative procedures that will facilitate accomplishment of their varied programs.

The Civil Service Commission and other government agencies each year conduct a large number of formal personnel action proceedings that involve charges of personal misconduct, poor job performance, or other behavior which reflects adversely on the individual employee. Each year several thousand adverse personnel action appeals are decided throughout the government; the Civil Service Commission alone adjudicates well over 1,200 appeals annually. The nature of these cases and the size of the caseload make it imperative both that proceedings be conducted with scrupulous fairness, and that procedures be neither too costly nor time-consuming. While existing adverse-action procedures have attempted to meet these objectives, the Conference believes that implementation of this recommendation will yield substantial improvements in many highly significant respects.

This recommendation is intended to apply only to those classes of federal civilian employment currently entitled to adverse-action procedures, as identified in Subchapter S2 of Federal Personnel Manual Supplement 752-1.

A. Definitions and Standards

1. *Adverse Action.* In all cases in which an employing agency takes a personnel action adversely affecting an employee on the basis of his conduct or performance, the employee should be afforded an opportunity for an evidentiary hearing and his case should be decided on the basis of the record made at the hearing.

Such procedures are inappropriate, however, for use in situations in which an agency action made on the basis of broad managerial considerations of agency structure or resource allocation (e.g., change in job classification, reduction in force) has incidental adverse effects on certain agency employees. The Civil Service Commission should seek legislation redefining the category of "adverse action" to exclude therefrom personnel actions not based on the individual employee's conduct or performance. However, in any proceeding to effect a personnel action assertedly based on managerial considerations, the employee should retain the right to challenge the bona fides of the agency's action.

2. *Efficiency of the Service.* The Civil Service Commission should publish regulations or interpretive rules elaborating in as much detail as practicable the statutory standard of "efficiency of the service."

B. Procedures for Agency Hearings

1. All employing agencies should establish procedures for personally advising an employee who has received a letter of proposed adverse action about the consequences of the action proposed and the procedures available for contesting it, which should continue to include the right to respond to the employing agency's charges prior to an evidentiary hearing.

2. An employee against whom an adverse action is proposed should have an opportunity for a prompt evidentiary hearing be-

fore the action becomes effective. However, if the employing agency determines that retention of the employee in his current duty assignment will adversely affect the ability of his office or installation to perform its functions, the employing agency should be able, pending its final decision, (a) to reassign the employee; (b) to place the employee on administrative leave with pay; and (c) if, for a cause attributable to the employee, the hearing is not commenced within thirty days after the agency notifies him of its readiness to proceed or has not resulted in a final agency decision within sixty days after such notification, to place the employee on leave without pay.

3. Except in extremely rare cases where an employing agency can establish good cause for keeping the hearing closed, an employee subject to adverse action should have a right to elect a hearing that is open to the public. An employee is entitled to a private hearing, however, at which he may be accompanied by an observer of his choosing, in addition to any representative. This recommendation is not intended to limit the hearing officer's traditional authority to exclude other witnesses during the taking of testimony, or to maintain order and decorum.

4. The Civil Service Commission should assign the hearing officers to conduct hearings before employing agencies. A hearing officer should be suitably equipped by training and experience to conduct such personnel hearings, and, unless he is an administrative law judge, should not be an employee of the charging agency. Ordinarily, hearing officers should be drawn from a pool established and employed by the Civil Service Commission, but when appropriate the Commission should be able to assign as hearing officers other persons with the prescribed qualifications.

5. Civil Service Commission regulations should make clear that at any hearing the employing agency has both the burden of coming forward with evidence and the burden of persuasion.

6. The hearing officer should use a prehearing conference or other means to identify and limit the hearing to the trial of material issues of fact as to which the parties genuinely disagree. The hearing officer should also be authorized to resolve summarily those

material issues of fact as to which he is satisfied there is no genuine disagreement.

7. The hearing officer should be authorized to order an employing agency to produce witnesses in its employ or documentary evidence that he believes may be relevant to an employee's case. He should be free to call witnesses himself, to question witnesses for both parties, and to provide guidance to employees who are not represented. With the completion of the hearing, the evidentiary record should be considered closed for purposes of the employing agency's decision and any appeal by the employee to the Civil Service Commission.

8. The hearing officer should make factual findings and prepare a proposed decision, which would be submitted to the official designated by the employing agency to make the agency decision and made available to the parties along with the transcript of the hearing. The parties should have an opportunity (e.g., ten days) in which to submit written argument, including objections to the proposed decision, to the deciding agency official. If the deciding official does not accept the hearing officer's proposed decision, he should prepare a formal agency decision that, among other things, states specifically the reasons for rejecting the hearing officer's findings or recommended disposition. The employing agency should be able to make its personnel action fully effective upon the issuance of its decision, and any subsequent appeal should not have the effect of postponing such effectiveness unless the employing agency otherwise directs.

C. Procedures for Appeals from Agency Decisions

1. Employing-agency appeals systems, apart from that required by paragraph B(8) (i.e., a final agency decision following the hearing at a level higher than that proposing the action) should be abolished.

2. An employee against whom adverse action is taken should have an opportunity for a single appeal outside his agency, to a central appellate authority within the Civil Service Commission.

3. The Civil Service Commission's appellate authority should customarily be limited in its review to the record compiled at the employing agency. Upon the motion of an employee, however, the authority should be able to admit, or remand to the hearing officer for the admission of, evidence that the employee could not reasonably have produced at the original hearing, subject to the employing agency's right to respond or rebut.

4. The Commission's appellate authority should have authority to affirm, or to reverse, or to modify the employing agency's disciplinary action in any appeal.

5. The Commission's appellate authority should assign cases for decision by lot or by rotation so far as practicable, and permit announcement of dissenting and concurring views.

6. The Civil Service Commissioners should retain discretionary authority to reopen and decide exceptional cases upon the petition of either the employing agency or the employee.

7. Employing agency and Commission decisions in adverse action cases should be publicly available after minimum editing necessary to protect employee privacy.

D. Ex Parte Communications

1. (a) At no time should officials of the Civil Service Commission who participate in or are responsible for the disposition of employee appeals provide advice to either party or to the hearing officer on the initiation, processing, or disposition of any adverse action.

(b) Other Civil Service Commission officials should not advise or consult with either party, or their representatives, regarding the merits of any case that has been formalized by the issuance of a letter of proposed adverse action.

2. Hearing officers who conduct agency hearings and Civil Service Commission officials who participate in or are responsible for deciding employee appeals should be free from all ex parte influence or advice—including communications from employing

agencies, employee representatives, and other Commission employees—relating to the factual issues or appropriate disposition of any adverse action or appeal. Expert professional advice on the facts or disposition of a case (such as the evaluation of a job classification specialist) should only be received on the record, subject to the right of both parties to respond.

E. Role of the Civil Service Commission

With the additional safeguards of the independence of the Civil Service Commission's appellate authority, proposed under C and D, above, it is not necessary to establish a new, independent agency to adjudicate adverse action appeals.

F. Effect on Employee Grievance Procedures

The provisions of this recommendation are not intended to supplant or preclude provision for employee grievance procedures in existing or future collective bargaining agreements.

Proposed Changes in Adverse Action and Appeals Systems United States Civil Service Commission Bulletin [Bulletin No. 752-5, March 30, 1973]

Action date: April 16, 1973

1. An intensive review of the systems governing adverse actions and appeals has been underway in the Civil Service Commission. The viewpoints expressed by agencies, unions, and other interested groups in response to our request for suggestions at the outset of the study were most helpful. The purpose of this letter is to request comments and recommendations from the headquarters offices of departments and agencies on proposed changes and possible courses of action now under consideration. Comments are also being requested from unions, veterans organizations, and other interested groups.

2. Attachment 1 to this Bulletin discusses certain aspects of our systems review and sets forth the modifications being considered. As that attachment indicates, we envision changes in the design of the appellate system, in its operation, and in the internal structuring of the appellate function within the Civil Service Commission. For purposes of comparison, the existing appellate system is charted in attachment 2 and the proposed revised system in attachment 3.

3. Some modifications can be made administratively by action of the Civil Service Commission, or by revision of Executive order. Others would require legislation. Our plan is to consider concurrently the full range of possibilities for systems improvement, acting first on changes which can be effected by administrative action, followed by recommendations for revision in Executive order, where so indicated, and submitting a legislative proposal covering those remaining.

4. Comments and recommendations should be as specific as possible and, where feasible, should be supported by factual analysis or examples to ensure our full understanding and consideration of the points being made. In particular, our proposal

to delete agency appeals systems has budgetary implications for both the agencies and the Civil Service Commission. Therefore, in responding on this aspect, agencies are asked to indicate their estimate of the annual workload and costs which would be shifted from the agencies to the Commission. In providing these estimates, agencies should separately indicate any offsetting additional agency costs they can foresee from other aspects of these proposals, especially proposal 4.

5. To facilitate the submission of comments, the specific proposals being considered are listed individually and numbered in the attached summary. Comments may be forwarded directly to:

Raymond Jacobson, Director
Bureau of Policies and Standards
U.S. Civil Service Commission
Washington, D.C. 20415

6. Responses from headquarters offices only of departments and agencies are requested by April 16, 1973.

Bernard Rosen
Executive Director

Attachment 1

Review of Adverse Action and Appeals Systems... A Summary

BACKGROUND

Adverse action and appellate processes have been the focus of increasingly high interest, not only to employees and agencies throughout the federal service, but to the Congress, to labor and veterans' organizations, and to the courts. The Civil Service Commission identified the adverse action and appeals system as an area for major Commissionwide emphasis during fiscal year 1972 and a top-to-bottom systems review was launched in the second half of that year.

Separate and independent studies of the process were undertaken also by the Administrative Conference of the United States and the General Accounting Office. The Commission cooperated with those studies, sharing data and informational inputs with both agencies, and providing needed statistical, program, and technical material to them.

OBJECTIVES—DATA—APPROACH

The objectives which a soundly designed adverse action and appellate system should satisfy were expressed by the Civil Service Commission at the outset of its review as a system that produces fair and just results; that avoids needless delay and complexity; and that is accepted by—and merits the confidence of—federal managers, employees, and the public alike. The systems study proceeded with those basic objectives in mind, and a format to facilitate the organization of comments around the identified objectives was developed for use by agencies, labor and veterans' organizations, and other interested parties from whom comments were solicited. The responses received were consolidated and evaluated carefully as part of the review.

To gain additional perspective on the functioning of the appellates system in actual operation, information was obtained by a special survey of appeals decided by agencies and Commission appellate offices. Fiscal year 1970 was selected as the base period to assure that only cases which had completed the full appellate cycle would be included. From that information a computerized data base was established which provided a statistical picture of such elements as:

> The demographic characteristics of those who appeal . . . from what actions...taken for what reasons.
>
> The frequency of hearings . . . the extent to which appellants are represented . . . the nature of representation.
>
> The outcomes of appeals . . . time in process . . . further appeals.

The data not only provided more information on appeals than had previously been available, but, importantly, and for the first time, permitted analysis of how the various elements involved related to each other.

Within the Commission, a high-level work group of program managers and key staff officials with functional responsibilities bearing on adverse action appellate policy was established. Throughout the study there were frequent consultations with the work group and the Civil Service Commissioners convened in several meetings to provide overall policy guidance.

TOWARD A REVISED APPELLATE SYSTEM

The tentative system revisions and opportunities for improvement identified in the study resulted from careful consideration of points of view from many different sources and from extensive study and analysis. The proposals for change emanating from the review seek a system that provides a full and fair appellate procedure; that, at the same time, is more open and independent in its operation; and that avoids excessive layering and delay. Accomplishment of that result requires changes in the design of the appellate system, in its operation, and in the internal structuring of the appellate function within the Civil Service Commission.

Some of the modifications can be made administratively by action of the Civil Service Commission. Others would require revision by Executive order. A third category will require legislative action. The proposed changes being considered are grouped below under these headings.

SPECIFIC PROPOSALS

I. Proposed Changes by Administrative Action or Executive Order

A. *Changes in System Design*

1. All appeals will be made directly to the Civil Service Commission. This proposal assumes that Executive Order 10987 requiring each agency to establish an appellate system for reconsideration of adverse actions will be revised. If the Executive order is modified, agencies will no longer maintain their own adverse-action appellate systems. A possible exception is, however, contemplated. The legislative proposal being considered by the Commission (see proposal 13, below) would authorize the use of negotiated procedures, where agreed to by an agency and a recognized labor organization for review of an adverse action. If enacted, the proposals would permit an adversely affected employee to request review by his agency under the procedures negotiated between the agency and a union representing his unit, or the employee could appeal to the Civil Service Commission, but not both.
2. The number of appellate levels in the Civil Service Commission will be reduced. The initial appellate decision under a new, unified appellate structure will complete Civil Service Commission action on an appeal, with further review available only if stated conditions (as described in proposal 3, below) are met.

3. Further review within the Commission of an appellate decision may be requested by either party on showing that there is new and material evidence not previously available; that the previous decision involves an erroneous interpretation of law or regulation or a misapplication of policy; or that the previous decision is of a precedential nature with effects beyond the case at hand. Unless further review is granted under those standards, the initial appellate decision will stand as the Commission's final determination of an appeal. The Civil Service Commissioners (as distinguished from the appellate body) would retain discretionary authority to reopen and reconsider any previous decision they deem to involve policy considerations sufficient to warrant their personal review.
4. The Commission's instructions to agencies will be revised to require that a management official other than the person who initiated an adverse action must consider the employee's reply to the notice of proposed adverse action and concur in the decision if it is adverse to the employee. In other words, it will not be possible for the same manager to propose an adverse action, receive the employee's reply, and then issue the decision without the matter being considered by a responsible official at a higher level of authority. The intent of this new provision is to assure that judicious consideration is brought to bear on a possible adverse action while it is still in the proposal stage, and that no adverse decision be placed into effect until it is determined by the reviewing official that all pertinent facts and evidence, including the employee's reply, are in the record and have been considered. The reviewing official will have the responsibility of determining whether additional fact-finding, investigation, personal discussion with the employee concerned, or other steps to establish the full facts are necessary.

B. *Changes in System Operation*

5. The prohibition in the Commission's regulations against open hearings will be removed. A hearing will be open

to the public if the appellant requests that it be open. A hearing officer may for good cause close all or part of a hearing to the public, and an agency may request that a hearing be closed if national security considerations or other compelling reasons preclude public attendance.

6. The evidentiary record will be closed at the conclusion of the hearing and subsequent Commission review (except for new evidence not previously available) will be on that record.
7. The Commission's instructions will make clear that in the consideration of an appeal the burden of proof and of proceeding rests with the agency, not with the appellant. The provision is not intended to be an invitation to frivolous appeals, however, and the obligations on an appellant for setting forth the basis for his appeal are not changed.
8. The terms "furlough" and "reduction in rank" will be redefined in Commission regulations to accord more closely with the intent of the Veterans Preference Act. Long-term furloughs, i.e., of more than thirty days, now treated as reduction-in-force actions, would be henceforth regarded as adverse actions requiring advance notice, opportunity to reply, etc. Short-term furloughs would be reviewable under agency grievance procedures. The concept of rank will be redefined to equate rank with grade. This would mean that no reduction in rank will be judged to have occurred where there is no loss in grade or pay.

C. *Proposed Organizational and Operational Changes*

9. The organizational independence of the appellate function in the Civil Service Commission will be increased. Commission appellate offices, including the Appeals Examining Office in Washington, D.C., will be organizationally attached to a restructured central appeals authority in CSC headquarters. Appellate offices at field locations will no longer report to the Commission's Regional Directors, nor the Appeals Examining Office to the Executive Director. A number

of other administrative modifications to increase the independence of appellate operations within the Civil Service Commission will be made.

10. Authority will be delegated to Commission appellate offices to modify penalties where it is shown that the penalty imposed is not in accord with agency policy or agency practice in similar situations.
11. Significant decisions of Commission appellate offices will be published.
12. Commission policy will be clarified to make it clear that those Civil Service Commission officials who participate in, or who are responsible for, the determination of adverse action appeals will not advise an agency or an employee on the initiation or futherance of an appeal. The policy will also make it clear that agencies or appellants and their representatives should not request advice regarding the merits of a case from other Commission officials once an appeal has been lodged with the Civil Service Commission.

II. Legislative Proposals

13. Legislation will be recommended to authorize the use of procedures negotiated between an agency and a recognized labor organization as an alternative to appeal to the Civil Service Commission (see proposal 1, above). The legislative proposal being considered contemplates that negotiated procedures may provide for binding arbitration, where mutually agreed to by the parties, with the Civil Service Commission retaining authority to review arbitration awards if they are contrary to law or regulation, and on other reasonable grounds as may be provided for by regulations of the Civil Service Commission. Under the proposal the choice of appeal either to the Civil Service Commission or to the agency under negotiated procedures would rest with the adversely affected employee.
14. Legislative action will be proposed to clarify the meaning of the statutory standard for adverse actions, "the

efficiency of the service," particularly as it relates to matters arising outside the employment setting. The "efficiency of the service" has remained as the legal basis for adverse actions by agencies since the term was introduced in the Lloyd-LaFollette Act of 1912. An updated expression of legislative intent may well be in order in the light of recent judicial rulings and of changed conditions during the more than sixty years the standard has been in effect.

15. Legislation to extend to nonveterans by statute the same adverse action protections and appeal rights accorded to veterans will be requested. (The adverse action appellate rights now possessed by nonveterans flow from Executive order, not from statute.)
16. Legislative redefinition of the enumerated categories of adverse action will be proposed. The existing statutory provisions do not distinguish between actions that are disciplinary in nature and result from delinquency, or misconduct, or other causes personal to the individual, and actions resulting from the application of a system (e.g., position classification) or other purely impersonal reasons. Neither do the current provisions differentiate between actions having a major effect on an employee's vital career interests (e.g., removal) and those having a temporary or relatively minor effect (e.g., some pay adjustments). They are all treated now under a single adverse action umbrella. Improved statutory distinctions between essentially different kinds of situations will provide a basis for relating procedures more appropriately to the nature and cause of a proposed action.

ADDITIONAL CONSIDERATIONS

In arriving at the above proposals for revision of the adverse-action appellate system, many recommendations and suggestions were taken into account. Obviously, the sense of direction indicated by the proposals reflects choices and judgments that have been made from among the various courses of action possible. Since the proposals are subject to change on the basis of comments received, some further elaboration on the basic considerations underlying them will be helpful in placing the proposals in perspective.

Predecision Hearings by Civil Service Commission—Employed Examiners

Various interested parties have urged that the Civil Service Commission amend its regulations to require an evidentiary hearing prior to the decision by the employing agency on a proposed adverse action. A companion recommendation is that the hearing be conducted by a Civil Service Commission examiner, who would submit either a recommended decision, or findings and recommendations, to the deciding official in the agency. These suggestions were treated as central issues in the systems review. And while they were considered most seriously, their adoption is not being proposed for reasons regarded as compelling.

The source statute affording a right of appellate review of an adverse action by the Civil Service Commission is the Veterans Preference Act of 1944. Its provisions nowhere contemplate a predecision hearing or injection of the Civil Service Commission into an agency's consideration of a proposal before an administrative decision is made. The procedures specified in the law are believed to be intrinsically fair, striking a proper balance between the interest of employees, the interests of the Government as an employer, and the public interest.

It is important, of course, that employees be adequately protected against unjustified or arbitrary adverse actions. But it is also essential to the effective functioning of any organization that management have a reasonable capacity to act expeditiously when the facts require.

If a decision is made only after judicious consideration of all available facts by a responsible official not a party to the action proposed, prompt and impartial appellate review provides the necessary balancing of interests. The system revisions proposed meet the conditions of providing for both full prior consideration, and an early appellate determination of the propriety of the administrative action.

Administrative action by the Civil Service Commission to require a hearing before a Commission examiner as a precondition to any adverse action decision would be an unreasonable limitation on the authority needed by an agency to maintain organizational effectiveness and discipline. Such action by the Commission would go beyond the bounds of prudence, as well as what the available statutory guidelines clearly intend.[1]

Negotiated Procedures

Interest has been expressed, particularly by labor organizations, in authorizing the use of negotiated procedures, including arbitration, as an additional avenue for review of adverse actions.

This suggestion assumes the continuation of the statutory appellate system for those employees who elect to use it, or for whom negotiated procedures are not available, and it poses, therefore, the basic issue of how the two systems would relate to each other. In view of the appellate entitlements currently provided by law and Executive order, specific legislative authorization is considered to be necessary for the use of negotiated procedures on this basis. If two different appellate review procedures are to be available concurrently, the authorizing legislation should clearly provide that the use of one is expressly in lieu of the other.

[1] Although a recent court decision has held that constitutionally guaranteed due-process protections require a hearing prior to an administrative decision to remove an employee, that decision is believed to be in error and Supreme Court review has been requested.

A proper relationship between two appellate avenues also requires that review under each should become available at a common starting point. Since, for example, the statutory system provides for appellate review after an adverse action has been effected, the proposal to authorize negotiated procedures assumes that review under such procedures will also become available only at the same point and under the same conditions. In other words, negotiated agreements are not visualized as altering or adding to the procedures that govern agencies in effecting an adverse action under the proposed statutory system.

Agency Appellate Systems

The review of the adverse-action appellate system establishes that the improvements most fundamentally needed hinge on solutions to the interrelated problems of the excessive length of time required to reach a final decision on an appeal, and the multiple layers of review. Currently, it takes over 300 days on the average to conclude action on an appeal that has gone through the three levels of review (one at the agency and two at the Civil Service Commission) that are automatically available. An average of 170 days is required (based on fiscal year 1972 experience) for completion of appellate review at the agency alone.

The existing appellate structure requires that each agency maintain a system for review of adverse action established under, and conforming to, the regulations of the Civil Service Commission. The proposals for systems revision would eliminate that requirement. It is recognized that this is a highly controversial part of our proposal. The basic argument for retention of the agency appellate system is that it gives higher administrative levels within an agency the opportunity to correct an error made at a lower level. The Commission fully recognizes the importance and validity of this argument. However, after careful consideration, it was concluded that elimination was necessary in order to greatly expedite final action on an appeal. Part of our consideration in coming to this conclusion was the knowledge that an agency could still exercise this discretion at any time during the process of CSC appellate proceedings and, if it decided that an error had been made at a lower level, it could cancel the adverse action prior to final CSC decision.

CONCLUDING STATEMENT

In sum, the object of the proposals is to produce an adverse-action appellate system that is simpler and faster, yet fair; and that functions with the maximum feasible degree of organizational independence and openness.

Following considerations of the responses received, the CSC will decide on the actions it will take under its own authority and what action it will recommend to the President and the Congress.

Existing Adverse Action Appellate System

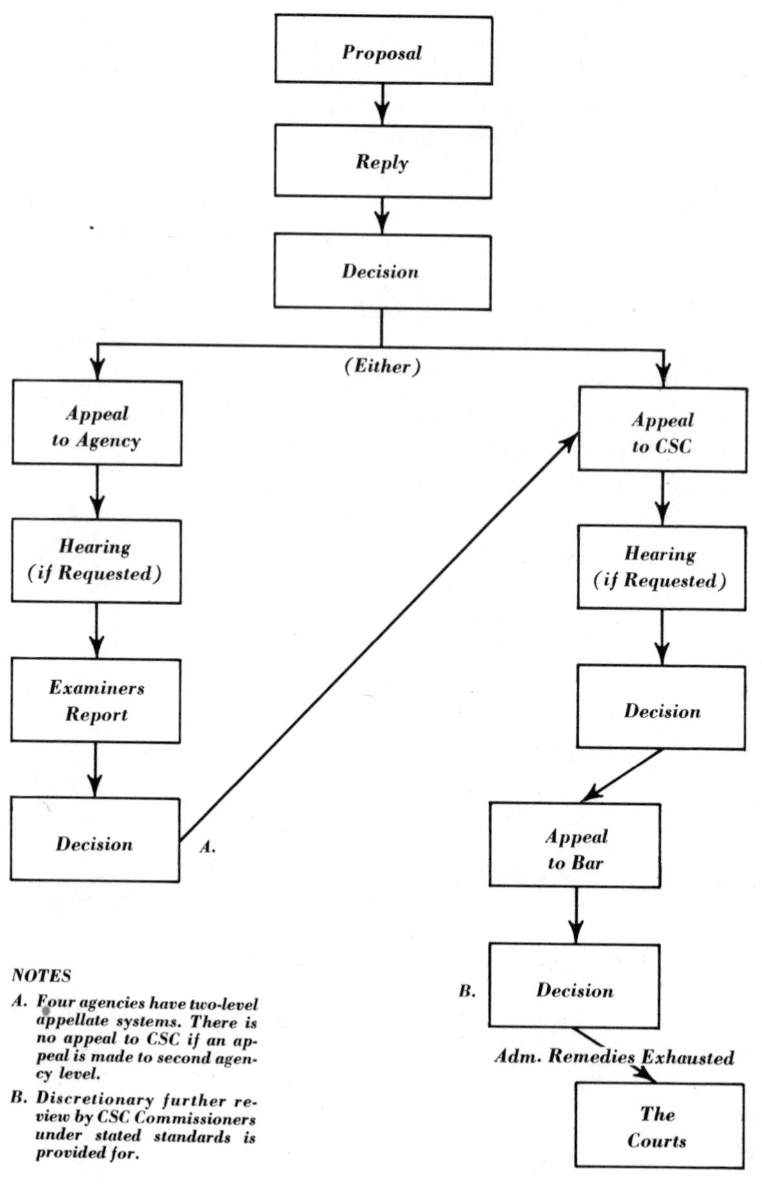

NOTES

A. *Four agencies have two-level appellate systems. There is no appeal to CSC if an appeal is made to second agency level.*

B. *Discretionary further review by CSC Commissioners under stated standards is provided for.*

Proposed Adverse Action Appellate System

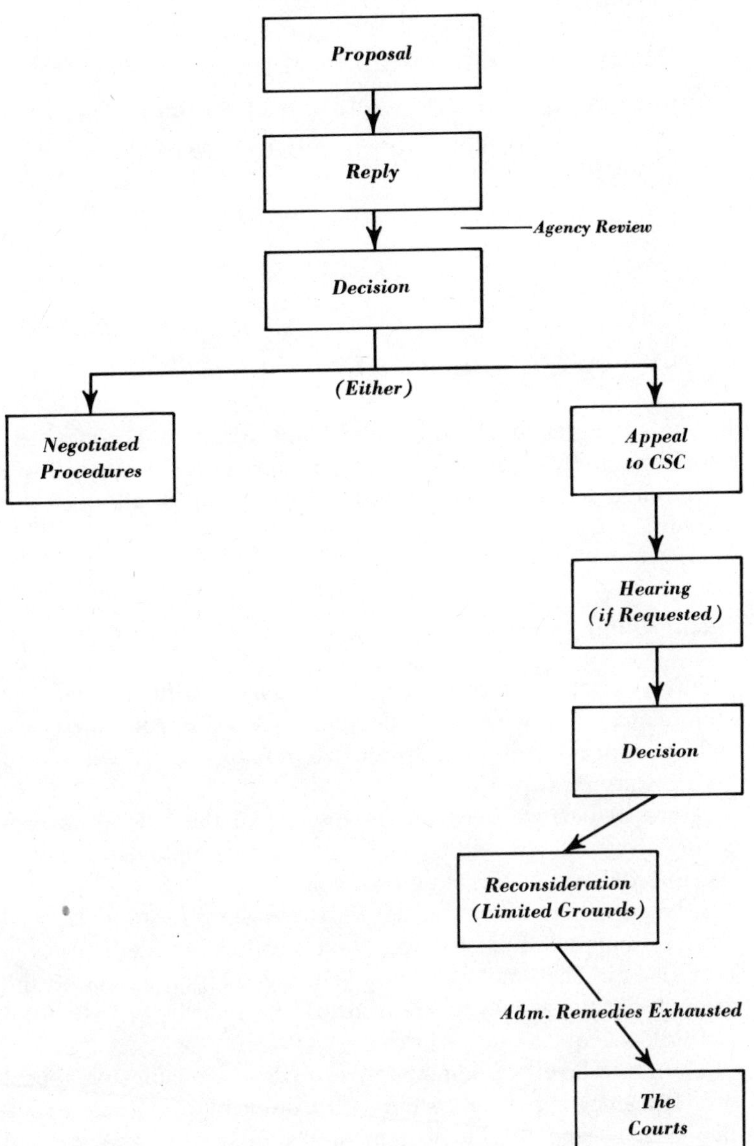

Comptroller General's Report to the Congress

Design and Administration of the Civil Service Commission's Adverse Action and Appeal Systems Need to be Improved B-179810

Digest

WHY THE REVIEW WAS MADE

Because congressional committees and others are concerned about the equity of the adverse action and appeal systems, GAO reviewed the Civil Service Commission's administration of the systems.

Background

Adverse actions provide federal managers with a means of maintaining an efficient and effective work force. An employee's right of appeal enables him to seek redress of actions believed to be arbitrary or capricious.

A proper balance between the interest of the federal government as an employer and the rights of federal employees is essential to an effective operating program.

Adverse actions involve removals, suspensions for more than 30 days, furloughs without pay for 30 days or less, and reductions in rank or pay. The employee can challenge such an action on the ground that the agency acted arbitrarily or unjustly or that it did not follow required procedures.

The three levels of administrative review available for appeal are (1) agency appellate systems, (2) Commission regional appellate offices, and (3) the Commission's Board of Appeals and Review.

FINDINGS AND CONCLUSIONS

The propriety of and need for agency appeal systems are questionable because of problems associated with:

The inexperienced and inadequately trained agency hearing officers.

The excessive time required to process appeals at agency level.

The duplicate effort involved in permitting employees hearings by both the agencies and the Commission.

Employees are concerned that the adverse action and appeal systems are unduly management oriented. Personnel managers are concerned that the systems inhibit their abilities to keep a quality work force.

GAO's review, as well as prior studies, identified the following factors creating these viewpoints.

Most employees were not granted hearings until after penalties were imposed.

Neither the Commission's regional appellate offices nor the Board of Appeals and Review had the authority to mitigate agency penalties.

Hearings were closed to the public.

The systems were designed in such a way that managers and supervisors often were reluctant to take justifiable adverse actions.

According to the concerned parties, the issue of the timing of the hearing is the most sensitive and controversial issue in the adverse-action and appeal systems. The systems should maintain a balance of fairness between management and employees. GAO has carefully considered the evidence and focused on the advantages and disadvantages of the alternatives of the timing of the hearing issue. Opinions of many concerned parties are divided and GAO is not in a position to resolve the controversy.

The Supreme Court will address the constitutional issue as to whether predecision hearings on adverse actions are constitutionally required.

The Commission appellate offices did not have authority to mitigate penalties generally. In a recent proposal, however, the Commission planned to grant its offices limited mitigation authority and to gain a reasonable amount of experience operating under this broadened authority. In view of this, GAO is deferring a formal recommendation on this matter.

As the personnel agency of the executive branch, the Commission establishes personnel policy and regulations and assists agency management in implementing them.

As administrator of the adverse-action and appeal systems, the Commission tries to protect federal employees from arbitrary and unjust agency actions.

The lack of a separate and distinct organization within the Commission for each of these activities creates doubt as to its objectivity and independence in administering the appeal system.

The Commission's objectivity and impartiality can be established and employee trust in the appeal system can be increased through a restructuring of the Commission's appellate organization. Such restructuring should be designed to centralize administration of the appeal program and to separate personnel management activities from adjudication of appeals, which would avoid the appearance of conflict that these dual functions create.

RECOMMENDATIONS

To avoid using inexperienced or inadequately trained hearing officers and to prevent delays and duplicate effort involved in processing appeals, the Commission should act on its proposal to eliminate agency appeal systems as soon as practicable.

GAO recommends that administration of the appeal program be centralized under the Board of Appeals and Review and that:

Regional appeals examiners and the Appeals Examining Office report directly to the Board.

Regional examiners and the Appeals Examining Office be

empowered to make decisions independently of the regional directors and the Executive Director.

The Bureau of Personnel Management Evaluation no longer coordinate the Commission's first level of appeal.

The Board, and not the Bureau of Policies and Standards, establish the Commission's appellate policy.

The administrative relationships between the Board and the Executive and Deputy Executive Directors be limited to matters of minor administrative support.

The Board be responsible solely to the Commissioners.

AGENCY ACTIONS AND UNRESOLVED ISSUES

The Commission stated that the proposed changes to the adverse action and appeal systems, announced in March 1973, attest to its agreement with GAO's overall evaluation that the design and administration of these systems need to be improved.

The Commission, like GAO, proposes eliminating agency appeal systems and allowing the employees the right to one hearing and one appeal before the Commission. The Commission proposes also giving employees the option of using negotiated procedures.

GAO believes that, when unions and management negotiate alternatives for settling adverse actions, employees should have the option of using such procedures.

GAO concurs with the Commission's recently adopted policy of having the adverse action hearing open to the public at the appellant's request.

The Commission is against the preaction hearing primarily because it feels that requiring management to hold a hearing as a precondition to discipline is an unreasonable limitation on the authority needed to maintain organizational effectiveness and discipline. In a recent report, the Administrative Conference of the United States adopted a recommendation favoring a preaction hearing in certain cases terminating an employee's pay. The Conference report also discussed many of the arguments for a preaction hearing.

The Commission recognizes the need for revising its appellate structure and has proposed realigning its organization to increase the independence of the appellate function. Although the Commission has not detailed all of its planned changes, GAO did note that it had included establishment of a new centralized appeal authority to which regional appeal offices and the Appeals Examining Office would report.

MATTERS FOR CONSIDERATION BY THE CONGRESS

This report attempts to focus attention on the controversial issue concerning the timing of the hearing.

In order to carry out certain Commission-proposed changes, legislation would be required.

Legislation would also be necessary to authorize the use of negotiated procedures to settle adverse actions.

Appendix C

Recommendations for Inspections and Investigations

Many of the failures of the Commission's inspection program are the result of an orientation and perspective that specific recommendations may do little to remedy. These basic assumptions must be changed. (See Chapter 6 for a discussion of ways in which inspection may be used to change the federal service.) The recommendations below are improvements that can be made in the present inspection program. Because the present direction of inspection carries with it the seeds of its failure, however, these recommendations are only ameliorative.

Recommendations Dealing with Public and Employee Access

Recommendation 1: The Commission should allow citizens, Congress, and employees to review its inspection reports.

Recommendation 2: Selected employees and employee representatives should be invited to attend closeout sessions conducted at installations.

Recommendation 3: More information concerning inspection results and planned follow through should be provided by the Commission to employees and employee representatives.

Recommendation 4: Greater employee involvement should be sought in the process of planning inspections. Interviews with employee groups might be conducted before a nationwide inspection plan is drafted.

Recommendation 5: Employees should be informed of violations affecting them which are discovered during an inspection.

Recommendations Concerning Inspection Techniques

Recommendation 6: New questionnaires should be designed for employees containing well-drafted questions dealing with Equal Employment Opportunity, the Federal Women's Program, and the appellate system.

Recommendation 7: A thorough review of personnel actions should be made during inspections.

Recommendation 8: In installations or agencies that have not been inspected within the past year, Commission inspectors should review personnel actions conducted during the period in which there was no Commission inspection or for at least three years. In separation actions, files or copies of the files should be retained at the agency for three years after a final administrative determination on the adverse action.

Recommendation 9: Notification procedures should be reexamined and enforced to insure adequate employee notification by agencies of planned Commission inspections.

Recommendation 10: Appointments for employees who wish to meet with Commission inspectors should not be scheduled by that agency's personnel.

Recommendation 11: The Commission should use statistics taken from the 29-A forms to determine more precisely how inspection time is being utilized and how to redirect it.

Recommendation 12: If the complaint office is to be used in the inspection process, greater publicity for the office is necessary. Reports should be given to employees on the inspection results coming from their complaints.

Recommendations Dealing with Agency Influence

Recommendation 13: Survey directors should be periodically rotated. Such rotation every two or three years would allow some familiarity with an agency and still avoid the development of relationships with agency personnel that could affect the objectivity of inspection reports.

Recommendation 14: The inspection agreements that have been signed with the armed forces should be completely reanalyzed.

These agreements should be abolished or be redrafted to assure that Commission inspections are not restricted. Present agreements are often inconsistent with the Commission's new policy of quality control of agency inspections.

Recommendation 15: Follow-through on inspections should rely less upon agency evaluation of its own progress.

Recommendations Concerning Investigation of Employees

Recommendation 16: The Congress and the Civil Service Commission should reappraise investigative programs and the standards used to judge employee suitability and loyalty. Such a reappraisal should consider the cost and benefits of the system and the predictive value of the standards that are used. In determining costs and benefits, the losses to the government and to individuals who are false-positives would be considered.

Recommendation 17: The Commission should apply to itself the requirements of the Fair Credit Reporting Act. In this area potential employees of private enterprises should not enjoy greater rights than potential federal employees. Clearly in suitability and qualification areas no sufficient reason exists for exclusion of federal employees from the coverage of the Act.

Recommendation 18: As part of the coverage of the Fair Credit Reporting Act, federal agencies should be required to inform an applicant if he has not been hired as the result of information contained in an investigative report and to inform potential employees within three days of the time that an investigative report is ordered.

Recommendation 19: The training program of investigators should contain seminars dealing with civil rights and civil liberties. In addition, as part of their training, investigators should participate in seminars with representatives of minority groups, civil liberties organizations, employees, and young persons. Such seminars should be periodically provided for all investigators.

Recommendation 20: The Commission should increase the representation of women and minority groups in the Bureau of Personnel Investigations.

Recommendation 21: More reinterviews should be conducted

and any disciplinary action taken as a result made available to the public.

Recommendation 22: A complaint procedure by which citizens may complain about investigative practices within the government should be established. As a minimum such a complaint procedure would require an investigation of the complaint and a response to the citizen or employee stating what was found, the disposition of the complaint, and the reasons for any action taken or not taken.

Recommendation 23: The standards for appraisal of agency internal-security programs should be more clearly defined and citizen and employee response invited.

Recommendation 24: For those agencies to which the Commission has delegated investigative responsibilities for the competitive service, additional criteria and standards should be established. Improved oversight, including increased manpower assigned to appraisal and increased reporting requirements, should be provided.

Appendix D

Commission Reports on Delay in Complaint-Processing

Following are copies of two Commission reports showing the reasons for delay in complaint-processing. The first is a report on April 1971 and the second on November 1973. Comments in parentheses are interpretation.

OFFICE OF THE ASSISTANT EXECUTIVE DIRECTOR

EEO HEARINGS—CASE AGE REPORT—DAYS IN PROCESS

4-week period ending 3/6/71

EEO Cases with CSC Hearing Examiners	
1–30 days	40
31–60 days	29
Over 60 days	14
Total	83

4-week period ending 4/3/71

EEO Cases with CSC Hearing Examiners	
1–30 days	33
31–60 days	35
Over 60 days	11
Total	79

COMMENTS

I. Analysis of Chart Data

38 new hearing requests received—3 more than last period

29 cases closed (hearing held—decision sent to agency)—2 more than last period

13 cases remanded to agencies for additional investigation—7 more than last period

Cases over 60 days old continue to decline—declined by 3 since last period

II. Problems Involving Workload Not Appearing on the Chart

Reasons for delays in cases (pending with EEO Appeals Examiners more than 60 days):

AT [Atlanta]—0

BN [Boston]—1 case

suspended awaiting policy decision on availability of performance appraisals at hearing from CSC. We have suggested to Examiner that identity of persons on certificate be disguised pending our formal decision on Navy request but Navy prefers to wait for formal reply to its inquiry. (This case previously reported overdue for flash report periods 1/9, 2/6, and 3/6/71.) [Commission and agency are responsible for the delay.]

CH [Chicago]—4 cases

1 case—hearing originally scheduled for 2/4/71—postponed at request of complainant's representative—representative subsequently withdrew from case—hearing held on 3/23/71—awaiting transcript. [The only case in which complainant is solely responsible for the delay in the processing time of his hearing—assuming that an Examiner was promptly assigned to the case and that there was no delay in originally scheduling the hearing. Note that complainant's delay is caused by representation problems.]

1 case—hearing originally scheduled for 2/3/71—postponed at request of complainant's representative—representative subsequently withdrew from case—hearing held on 3/16/71—awaiting transcript. [Agency and complainant are responsible for the delay. Since the hearing was held on 3/16/71, the transcript is slow as of 4/3/71, and agencies are usually responsible for transcription. In the New York case

below, a hearing ended on 3/16, and the transcription by the agency is considered slow in that case. Note that complainant's contribution to the delay is caused by representation problems.]

1 case—hearing held on 2/9/71—slow transcription by agency—transcript has now been received—Examiner currently preparing recommended decision. [Agency is responsible for delay.]

1 case—assigned to Examiner 1/4/71—hearing held 2/2/71 —transcript received 2/15/71—Examiner was involved in other appeals work—currently preparing recommended decision. (Region has now restricted Examiner to EEO hearings work only.) [Commission is responsible for the delay. Note that Examiner held a hearing almost a full month after being assigned the case and had not prepared a decision as of 4/3/71, more than two months after the hearing. Somewhat belatedly the Commission, as indicated in its note in the parenthesis, has allocated more manpower in this region to the hearing of EEO complaints.]

DA [Dallas]—0

DE [Denver]—0

NY [New York]—1 case

assigned to Examiner 1/30/71—hearing held 3/9, 11, and 16/71—slow agency transcription—awaiting transcript. [Commission and agency are responsible for the delay. Commission's Examiner set a hearing date more than a month after the case was assigned to him.]

SF [San Francisco]—1 case

prehearing conference held on 2/23/71—agency representative not available for hearing until 3/9/71—complainant requested delay to obtain legal assistance—hearing rescheduled for and held on 4/8/71. [Agency and complainant are responsible for the delay. Note that complainant's contribution to delay is caused by representation difficulties.]

CO*[Central Office]—4 cases

1 case—assigned to Examiner 11/5/70—delayed at agency request until beginning of 1971 due to unavailability of witnesses—further delayed by complainant and agency because of unavailability of their respective representatives—hearing held on 3/18-19/71—awaiting transcript. (This case previously reported overdue for flash report periods 2/6 and 3/6/71.) [Agency and complainant are responsible for the delay. Note that complainant's contribution to delay is caused by representation difficulties.]

1 case—assigned to Examiner 12/1/70—hearing delayed at agency request due to unavailability of witnesses—hearing delayed by Examiner as agency EEO Officer transferred—Assistant Executive Director advised agency headquarters of situation and new EEO Officer appointed—hearing held 3/11/71—awaiting transcript. (This case previously reported overdue for flash report periods 2/6 and 3/6/71.) [Agency is responsible for delay.]

1 case—assigned to examiner 11/23/70—file reviewed 12/4/70—supplemental information requested from agency received 12/22/70—hearing delayed at complainant's request to allow her time to obtain a representative—hearing held 2/22-23 and 3/3/71—transcript received 3/18/71—Examiner (part-time) involved in duty station move—currently preparing recommended decision. (This case previously reported overdue for flash report periods 2/6 and 3/6/71.) [Commission and complainant are responsible for delay, with perhaps some responsibility to the agency. Agency contributed to delay if requested "supplemental information" should have been in its investigative report or if excessive time was spent gathering the "supplemental informa-

*C.O. [Central Office] cases reported here are being handled by part-time EEO Appeals Examiners (CSC employees). Full-time Examiner reported for duty on 1/25/71 and another full-time Examiner has been selected. [This note in original. Everything not in brackets is in the original.]

tion." Note that complainant's contribution to delay is caused by representation difficulties.]

1 case—assigned to Examiner 12/2/70—file reviewed 12/11/70—Examiner took no action on scheduling hearing as he learned that activity had no EEO Officer—Assistant Executive Director informed of this on 2/5/71 and advised agency headquarters of situation—new EEO Officer appointed—hearing held 2/23–25 and 3/4/71—slow transcription—awaiting transcript. (This case previously reported overdue for flash report periods 2/6 and 3/6/71.) [Commission and agency are responsible for delay. Commission's Assistant Executive Director Kator was allegedly not informed of the causes of delay until the commission's Examiner had been assigned to the case for more than two months.]

OFFICE OF FEDERAL EQUAL EMPLOYMENT OPPORTUNITY DISCRIMINATION COMPLAINT HEARINGS CASE AGE REPORT—DAYS IN PROCESS

4-week period ending 10/27/73

EEO Cases with CSC Complaint Examiners	
1–30 days	64
31–60 days	69
Over 60 days	55
Total	188

4-week period ending 11/24/73

EEO Cases with CSC Complaint Examiners	
1–30 days	55
31–60 days	61
Over 60 days	50
Total	166

COMMENTS

I. Analysis of Chart Data

58 hearing requests received; 9 less than last period, 4 more than corresponding period one year ago.

78 cases closed; 14 remanded to agency, one more than last period, 11 more than corresponding period one year ago; 64 decisions sent to agencies, 19 more than last period; one more than the number closed during the corresponding period one year ago.

Overdue cases* currently represent 30.1% of the workload compared with 29.2% last period and 19.4% during corresponding period one year ago.

II. Data on Cases Pending over 60 Days Not Reflected on the Above Chart

OFFICE OF FEDERAL EQUAL EMPLOYMENT OPPORTUNITY

*Any case with complaints examiner over 60 days.

OFFICE OF FEDERAL EQUAL EMPLOYMENT OPPORTUNITY
DATA ON CASES PENDING OVER 60 DAYS

Region	# of Cases Pending	Date Case Received	Date Hearing Scheduled	Date Hearing Held	Date Transcript Received	Comments
AT	1	9/17/73	10/17 11/14	. . . . . .	. . . . . .	Hearing delayed to allow complainant to obtain attorney; agency failed to notify witnesses. Not rescheduled, complainant's attorney hoping to settle thru negotiations.
BN	1	9/5/73	9/27 10/24	10/24	11/12	Hearing postponed at complainant's request. Draft decision required rewrite, expect to issue by 12/23/73.
CH	12	8/22/73 (10 complaints)	9/11	9/11 thru 9/20	11/2	Group of 10 individual hearings. Court reporter is employee of Provost Marshal. Decisions being written.
		9/12/73	10/2 10/10	10/10 and 11	11/2	Hearing delay due to complainant's representative's court calendar conflict. Draft decision being rewritten.
		9/20/73	10/16 10/23	10/23, and 24, 30	. . .	Attorney for the complainant in court on scheduled hearing date.

Region	# of Cases Pending	Date Case Received	Date Hearing Scheduled	Date Hearing Held	Date Transcript Received	Comments
DA	7	9/6/73	9/24	9/24	11/26	Illness of reporting firm's court typist delayed transcript.
		9/7/73	10/14	10/14	11/12	Complaint Examiner's illness has delayed writing the decision.
		9/10/73	9/27	9/27	10/15	Interrogatory still pending—witness in hospital, agency does not want decision issued without interrogatory.
		9/14/73	10/4	10/4, 5	11/12	Decision delayed due to Complaint Examiner's prescheduled leave. CX now in prescheduled training course.
		9/10/73 and 9/21/73	10/9	10/9	11/12	Case file was not received until 9/21. Hearing date was earliest available date CX could schedule hearing.
		9/19/73	11/13	11/13	. . .	Complainant's attorney not available due to court calendar.
		9/25/73	10/30 11/8	11/18	. . .	Hearing delayed at request of the agency and the complainant.
NY	2	8/20/73	10/2	10/2	11/19	Hearing delayed at request of com-

						plainant and his representative. Decision being typed.
		7/26/73	8/29 10/3	10/3, 4, 5	10/26	Hearing postponed to October at complainant's request. Complaint Examiner involved with other EEO hearings and conducting a training session.
PH	6	7/10/73	Prehearing 7/24 cancelled 8/8 9/12	8/8 9/12	11/5	Complainant on Travel Duty in Europe. Assistant Commissioner and other witnesses difficult to obtain. Decision to be issued by 11/30.
		8/1/73	8/29	8/29	9/13	Decision written 10/3. New information received from both agency and complainant. Decision redrafted 10/24.
		8/13/73	Prehearing 8/29 Hearing 10/17	10/9, 10	11/16	Agency and complainant requested postponement. Transcript faulty; meeting with parties scheduled 12/5 to reconstruct faulty transcript.
		9/5/73	Prehearing 10/4 Hearing 10/17	10/17, 18 19, and 11/7, 8	. . .	Awaiting transcript.

Region	# of Cases Pending	Date Case Received	Date Hearing Scheduled	Date Hearing Held	Date Transcript Received	Comments
		8/16/73	Prehearing 9/6 Hearing 9/20	9/20	. . .	Awaiting transcript.
		8/20/73	9/5 9/24	9/24, 25, 26, and 10/1, 2, and 11	10/29	Hearing postponed at complainant's request. Decision being drafted.
SF	12	5/17/73	6/5 6/27	6/27, 28, and 7/16, 17, 18, 19, 20	8/13	Hearing postponed at complainant's request. Case reassigned to new Examiner 6/18/73. Decision delayed due to Examiner's involvement in top priority investigation, directed by Central Office. Expect to complete draft by 11/30/73.
		6/29/73	8/8 and 9/17	8/8, 8/28, 9/17, and 10/12	11/5	Hearing delayed to give complainant opportunity to come from Canada. Key witness unavailable until 9/4/73. Case reassigned to another Examiner. Hearing commenced 9/17 continued

					to 10/12 in order to obtain testimony of key witness. Decision awaiting information from agency.
	7/5/73	7/25 8/7 9/6 10/4	10/6, 17, 18, 19	11/6	Agency representative unavailable at first scheduled hearing; complainant ill at second scheduled hearing; agency official hospitalized—unavailable for third scheduling. Decision being written.
	8/19/73	9/10	9/10, 11	10/5	Complaints Examiner detailed, working on investigative backlog and other EEO work.
	8/23/73	9/14 9/27	9/27 continued to 11/5	. . .	Agency has only one representative handling all its EEO hearings. Hearing delayed to accommodate his schedule. Agency has been instructed to train or otherwise provide other representatives.
	7/18/73	8/8 8/20	8/20, 9/4, 10, 11, 12, 13, 17, 24, 25,	11/26	Complainant requested additional time to obtain representative and prepare his case. Witnesses unavailable for second scheduled hearing—long hearing, large transcript.

Region	# of Cases Pending	Date Case Received	Date Hearing Scheduled	Date Hearing Held	Date Transcript Received	Comments
				26, 27 10/1, 2, 9, 10, 11, 12, 15, 16, 17, 18, 19, 23, 24, 25, 29		
		7/19/73	8/21 9/5 10/2	10/2, 3, 4, 5 10/16, 17, 28, 29	11/14	Hearing postponements due to Agency's representative involvement with other EEO cases. Agency has only one representative.
		8/13/73	9/18	9/18, 19, 21, 24, 26	10/5	Decision writing delayed due to other EEO cases and training.
		8/27/73	9/5	9/5, 7, 10, 11, 12, 14, 18, 19, 20, 21, 24, 25	11/26	Transcript being reviewed.

				10/15, 16, 29, 30, 31 11/1, 2, 6, 7		
		8/30/73	10/2 10/30	10/30, 31	11/19	Complainant's representative not available on first hearing date, arranging for witnesses from overseas.
		9/7/73	10/16	10/16, 17, 18, 19	11/16	Hearing delayed due to conflict with other EEO hearings. Writing delayed due to involvement with other EEO case.
		9/10	10/9	10/9, 10	10/29	Decision being rewritten.
CO	9	6/27/73	7/26 8/8 10/10	10/10	Partial 11/19	Complainant at New York duty station, hearing scheduled for D.C. Complainant's representative, then agency, requested delays; witnesses unavailable, representative unable to appear. Examiner on prescheduled leave. Awaiting complete transcript.
		7/12/73	8/21	8/21, 22	9/10	Recommended decision delayed—Examiner involved with older EEO cases. Expected release date 12/3/73.

Region	# of Cases Pending	Date Case Received	Date Hearing Scheduled	Date Hearing Held	Date Transcript Received	Comments
		8/9/73	9/11 9/25	9/25 10/2, 10	10/2, 15, 23	Examiner involved in extended EEO hearing. Expected release date 12/20/73.
		8/13/73		10/16, 17, 18	11/1	Hearing delayed because of Complaints Examiner's prescheduled leave and other hearing schedules. CX requested additional information from agency and gave complainant's representative opportunity to comment. First draft submitted. Expected release date 12/5/73.
		8/17/73		9/25, 26	10/5	First draft required rewrite. Returned to Examiner 10/26. Second draft has been submitted. Expected release date 12/3/73.
		9/5/73	10/3 10/30	10/30, 31 11/1, 7, 8, 9, 15, 16	. . .	Hearing postponed at agency request. Awaiting transcript.
		9/24/73		10/24, 25	11/5	Examiner involved in another EEO

					hearing and drafting older cases. Expected release date 12/14/73.
	9/24/73		10/24 cont'd to 11/19	Partial	Hearing continued due to unavailability of witnesses. Awaiting last day's transcript. Expected release date 12/20/73.
	9/12/73	10/1	10/1, 2	10/12 and 16	Examiner engaged in preparing reports on older cases, also engaged in other types of hearings. Expected release date 12/10/73.

Appendix E

Bureau of Personnel Investigations' Review of Publications

Following is an exact copy of the list, provided by Mr. Johnson, of publications regularly received by the Security Research Section of the BPI. The opinions expressed about the publications are those of the BPI.

Name of Publication	*Commission Description of Publication*
AMERICAN DIALOG Pub: Dialog Publications, Inc. Room 804, 32 Union Square New York, N.Y. 10003	First issue August–September 1964, replacing *Mainstream,* which, in turn replaced *Masses and Mainstream* and the earlier *New Masses:* Devoted to the cultural offensive.
DAILY WORLD Pub: Longview Publishing Co., Inc. P.O. Box 544 Old Chelsea Station New York, N.Y. 10011	Communist Party, USA, propaganda vehicle from July 4, 1968, replacing *The Worker* (weekly) and the earlier *Daily Worker,* first issued January 3, 1924.
FREEDOMWAYS Pub: Freedomways Associates 799 Broadway New York, N.Y. 10003	"A Quarterly Review of the Negro Freedom Movement," initiated with the Spring issue, 1961.
HORIZONS (Defunct) Pub: Progress Books 487 Adelaide St. West Toronto 2B Ontario, Canada	Canadian Communist theoretical quarterly with moderate circulation in the United States.

Name of Publication	*Commission Description of Publication*
INSURGENT (Defunct) Pub: W. E. B. Dubois Clubs of America 1853½ McAllister St. San Francisco, Ca. 94115	Official monthly publication of the W. E. B. DuBois Clubs of America.
JEWISH CURRENTS Pub: Jewish Currents, Inc. 22 E. 17th St., Suite 601, New York, N.Y., 10003	Specialized monthly periodical; replaced *Jewish Life.*
NEW WORLD REVIEW Pub: New World Review Publication, Inc. 156 5th Ave., Suite 308 New York, N.Y.	Prime quarterly propaganda vehicle, formerly *Soviet Russia Today.*
PEOPLE'S WORLD Pub: People's World 81 Clementine St., San Francisco, Ca. 94105	West Coast (weekly) newspaper of the Communist Party, U.S.A.; formerly the *Daily People's World.*
POLITICAL AFFAIRS Pub: Political Affairs Publishers, Inc. 799 Broadway, Rm. 618 New York, N.Y. 10003	Official Communist Party theoretical organ, replacing *The Communist* in January 1945.
WORLD MARXIST REVIEW Pub: Progress Books 487 Adelaide St. West Toronto 28, Ontario, Canada	The North American edition of the monthly journal, *Problems of Peace and Socialism,* published in Prague, Czechoslovakia.
GLOBAL DIGEST (Defunct)	Published monthly under Chinese Communist auspices.

Name of Publication	Commission Description of Publication
Pub: Global Digest #4—Fung Fai Terrace, 1st Floor Happy Valley, Hong Kong	
MILITANT Pub: Militant 873 Broadway New York, N.Y. 10003	Official weekly newspaper of the *Socialist Workers' Party* (Trotskyite offshoot of the Communist Party, U.S.A.)
MINORITY OF ONE (Defunct) Pub: Minority of One, Inc. 155 Pennington Ave. P.O. Box 544 Passaic, N.J. 07055	An "independent monthly," strongly oriented to the Chinese Communist position in practice.
MONTHLY REVIEW Pub: Monthly Review, Inc. 33 6th Ave. New York, N.Y. 10014	Trotskyite monthly periodical, with strong anti-Russcom, pro-Chicom leanings.
PEKING REVIEW Pub: Peking Review Guozi Shudian P.O. Box #399 Peking, China	Published every Friday by the Chinese Communist government.
PROGRESSIVE LABOR Pub: Progressive Labor G.P.O. Box 808 Brooklyn, N.Y. 11201	Official monthly organ of the Progressive Labor Party, militant Chinese Communist-oriented organization.
GUARDIAN Pub: Guardian Associates 197 E. 4th Street New York, N.Y. 10009	Weekly newspaper of the "instant revolution" variety, covering Movement and New Left activities with high priority on SDS publicity. Replaced the *National Guardian.*
NEW UNIVERSITY THOUGHT	Theoretical journal, irregular publication.

Name of Publication	*Commission Description of Publication*
Pub: New University Thought Publishing Company P.O. Box 7431 18112 N. Lawn Detroit, Michigan 48221	
RAMPARTS MAGAZINE Pub: Ramparts Magazine, Inc. 301 Broadway San Francisco, Ca. 94133	Sensational in character; widely circulated monthly.
RIGHTS Pub: National Emergency Civil Liberties Committee (NECLC) 25 E. 26th Street New York, N.Y. 10010	Official monthly of the NECLC, with a strong libertarian pitch.

Appendix F

Participants in Personnel Interchange Program (1971) (Supplied by the President's Commission on Personnel Interchange)

1971

NAME	TITLE AND SPONSORING COMPANY	LOCATION	TITLE AND HOST AGENCY	AGENCY SALARY	GRADE
Allison, John H.	Assistant Vice President—Public Relations Bell Telephone Company of Pa.	Pittsburgh, Pa.	Senior Program Officer Dept. of HUD	$31,477	15
Armacost, Samuel S.	Vice President—London Bank of America NT & SA	San Francisco, Ca.	Foreign Service Reserve Officer Dept. of State	$25,087	FS3
Bradley, Frank W.	President & Chairman, Board of Directors Standard Oil of California (Iran Oil Company—London)	San Francisco, Ca.	Special Asst. to Director, Resources Utilization Dept. of HUD	$27,433	15

Bradshaw, John W.	Division Industrial Relations —Manager GTE Sylvania Inc. (Eastern Division)	Needham Hgts., Ma.	Executive Fellow Dept. of Labor	$26,675	15
Broughman, James R.	Manager, Program Control The Bendix Corporation (Aerospace Systems Div.)	Ann Arbor, Mi.	Special Asst. to Director of Evaluation Dept. of HUD	$20,815	14
Cartwright, Jon S.	Manager, Manpower Planning IBM Corporation	White Plains, N.Y.	Special Asst. To Asst., Sec. for Admin. Dept. of Commerce	$30,715	15
Daly, William N.	Planning & Financial Programs Manager Mobil Oil Corporation	New York, N.Y.	Program Officer Dept. of Commerce	$25,673	14
DeSio, Anthony W.	Assistant Program Manager Lockheed Missiles & Space Corp.	Sunnyvale, Ca.	Space Assistant NASA	$26,400	15
Donnelly, Richard H.	Deputy Director—Personnel Douglas Aircraft Company McDonnell-Douglas Corp.	Long Beach, Ca.	Labor Management Relations Spec. U.S. Civil Service Commission	$26,675	15
Erickson, Richard L.	Manager, Guidance & Control Systems Engineering General Electric Company	Syracuse, N.Y.	Program Analyst Dept. of Trans.	$24,251	15
Geil, Fred G.	Senior Engineer Sonic Technology Dept. Westinghouse Research Lab.	Pittsburgh, Pa.	Consultant Naval Undersea Research & Develop. Ctr. (Calif.) Dept. of the Navy	$22,203	14

NAME	TITLE AND SPONSORING COMPANY	LOCATION	TITLE AND HOST AGENCY	AGENCY SALARY	GRADE
Harrison, Otto R.	Engineering Manager Humble Oil & Refining Co. (Midcontinent Div.)	Houston, Texas	Petroleum Engineer Environmental Protection Agency	$28,291	15
Hawkes, Sidney G.	Government Affairs Representative The Mead Corporation	Dayton, Ohio	Supervisory Auditor General Accounting Office	$22,203	14
Ingersoll, John T.	Programming Manager Owens-Illinois, Inc.	Toledo, Ohio	Management Systems Officer Dept. of HUD	$23,591	14
Joyner, Nelson T.	General Manager American Standard Inc.	New York, N.Y.	Program Officer Bureau of Int'l Commerce Dept. of Commerce	$25,867	15
Kelly, James F.	Program Develop. Manager Rocketdyne Division North American Rockwell	Canoga Park, Ca.	Special Assistant Division of Placement Dept. of Labor	$24,251	15
Kumm, William H.	Manager, Advanced Concept Engineering Ocean Research & Engrg. Ctr. Westinghouse Electric Corp.	Annapolis, Md.	General Physical Scientist NOAA Dept. of Commerce	$24,285	14
Lancaster, Thomas A.	Project Engineer Aerospace Systems Div. The Bendix Corporation	Ann Arbor, Mi.	Deputy to the Special Projects Director Urban Mass Trans. Dept. of Trans.	$22,203	14

Levin, Barton J.	Special Assistant to the V.P.—Operations AT & SFe Railway Co.	Chicago, Ill.	Transportation Spec. Federal Railroad Adm. Dept. of Trans.	$18,945	13
Meuser, Kenneth G., Jr.	Manager, Corporate Community Relations TRW Inc.	Cleveland, Ohio	Special Ass't. to Director of Commun. Environmental Protection Agency	$18,353	13
Nutant, John A.	Manager, Engineering Analysis Westinghouse Electric Corporation	Pittsburgh, Pa.	Manager, Engineering Analysis Environmental Protection Agency	$23,591	14
Smarz, Thomas R.	Manager, Labor Relations AVCO Corporation	Stratford, Conn.	Attorney Advisor FAA (General Counsel Department) Dept. of Trans.	$21,509	14
Stauffer, C. Hoff	Consultant McKinsey & Company, Inc.	Washington, D.C.	Program Analyst Environmental Protection Agency	$24,251	15
Wakefield, James T.	Staff to Director of Guidance Systems LTV Electrosystems	Dallas, Tex.	Computer Systems Analyst NASA	$20,815	14
Carson, C. Wesley	IBM Corp. (Management Systems Analyst) Armonk, N.Y.	Washington, D.C.	Bureau of Int'l Commerce Dept. of Commerce (Special Assistant)	$24,251	15
Fote, William D., Jr.	Con Edison (Staff Assistant, Central Construct. Dept.) N.Y., N.Y.	Washington, D.C.	Veterans Administration (Project Supervisor & Senior Project Supervisor)	$21,608	14

NAME	TITLE AND SPONSORING COMPANY	LOCATION	TITLE AND HOST AGENCY	AGENCY SALARY	GRADE
Graner, Ralph H.	Bank of America NT&SA (Executive Trainee) San Francisco, Ca.	Washington, D.C.	Dept. of State (Foreign Service Officer —Int'l Economist)	$18,945	Class 4
Mabbatt, Frederic S.	AVCO Corporation (Special Assistant Communications) Greenwich, Conn.	Sao Paulo, Brazil	USIA (Information Officer)	$17,319	Class 4
Morris, James P.	Mobil Oil Corporation (Management Sciences Associate) New York, N.Y.	Washington, D.C.	Department of Defense (Program Analyst—Assistant for Strategic Analysis)	$26,675	15
Ridgell, James N.	North American Rockwell (Audit Executive) El Segundo, Ca.	Washington, D.C.	U.S. Air Force (Data Automation Plans Officer)	$22,203	14
Sonefeld, Otto F.	AT&SFe Railroad Co. (Special Assistant to V.P.—Operations) Chicago, Ill.	Washington, D.C.	Federal Railroad Admin. Dept. of Transportation (Transportation Special.)	$22,897	14
Thomas, Alvin L.	Std. Oil of S. Calif. (Senior Computer Analyst) San Francisco, Ca.	Washington, D.C.	Defense Info. Agency (Computer Systems Anal.)	$18,945	13

Butler, Jack E.	Mobil Pipe Line Company Mobil Oil Corporation (Manager of Accounting)	Dallas, Tex.	Bureau of Int'l Commerce, Dept. of Commerce (Program Director)	$24,411	15
Coupe, John R.	LTV Electrosystems, Inc. (Advanced Plans/Programs)	Dallas, Tex.	Post Office Dept. (Associate Director of Marketing)	$24,566	14
Custer, W. Eldridge	Humble Oil & Refining Co. (Senior Staff Supply Analyst)	Houston, Tex.	Dept. of the Treasury (Staff Assistant,Office of Assistant Sec. for Int'l Affairs)		15
Dresser, David I.	Motorola (Manager, Long Range Planning—Communications and Electronics Ins.)	Washington, D.C.	Model Cities Admin., Dept. of HUD (Human Resources Officer)	$24,500	14
Flanagan, John F., Jr.	American Airlines (Manager, Operations Planning)	New York, N.Y.	FAA, Dept. of Transportation (Fleet Requirements Specialist)		14
Frankel, Michael L.	TRW Systems Group (Senior Staff Engineer)	Washington, D.C.	Dept. of Interior (Program Coordinator in Office of Environmental & Program Planning—now EPA)	$26,100	14
Frannea, John A.	Mobil Oil Corporation (Senior Analyst, Midland E & P Division)	Midland, Tex.	Office of OEO, Executive Office of the President (Community Action Spec.)	$18,400	13

NAME	TITLE AND SPONSORING COMPANY	LOCATION	TITLE AND HOST AGENCY	AGENCY SALARY	GRADE
Johnson, Richard D.	Syntex Laboratories (Associate Director, Regulatory Affairs)	Palo Alto, Ca.	Nat'l. Bureau of Standards, Dept. of Commerce (Physical Sciences Administrator)	$24,000	15
Lehman, David A.	IBM Corporation (Program Manager)	Los Gatos, Ca.	U.S. Dept. of Trans. (Marketing Analyst, Civil Aviation Research & Develop. Policy Study (Office of the Sec.)	$29,000	15
Livaudais, Emanuel F., Jr.	Atlantic Richfield (Staff Landman)	Dallas, Tex.	U.S. Postal Service (Real Estate Appraiser, Bureau of Facilities)	$21,700	14
Macmanus, Thomas H.	General Electric Co. (Manager, Special Market Sales, Radio Receiver Dept.)	Utica, N.Y.	Bureau of Int'l Commerce, Dept. of Commerce (Project Officer, Int'l Business Assistance Service)	$20,813	14
Million, E. Z.	Computer Congenerics Corp. (Vice-President)	Oklahoma City, Okla.	USAF, Dept. of Defense (Operations Research Analyst)	$25,673	15

O'Shea, Timothy J.	Westinghouse Electric Corp. (Assistant Manager, Electric Components Sales Dept.)	London, England	Dept. of Commerce (Special Assistant to Dir. of Overseas in Emergency Markets Exports Operations)	$25,000	15
Rapp, Brian W.	McKinsey & Company (Consultant)	Washington, D.C.	Dept. of State (Management Analyst)	$24,349	15(FSO)
Salay, Stephen G.	Consolidated Edison (General Supervisor)	New York, N.Y.	Dept. of Interior (Staff Assistant Office of Asst. Sec.)		15
Scieszka, Jerry F.	State Street Bank and Trust Co. (Marketing Officer)	Boston, Ma.	Department of HUD (Staff Assistant, Model Cities)	$23,462	14
Toffel, Alvin E.	North American Rockwell Corp. (Director of Mgmt. Systems, Aviation Division Office)	Los Angeles, Ca.	OMB, Executive Office of the President (Systems Analyst)	$24,000	15
Wilson, Ralph L.	Owens-Illinois (Administrative Manager)	Toledo, Ohio (Home Office) Bahamas	General Services Administration (Labor Relations Specialist)	$22,900	14
Gillespie, Joseph S., Jr.	C&P Telephone Co. of Md. (General Traffic Supervisor)	Baltimore, Md.	Model Cities Admin. Dept. of HUD (Human Resources Officer)	$29,099	15

Appendix G

Analysis of 29-A Forms

The 29-A forms are time and manpower records completed on each Commission inspection. These reports are used by the Bureau of Personnel Management Evaluation for budget and planning purposes. Officials of the Bureau gave our group access to the 29-A forms for fiscal year 1970 and to selected forms for fiscal year 1969. From the 29-A forms data were transferred to prepared forms for analysis.

The statistics used in Chapter 6 are taken from an analysis of data copied from the 29-A forms for fiscal year 1970. In analyzing the Commission's inspection program only the data for nationwide and other general inspections were used. Nationwide and other general inspections were chosen because these inspections are the most comprehensive, using all of the inspection techniques, questionnaires, interviews, and review of personnel folders.

The primary technique used in analyzing the data was comparison. For example, the number of questionnaires examined was compared to the amount of time spent examining these questionnaires. Some of the 29-A forms from which we took data might list the number of interviews or the number of questionnaires covered but failed to list the amount of time spent on review. More often the 29-A forms would list the amount of time spent in reviewing questionnaires or conducting interviews but failed to list the number of questionnaires or interviews covered.

To use data from a form which itself did not list both the number of items covered and the amount of time involved would create inaccuracies in comparisons. For example, in determining the amount of time spent on employee interviews from a form which did not list the amount of time spent but which listed the number of interviews would understate the amount of time spent for interviews. (The assumption was made that some interviews had been conducted and that through inadvertance they had not been re-

(TYPED COPY OF 29-A FORM) A-18

United States Civil Service Commission

INSPECTION STATISTICS

PART I

A. Inspecting Office:__________ B. Date of Report to Agency:__________
C. Type of Inspection: ___ Nationwide ___ Other General ___Post Office
___ Special (Specify)__________

D. Establishment and Location:

E. Dates at Installation:

F. No. of Man-days On-site:

G. Date of Close-Out:

	Class. Act	Wage Board	Other	Total
H. No. Of Employees at Establishment:				
I. No. of Employees Covered by Inspection:				

PART II	No. Processed		Man-Hours		Total
A. Preparation					A.______
B. Opening Conferences					B.______
C. Review of Management Responsibilities					C.______
1. Management Interviews		____		____	
2. Review of Mgt. Policies & Programs				____	
D. Review of Personnel & Staff Admin.					D.______
1. Interviews with Personnel staff members		____		____	
2. Interviews with Other Mgt. staff members		____		____	
3. Personnel actions reviewed		____		____	
4. Class determinations reviewed		____		____	
a. Documentary review	(__)		(__)		
b. Position review	(__)		(__)		
E. Review of Personnel Mgt. at Supervisory Levels					E.______
1. Supervisory Interviews		____		____	
2. Employee interviews		____		____	
a. CSC selected	(__)		(__)		
b. Employee requested	(__)		(__)		
3. Employee Rep. interviews		____		____	
4. Questionnaires		____		____	
a. Employee questionnaires	(__)		(__)		
b. Supervisory questionnaires	(__)		(__)		
F. Closing Presentations					F.______
1. Preparation				____	
2. Pres. at personnel staff level				____	
3. Pres. at top management level				____	
G. Report Writing					G.______
1. Preparing report				____	
2. Reviewing report				____	
H. Misc. Activities (not otherwise covered)					H.______
Total Inspection Time				Total	______

A-19

PART III

A. Number of CSC staff participating in inspection ______
  1. No. full-time ______
  2. No. part-time ______
  3. No. in trainee status ______

PART IV

A. Review of Personnel Actions	Career, Cond.-Conv.	Temporary, Ext. & Conv.	Excepted Appointment	Transfer	Reinstatement	Reemployment	Promotion	Reassignment	Change to Lower Grade	Suspension	RIF-Incl. Furl, & Res.	Removal & Separation	Retirement (Age)	Performance Rating	Other		Total
1. No. Actions Covered																	
2. No. Cases Examined																	
3. Violations																	

B. Review of Agency Classification Actions	Documentary Review	Position Review	Total
1. Total Classification Act Positions Covered			
2. Number Positions Reviewed*			
3. Total Classification Changes Recommended*			
a. Grade Change-Up*			
b. Grade Change-Down*			
c. Series Change (Without Grade Change)*			
d. Title Change (No. Grade or Series Change)*			
4. No. of Recommendations for Agency Review or any other Agency Action			
5. No. of Recommendations for Preparing New P.D. or Revising Present P.D. (no other classification change involved)			

(Include all IA's)

corded.) Likewise to list 5 man-hours interviewing on a form which did not list the number of interviews would overstate the amount of time spent. Therefore, on any comparison only data from those forms which listed both the number of items covered and the amount of time spent were used. For each comparison all the data sheets were examined and those which did not contain both a listing of the number of items covered and the amount of time spent were culled. For each comparison the data from different forms might be culled and a varying number of form data sheets used. Although this procedure might lead to some discrepancies between comparisons, it did ensure that each comparison was more accurate than if all the forms had been used.

As pointed out in Chapter 6, officials of the Bureau of Personnel Management Evaluation had reservations about the value of some data recorded on the 29-A forms. Several officials said that questionnaire evaluation, interviewing, and other work was done "off the clock" and not recorded on the 29-A forms. Officials also said that previsitation activity was not properly broken down to indicate review work that was done prior to on-site visitation. In reviewing the 29-A forms we did find confusion in filling out items, e.g., how group interviews were recorded, and we did note occasional blank spaces. The forms also indicated confusion on how to record and break down the time of agency personnel who accompanied Commission inspectors and participated in the inspection. The Bureau of Personnel Management Evaluation has now adopted a revised form to record inspection time and manpower information.

On each 29-A form was a section listing the types of personnel actions of a particular type subject to review, the number of personnel actions reviewed, and the number of violations found. From this section in the forms covering nationwide, other general, and post office inspections the specific examples of coverage of personnel files used in Chapter 6 were taken.

Appendix H

Draft of Employee Rights and Accountability Act

TENTATIVE DRAFT OF AN EMPLOYEE RIGHTS AND ACCOUNTABILITY ACT

by Peter J. Petkas and Robert G. Vaughn

A bill to expand the rights of federal employees and to ensure the accountability of such employees to the citizens of the United States

Be it enacted by the Senate and House of Representatives of the United States of America in Congress assembled, that this Act may be cited as the "Federal Employee Rights and Accountability Act of 1972."

TITLE I—Findings and Declaration of Purpose

Sec. 101. Findings
The Congress hereby finds that

(a) Employees of the federal government risk substantial damage to their careers, possible loss of their livelihoods, and other forms of harassment if they express their views about

(1) the management of their agencies;
(2) the failure of their agencies to serve their statutory functions;
(3) the direction of agency policy;
(4) conflicts of public and private interest within their agencies; or
(5) illegal conduct by the agency or its employees.

(b) These risks exist to a large extent without regard to whether views are expressed through appropriate channels within the agency, to committees of Congress which have jurisdiction over the subject matter involved, through the fulfillment of lawful obligations of employees, or to the public at large;

(c) Existing laws, rules, and regulations of the separate agencies and of the Civil Service Commission have proven seriously deficient both for employees and for citizens;

(d) Similarly, citizens, under present laws, rules, and regulations do not have adequate access to the courts to seek the removal of employees and officials who fail to discharge their duties either under the laws which prescribe the responsibilities of federal agencies or those which regulate the conduct of federal employees; and

(e) The failure of agencies and their employees to fully implement Congressional enactments is frequently due to the inability of knowledgeable employees to communicate to the Congress and to the public information vital to the oversight functions of Congress and to the public's right to know;

Sec. 102. Declaration of Purpose

The Congress finds the purpose of this Act to be

(a) To enhance the rights of federal employees to challenge the actions or failures of their agencies and to express their views, without fear of retaliation, through appropriate channels within the agency, through complete and frank responses to congressional inquiry, through free access to law-enforcement officials, through oversight agencies of both the executive and legislative branches of government, and through appropriate communication with the public;

(b) To broaden remedies available to citizens to hold government employees accountable for the performance of their duties;

(c) To ensure that Acts of Congress enacted to protect individual citizens are properly enforced; and

(d) To provide new rights and remedies to guarantee that citizens can have confidence in their government and to ensure that public offices are truly public trusts.

TITLE II—Protection of Employees and of Congressional Access to Information

Sec. 201. Definitions

(a) For the purposes of the Act, "employee" (except as otherwise provided by this Act or when specifically modified) is defined as in 5 USC §2105 except that

(1) an employee paid from nonappropriated funds of the Army and Air Force Exchange Service, Army and Air Force Motion Picture Service, Navy Ship's Stores Ashore, Navy exchanges, and other instrumentalities of the armed forces conducted for the comfort, pleasure, contentment, and mental and physical improvement of personnel of the armed forces is deemed an employee for the purposes of this Act;

(2) an employee appointed by the President with the advice and consent of the Senate or any employee in a position of a confidential or policy-determining character as enumerated in 5 C.F.R. §213.3276 is not an employee for purposes of this Title.

(b) For purposes of this Act, "dismissed" (except as otherwise provided by this Act or when specificially modified) shall mean any personnel or manpower action which separates an employee or abolishes his position.

(c) For purposes of this Act, "agency" shall include every authority of the United States subject to the Administrative Procedures Act and shall also include any organization which has one or more corporate directors, commissioners, chief executive officers, or members of a governing body appointed by the President or an appointee of the President.

Sec. 202. Employee Bill of Rights

Employees shall have the following rights which the Employee Rights and Accountability Board, established in Title IV of this Act, and its agents shall have the duty to defend, protect, and enforce:

(a) The right to freely express their opinions on all public issues, including those related to the duties they are assigned to perform, *provided, however,* that any agency may promulgate reasonable rules and regulations requiring that any such opinions be clearly disassociated from agency or administration policy.

(b) The right to disclose information unlawfully suppressed; information concerning illegal or unethical conduct which threatens or which is likely to threaten public health or safety or which involves the unlawful appropriation or use of public funds; and information which would tend to impeach the testimony of officers or employees of the government before committees of Congress or the responses of such officers or employees to inquiries from members of the Senate or House of Representatives concerning the implementation of programs, the expenditure of public funds, and the protection of the constitutional rights of citizens and the rights of government employees under this Act and under any other laws, rules, or regulations for the protection of the rights of employees; *provided, however,* that nothing in this section shall be construed to permit the disclosure of the contents of personnel files, personal medical reports, or the disclosure of any other information in such a manner as to invade the individual privacy of an employee or citizen of the United States.

(c) The right to communicate freely and openly with members of Congress and to respond fully and with candor to inquiries from committees of Congress and from members of Congress, *provided, however,* that nothing in this section shall be construed to permit the invasion of the individual privacy of other employees or of citizens of the United States.

(d) The right to assemble in public places for the free discussion of matters of interest to themselves and to the public; and the right to notify fellow employees and the public of such meetings.

(e) The right to due process in the resolution of grievances and appeals including, but not limited to

(1) the right to counsel;

(2) the right to a public hearing and a copy of the transcript of such hearing;

(3) the right to cross-examine witnesses and to compel the attendance and testimony of witnesses and to compel the production of all relevant documents in the course of such a hearing or other similar proceeding; and

(4) the right to testify and submit evidence on behalf of other employees and of other citizens seeking redress in the courts or in the administrative process.

(f) The right to humane, dignified, and reasonable conditions of employment which allow for personal growth and self-fulfillment, and for the unhindered discharge of job and civic responsibilities.

(g) The right to individual privacy, *provided, however,* that nothing in this section shall limit in any manner an employee's access to his own personnel file, medical report file, or any other file or document concerning his status or performance within his agency.

Section 203. Complaints of Criminal Harassment for Congressional Testimony

(a) Any complaint alleging violations of 18 U.S.C. §1505 (which prohibits coercion and harassment of Congressional witnesses) shall be promptly investigated by the Justice Department. Within six months after filing of a complaint, the Justice Department shall render a decision on whether or not prosecution under that section is warranted. If the Department decides prosecution is not warranted, it shall state with specificity the facts and reasons upon which such decision is based.

(b) If the Justice Department renders a decision pursuant to this section that prosecution is not warranted or if it fails to render a decision as required by this section, any citizen may petition the United States District Court for the district in which the alleged violation took place or the United States District Court for the District of Columbia for an order to compel prosecution. If the court finds, after an independent review of the evidence, that a prima facie case exists, it shall order prosecution to be commenced.

(c) In its independent review of evidence the court shall have access to the enforcement file of the Justice Department and to all other relevant documents or files within that department or any agency thereof.

TITLE III—Accountability of Employees

Sec. 301. Definitions

(a) For purposes of this Title, "conflicts of interest" shall include behavior proscribed by 18 U.S.C. §§201–224. In addition, "conflicts of interest" may include behavior which the court in the exercise of sound discretion proscribes. In the exercise of its discretion, the court may consider Executive Orders addressed to the subject, rules and regulations governing employee conduct, and principles of fiduciary law.

(b) For purposes of this Title, "employee" shall be defined as in Section 201 of this Act, except that an employee appointed by the President with the advice and consent of the Senate or an employee in a position of a confidential or policy-determining character as enumerated in 5 C.F.R. § 213.3276 shall be an employee for purposes of this Title.

(c) For purposes of this Title, an "employee responsible" is one to whom Congress has delegated authority and any employee to whom such authority has been redelegated.

(d) For purposes of this Title, "consumer protection law" shall include any law intended to protect or which does in fact protect individual consumers from unfair, deceptive, or misleading acts or practices; anticompetitive acts or practices; or nondisclosure of product quality, weight, size, or performance.

Sec. 302. Public Employees as Fiduciaries

(a) Any employee who administers, enforces, or implements any health, safety, environmental, or consumer protection law or any rules or regulations promulgated for the enforcement of such laws is a fiduciary to any individual or class of individuals intended to be protected or who are in fact protected from injury or harm or risk of injury or harm by such laws, rules, or regulations, and, as a fiduciary, is obligated to protect such individual or class of individuals.

(b) Any individual or class of individuals may commence a civil action on his or their own behalf against any employee or employees in any agency for breach of a fiduciary duty upon showing that said employee or employees by their acts or omissions have exposed said individual or class of individuals to an injury or harm or risk of injury or harm from which they are to be protected by the employee or employees. Such action may be brought in the United States District Court for the district in which the employee or any one of the employees reside or in the United States District Court for the District of Columbia. The District Court shall have jurisdiction to entertain such action without regard to the amount in controversy or the diversity of citizenship of the parties. The United States through the Attorney General shall defend any employee or employees against whom such action is commenced. Such employee or employees may, however, at his or their option, provide for his or their own defense.

(c) If the court finds that any employee or employees have breached their fiduciary duty by any act or omission or by any series of acts or omissions, the court

(1) shall order performance or cessation of performance, as appropriate;

(2) may temporarily suspend any person or persons without pay from the Agency for a period not exceeding three months; and

(3) may remove an individual or individuals from the Agency; or

(4) may take any other appropriate action against any employee or employees within the Agency who have breached the duties of the fiduciary relationship.

Sec. 303. Curbing Fraud and Conflicts of Interest

(a) (1) Any citizen shall have a right to commence a suit in the U.S. District Court of the district in which he resides or in U.S. District Court for the District of Columbia on behalf of the United States to recover funds which have been improperly paid by the United States while there exists any conflict of interest on the part of the employee responsible for such payment.

(2) It shall be an affirmative defense to any action under this Section that the defendant did not know or have reason to know of the conflict of interest.

(b) Any citizen who commences a suit under this section shall be entitled to 30 percent of the amount recovered for the government plus attorney's fees and other costs incidental to the action.

(c) The right of a citizen to commence and maintain a suit under this section shall continue notwithstanding any action taken by the Justice Department or any U.S. attorney, *provided, however,* that if the United States shall first commence suit, a citizen may not commence a suit under this section, *provided, however,* that if the United States shall fail to carry on such suit with due diligence within a period of six months or within such additional time as the court may allow, a citizen may commence a suit under this section and such suit shall continue notwithstanding any action taken by the Justice Department or any U.S. attorney.

Sec. 304. Intent of Congress in Section 303

In §303 of this Title, it is the intent of Congress to create a right of citizens to commence and maintain suits under the provisions of this Title.

TITLE IV—Employee Rights and Accountability Board

Sec. 401. Definition

For purposes of this Title, "employee" shall be defined as in Section 201 of this Act, except that an employee appointed by the

President with the advice and consent of the Senate or an employee in a position of a confidential or policy-determining charcater as enumerated in 5 C.F.R. §213.3276 shall be an employee for purposes of this Title.

Sec. 402. Establishment of the Employee Rights and Accountability Board

(a) There is hereby established an Employee Rights and Accountability Board (hereinafter referred to as the "Board"). The Board shall be composed of five members, to be appointed as hereinafter directed. No more than three members of the Board may be of the same political party. No more than two members of the Board may have ever served in personnel, management, or administrative positions in any agency. Three members of the Board shall be attorneys admitted to practice before the bar of any jurisdiction in the United States for three years at the time of appointment. No member shall be eligible for reappointment.

(b) The term of office of each member of the Board shall be six years, except that (1) of those members first appointed, two shall serve for two years and two shall serve for four years respectively, from the date of appointment, and (2) any member appointed to fill a vacancy occurring prior to the expiration of the term for which his or her predecessor was appointed shall be appointed for the remainder of such term.

(c) The Chairman of the Board shall be elected by the Board to serve a two-year term. The Chairman shall be the chief executive and administrative officer of the Board.

(d) All members of the Board shall be compensated at the rate provided for in Executive Level 2 as set out in section 5313 of Title 5 of the United States Code.

(e) Three members of the Board shall constitute a quorum for the transaction of business.

(f) The Board may appoint and fix the compensations of such officers, attorneys, and employees, and make such expenditures as may be necessary to carry out its functions.

(g) Notwithstanding Section 206 of the Budget and Accounting Act of 1921 (31 U.S.C. 15), the Board shall transmit its estimates and requests for appropriations (including any requests for increases therein) directly to the Senate and House of Representatives.

(h) One member of the Board shall be appointed by the President with the advice and consent of the Senate, two members shall be appointed by the president pro tempore of the Senate, and two members shall be appointed by the Speaker of the House of Representatives; *provided that* the first member appointed by the President shall serve six years, the first members appointed by the president pro tempore of the Senate shall serve two and four years respectively, and the first members appointed by the Speaker of the House of Representatives shall serve four and two years respectively.

Sec. 403. Office of Inspection and Complaint

(a) The Board shall establish an Office of Inspection and Complaint which shall perform the following functions:

(1) Conduct inspections of all agencies to ensure compliance with orders of the Board;

(2) Conduct inspections to provide information on the implementation of rules and regulations of the Board;

(3) Conduct inspections to discover violations of rules and regulations of the Board;

(4) Investigate complaints filed with the Board by citizens and employees pursuant to this Title;

(5) Initiate actions against employees for violations of this Title or rules and regulations promulgated hereunder; and

(6) Perform such other investigative functions as the Board may prescribe.

(b) The Office of Inspection and Complaint shall be administered by an Inspector General who shall be appointed by the Board for a term of seven years and who shall be removable only for good cause.

Sec. 404. Office of Trial Examiners

(a) The Board shall establish an Office of Trial Examiners which shall hear and adjudicate complaints filed under this Title.

(b) No person may serve as a Trial Examiner or perform any of the duties of a Trial Examiner, who is not admitted to practice before the bar of any jurisdiction in the United States.

(c) The Office of Trial Examiners shall be administered by a Chief Examiner appointed by the Board for a six-year term.

(d) The Office of Trial Examiners shall not be subordinate to any other office under the Board, but shall receive its authority and direction directly from the Board.

Sec. 405. Powers of the Board

The Employee Rights and Accountability Board (hereinafter referred to as the "Board") shall have, in addition to the authority necessary and proper for carrying out its duties and the duties of its subordinate agencies and officers as specified elsewhere in this Title, the authority to

(1) Inspect and investigate all aspects of the federal personnel system, including but not limited to the effectiveness of disciplinary procedures and violations of employee rights;

(2) Appoint and remove all subordinate officials and employees, subject to the rules and regulations of the Board applicable to all civil servants; *provided, however,* that the Inspector General and the Chief Examiner shall be removable only for good cause;

(3) Hear and adjudicate complaints received from federal agencies and departments, from employees, and from citizens, including employee complaints alleging wrongful dismissal;

(4) Reprimand any government employee, suspend any government employee, fine any government employee, remove any government employee, or take other appropriate disciplinary action, *provided, however,* that any such action shall be taken pursuant to duly promulgated regulations of the Board and shall not be inconsistent with the rights of government employees granted by the Act, *provided further, however,* that the Board shall have the power to order any fines or portion thereof assessed pursuant to this section paid to the person, persons, or government agency damaged by the employee hereunder fined, upon application and proof of loss;

(5) Establish standards of conduct for all government employees pertaining to the performance of duties, conflicts of interests, and improper use of personnel management authority;

(6) Conduct and manage its own litigation without review, clearance, or participation by any agency of the executive branch, including the Department of Justice;

(7) Review employee complaints filed with the Office of Inspection and Complaint which allege that a transfer, reassignment, or manpower separation or readjustment was motivated

by malice or taken in retaliation for the exercise of an employee's rights as an employee or as a citizen.

(8) Promulgate any rules and regulations necessary for the fulfillment of its duties under this Act.

Sec. 406. Complaint Procedures

(a) The Board shall establish a citizen complaint procedure and shall receive and consider complaints from any citizen alleging violation by an employee of any federal law or any rule or regulation promulgated under any federal law; violation of any employee code of conduct or standard, including but not limited to those promulgated pursuant to this Act, or any rules or regulations promulgated by the Board; failure of any employee to carry out his duty under any federal law, rule, or regulation; negligent or improper performance of his duty by any employee.

The citizen complaint procedure established under this section shall include the following provisions:

(1) Complaints shall be filed with the Office of Inspection and Complaint, which shall within sixty days of the receipt of the complaint render a written decision setting forth findings of fact and including an order either dismissing the complaint or initiating prosecution before the Office of Trial Examiners; *provided, however,* that an order of dismissal under this section shall not bar or otherwise limit any other rights of the complainant to raise the same or similar issue before the Board or before any other federal agency; *provided further, however,* that any order of dismissal shall refer the complainant to any other appropriate federal, state, or local agency.

(2) If the Office of Inspection and Complaint orders the complaint dismissed, the citizen complainant or any other citizen may appeal the order to the Board within thirty days of the entry of such order.

(3) If upon review of any order of dismissal appealed under this subsection, the Board upholds the order of dismissal, the citizen complainant or any citizen may appeal the order of the Board upholding such dismissal to the United States Court of Appeals of the District of Columbia or the United States Court of Appeals for the district in which the complainant resides.

(4) The Office of Inspection and Complaint shall prosecute all complaints which a trial examiner finds meritorious, or

which the Board has found meritorious, or which an appropriate appellate court has found meritorious. All such complaints shall be adjudicated as set out in Sections 407 and 408.

(b) The Board shall establish an employee complaint procedure and shall receive and consider employee complaints alleging any misconduct enumerated in Section 406(a) of this Title as well as violations of any rules or regulations of the Board relating to the rights of employees and any action against an employee or against the interests of any employee by his employer agency motivated by malice.

The complaint procedure established under this subsection shall include the same provisions enumerated in subsection (a) of this section for citizen complaints.

(c) The Board shall establish an agency complaint procedure and shall receive and consider complaints from federal agencies and departments alleging any misconduct enumerated in Section 406(a) of this Title as well as cause for removal or discipline as specified in the rules and regulations of the Board.

The complaint procedure established under this subsection shall include the following provisions:

(1) Agency complaints against employees shall be presented directly to the Office of Trial Examiners and shall not be subject to review or consideration by the Office of Inspection and Complaint.

(2) Before any complaint is accepted by the Office of Trial Examiners under this subsection the agency shall

(a) Give advance notice ten days prior to filing the proposed complaint stating specifically and in detail any and all reasons for the proposed action.

(b) At the time of notice thus required, inform the employee of his right to answer personally and in writing and to submit affidavits in support of his answer.

(c) Provide the employee with a decision on whether or not a complaint will be filed stating the reasons which have been sustained and informing the employee of his rights before the Office of Trial Examiners, which notice and statement of rights shall have been approved by the Board.

(d) File the complaint within five days of notification of the employee of the decision to file.

Provided, however, that the employee against whom a complaint has been filed may be suspended with pay during the period herein provided for agency action and such additional time as may be necessary for the agency to obtain a ruling from the Trail Examiner as prescribed in subsection (3) for suspension pending a final decision on the merits, if his continued presence poses a substantial risk of harm to himself, to his fellow employees, or to the public.

(3) If the employee does not object to the Office of Trial Examiners within fifteen days of receiving a decision that a complaint will be filed, the Trial Examiner to whom the complaint has been assigned shall order the action sought by the agency complainant.

(4) If the employee objects to the action requested by the agency, the Trial Examiner to whom the complaint has been assigned shall order a hearing; *provided, however,* that the Trial Examiner, if he finds that the facts alleged in the complaint would, if true, support the conclusion that the employee's continued presence poses a substantial risk of harm to himself; to his fellow employees, or to the public, the Trial Examiner may also order that the employee be suspended with pay pending a final decision on the merits by the Trial Examiner.

Sec. 407. Hearing Procedures

(a) Hearings on any complaints prosecuted by the Office of Inspection and Complaint or by any agency shall be conducted by a Trial Examiner provided by the Office of Trial Examiners.

(b) Complaint hearings shall conform to the requirements of 5 USC §554 as in effect at the time of approval of this Act.

(c) Any hearing conducted by a Trial Examiner pursuant to this Title shall be open to the public

(d) For the purpose of any hearing under this Title, any Trial Examiner is empowered to administer oaths and affirmation, subpoena witnesses, compel their attendance, take evidence, and require the production of any books, papers, correspondence, memoranda, contracts, agreements, or other records which he deems relevant or material to the inquiry. Such attendance of witnesses and the production of any such records may be required from any place in any State or in any Territory or other place subject to the jurisdiction of the United States at any designated place of hearing.

(e) In case of contumacy by, or refusal to obey a subpoena issued to any person, the Board may invoke the aid of any court of the United States within the jurisdiction of which such hearing is carried on, or where such person resides or carries on business, in requiring the attendance and testimony of witnesses and the production of books, papers, correspondence, memoranda, contracts, agreements, and other records. And such court may issue an order requiring such person to appear before the Trial Examiner, there to produce records, if so ordered, or to give testimony touching the matter under investigation or in question; and any failure to obey such order of the court may be punished by such court as a contempt thereof. All process in any such case may be served in the judicial district whereof such person is an inhabitant or wherever he may be found. Any person, who, without just cause, shall fail or refuse to attend and testify or to answer any lawful inquiry or to produce any records, if in his or her power to do so, in obedience to the subpoena of the Trial Examiner, shall be guilty of a misdemeanor and, upon conviction, shall be subject to a fine of not more than $10,000 or to imprisonment for a term of not more than one year, or both.

(f) At least three members of the Board must participate in the deliberation preceding a decision and the decision of any appeal brought before the Board pursuant to this Title.

(g) All decisions of the Board, of Trial Examiners, and of any other official or employee of the Board required to issue findings of fact or written decisions under this Act or under the rules or regulations of the Board shall be published in a convenient form and made available to the public at reasonable cost.

(h) Any person against whom a complaint has been brought under this section may be represented by counsel or by his agency or both.

Sec. 408. Appeal Procedures

(a) Any employee or agency party to an action before the Office of Trial Examiners, or any complainant, may appeal the decision of a Trial Examiner to the Board, *provided, however,* that, with respect to citizen complaints, any citizen who is a member of the class of individuals intended to be protected by the law, rule, or regulation on which the complaint is based and who is affected by the alleged violation, omission, or negligent act, or any employee affected by the alleged violation, omission, or negligent act may appeal a decision to the Board.

(b) In any appeal taken pursuant to this section, the Board shall review the record and uphold, reverse, or modify the decision of the Trial Examiner. The Board may order oral argument, on its own motion or on motion timely filed by any party, and provide such other procedures or rules as it deems practicable or desirable in any appeal under this section and consistent with the Employee Bill of Rights in Title II of this Act.

(c) Any employee or agency party to an appeal to the Board, any complainant, any citizen or employee affected by an alleged violation may appeal the decision of the Trial Examiner, and any other citizen or employee affected by an alleged violation may appeal the decision of the Board to the United States Court of Appeals for the District of Columbia or the United States Court of Appeals for the district in which the appelant resides, *provided, however,* that the venue for such appeals shall not be such as to cause undue hardship to any employee or citizen.

(d) In any appeal in which official dereliction that may threaten public safety has been alleged, the court may remand the appeal to an appropriate district court for a hearing on the facts.

Sec. 409. Congressional Intent

It is the intent of Congress that the Board effectuate the following policy through its regulations and decisions:

1. That public employees be made personally accountable for failure to enforce the laws and for negligence, incompetence, or improper performance of their public duties;

2. That the rights of employees to expose corruption, dishonesty, incompetence, or administrative failure be protected;

3. That the rights of employees to contact and communicate with Congress be protected;

4. That employees be protected from reprisal or retaliation for the performance of their duties; and

5. That civil servants be motivated to do their duties justly and efficiently.

Appendix I

Civil Service Commission's Analysis of Nader Reports

Following is the Commission's analysis of the Nader Reports and the author's answers to written questions posed by Congressman John Rousselot. The questions, contained in the record of hearings before the House Post Office and Civil Service Committee, mirror many of the concerns expressed in the Commission's analysis. Although the original report has been edited for publication, the exchange highlights many of the major points of disagreement between the Commission and the author. A brief comment by the author concerning the Commission's analysis concludes this appendix.

U.S. Civil Service Commission Analysis of the Nader Reports

INTRODUCTION

This paper deals with two reports issued in June 1972 by the "Public Interest Research Group," under Mr. Ralph Nader. The first report, entitled *The Spoiled System: A Call for Civil Service Reform,* is intended to be a comprehensive examination and assessment of the Federal civil service as a whole, and of the U.S. Civil Service Commission as an institution. The second report, *Behind the Promises,* deals with the governmentwide Equal Employment Opportunity program.

Their Approach

The study methodology started with preconceptions and followed with a search for findings to support the preconceptions.

The reports are caustically critical of civil servants, personnel policies, and Commission operations as they impact on bureaucratic behavior and, in turn, the public they serve. They attack the basic mission orientation of the Commission and follow with rather severe, frequently unsupported and ill-informed criticisms of individuals, program performance in appeals, "inspections," personnel investigations, and equal employment opportunity.

The reports are unprofessional in documentation; more often than not they support conclusions with impressions rather than with hard facts. They are replete with distortions that show up not only in the factual errors, which we point out in this paper, but also in their repetitive use of a few carefully selected but totally unrepresentative "horror stories" that they use to prove their points.

The frequently unsupported and partisan allegations taken from these cases (some of which are currently in litigation) are used to draw conclusions based on gross generalizations. The oft-repeated charge of "bureaucratic lawlessness" is simply not credible in the face of the tens of thousands of public employees, from the bottom to the top of Government, who faithfully and honestly perform admirably, day in and day out. A few problem cases, described from one point of view only, certainly do not form a basis for branding the entire Federal service as a "spoiled system." There are some limits to how many times one or two names can be invoked to support an allegation that 2.8 million Federal employees have no protections from a "venal" management, and no rights to speak out. The thousands of Federal employees who each day bring significant problems to light successfully are wholly ignored. The charge of irresponsible management is not supported, nor are the allegations of "bureaucratic lawlessness." Both of these major themes of the report are based on the grossest of generalizations.

At best, this kind of fact-finding and reporting is unprofessional; at worst, it is irresponsible. It misrepresents the Federal personnel system. And it fails to recognize the appropriate employee safeguards that are present, as well as the basic integrity of the vast majority of Federal managers. In so doing it directly insults the millions of public employees who are serving the public faithfully and well.

Our Approach

In analyzing these reports, we have taken a substantially different approach. We have attempted to discuss the recommendations on a higher plane and on their merits. We have elected not to argue over the inaccuracies and distortions. We have tried to look at the recommendations objectively and, whether supported by fact or not, fully consider their worth in terms of improving our operations. We find that some of the recommendations are useful and we agree with them; in most such instances we had already identified the problem and were working on solutions.

The First Report—The Spoiled System

This report deals with the civil service system overall, the Civil Service Commission as an organization, and with three main program areas: appeals, evaluations, and investigations. The stated purpose is to seek ways in which high-level Federal employees can be held accountable for dereliction of duty, and by which public-spirited employees can be protected. To understand the thrust of the report and its prescriptions for change in the current civil service system, it is necessary to appreciate three basic concepts which provide the foundation for the author's analysis, conclusions, and recommendations. These concepts deal with the issue of accountability, the role of the Civil Service Commission, and the matter of how authority to manage is delegated and exercised in the executive branch of the Government.

Accountability.—In an introduction to the report, Mr. Nader expresses concern about "monolithic, nonaccountable government processes." He regards as one of several "centrally important questions" the "ways in which the civil service . . . can be held accountable for its actions as agencies and, particularly, as individual public officials." The report suggests that procedures do not exist permitting "citizens to initiate a review of personnel behavior," or "employees to raise violations of personnel policies." It also suggests that "Congress is unable to respond effectively" to frustration of its policies by bureaucrats "because no means exist to impose personal responsibility on administrators." That the report offers no factual support for these assertions is less important than the fact that they are totally in error. There are a good many ways in which Federal agencies and individual Federal officials and employees can be and are held accountable for their actions, as well as for their failure to act.

In a general way the Commission is of course accountable to the American public at large. To the extent that this accountability is direct, it is reflected by the publication and wide distribution of many Commission materials. This general notion of accountability is also channeled through other entities, such as the President and Congress, which are themselves directly accountable to the public as citizens and voters. In addition, the Commission satisfies a measure of its accountability by direct contact, typically in the forms of consultation and publication, with large and small groups of special interest publics: unions, veterans' organizations, civil rights groups, professional associations, employees, public administration associations, and many smaller groups.

The Commission also fulfills a very direct obligation of accountability to the Congress and its committees which publish all manner of information about our operations so that the public may be informed. This accountability takes many forms. Congress can, of course, pass, amend, or repeal any of the enabling legislation under which the Commission operates. Its appropriation committees, through control of our purse, exercise absolutely compelling power over the range and nature of our activities. Congressional inquiries concerning our operations on many fronts occur almost constantly. Moreover, one cannot ignore the statutory right of employees, individually or collectively, to petition or to furnish information to Congress.

Finally, a most important force in assuring public accountability of the Commission and other agency officials is the media. The newspapers in particular, through their Federal columnists, are almost daily raising searching questions—and demanding and receiving answers—about Federal personnel practices. They play a key role in highlighting personnel issues and cases which bear directly on the accountability of managers and personnel officials for their actions.

It is a simple matter to focus attention on any form of abuse of official power exercised by Federal officials or employees. The means of accountability do exist, and they are used.

The report reflects this notion of accountability: it assumes not only that any citizen has the right at any time to ask any Government official to account to him for any act (or any failure to act), but also that if the official is regarded by the citizen as in any way wanting or culpable in the exercise of his responsibilities, he should be publicly pilloried and disgraced, as well as discharged or otherwise disciplined. Its underlying assumption of public interest and accountability that venality and irresponsibility are the prevailing characteristics of those to whom public responsibility has been entrusted is simply not valid.

Role of the Commission.—A second basic concept in this report is a misunderstanding of the proper role of the Civil Service Commission. While the report is ambiguous, the thrust appears to be toward a mission aimed at direct control of the personnel management environment in the Federal service. This is followed by recommendations to, (1) change the "Basic assumptions surrounding the inspection function..." away from a "bargaining game," and (2) even more broadly, strip the Commission of all regulatory, complaint, and appellate functions and place them in a proposed "Employee Rights and Accountability Board." "Service oriented functions could be left in a revitalized Civil Service Commission which could serve as a management consulting firm, reducing the need of Federal agencies to rely heavily on outside consultants such as Booz, Allen and Hamilton, or McKinsey."

We take sharp issue with this basic theme that the Commission can only be effective if "pure"—i.e., purely regulatory or purely consultative. The point is, this should not be an "either/or" proposition. The Commission can and does perform both functions daily in its personnel management surveys and in other program areas. The two functions are, in many ways, closely interrelated. Since much of the Federal personnel system is based on regulations and standards, our required actions for correcting violations have a direct and broad tie-in to our function of providing management advice on how to improve all personnel operations within the framework of the system. Simple case correction does not solve the broader problem—the question of why the violation occurred in the first place. The report sees in this a role conflict; we see a relationship. Moreover, in today's complex society it is a rare institution or person that has only one single role, or mission, to perform.

Consequently, we view this report as reflecting both a limited and inaccurate perception of the Commission's role. It is limited in its underlying notion that the protection of employee rights is not an important management concern and responsibility. And it is inaccurate in its implication that our policies, and the manner in which we administer them, fail to recognize and fully protect employee rights. In carrying out our long-standing and clearly defined responsibilities as the central personnel agency for the executive branch, and as a management arm of the President, we have not overlooked or neglected our responsibilities directly related to protecting employee rights.

Finally, one sweeping report theme regarding the role the Commission has been playing needs unmistakable correction. That is the charge that the Commission is principally concerned with defending the status quo; that it is unchanging, stodgy, unimaginative, and lacking in innovation. The record of the past years belies this charge. The fact is, this has been a self-reforming Commission, progressive, and strong on taking new initiatives. We could list many examples to prove the point; a few will suffice.

The initiatives have been endless: the Intergovernmental Personnel Act has been brought into being, modern and streamlined examining and referral systems have been developed, the scope of our labor relations assistance has been greatly enlarged, the evaluation program has been revitalized and evaluation has been made mandatory governmentwide. Also,the Commission has come forth with new concepts for enlarging equal opportunity such as upward mobility and has developed and pushed imaginative programs for providing jobs for returning veterans, the disadvantaged, the handicapped and other groups. We are continuously studying our programs to see how they might be improved; the current broad scale appellate study and our Federal Executive Service proposal being immediate cases in point.

Rather than defenders of the status quo, the Commission could more accurately be described as disturbers of it.

Delegation of Authority.—Once again the report seems to find something conceptually wrong and administratively impractical about the whole matter of delegations of personnel authority to the agencies. It seems to ignore the fact that the basic powers of appointment and removal are lodged in the agency heads, and that the permissible intervention of the Commission in personnel matters is regulated by statute. It is alleged that, once the decision for decentralization of various elements of authority over personnel matters was made, we lost regulatory control and became an agency without a "clearly defined mission," thus developing a "role which stresses consultation and support." We find it difficult to understand why consultation and support are inherently undesirable, or are not mission-related.

Although the rationale and rhetoric are equally difficult to follow, the report seems to be saying three things: (1) that when agency managers possess the authority to manage that is commensurate with their legal responsibilities, they will abuse it; (2) that we grant agencies too much personnel authority beyond that which they are given in their enabling statutes; and (3) that we do not police these delegations adequately.

We find these assertions to be without merit and unsupported by the limited evidence in the report. The entire personnel management evaluation program belies the latter charge. In addition to the fact that no practicable alternative arrangements are offered, these observations show a rather limited understanding of the practicalities of managing public programs and activities under our constitutional form of government.

Although opting for the "comprehensive restructuring" of the Federal service outlined above, the report offers a series of "temporary pallatives" [sic] that presumably would enable the Commission to take some quick steps to improve itself. These steps or recommendations, which the report described as "only ameliorative," are fifty-three in number, of which fifty-one are discussed in detail in this paper. The remaining two treated actions the report recognized as already having been taken by the Commission.

The Second Report—Behind the Promises

This report deals exclusively with the matter of equal employment opportunity. Unlike its predecessor, however, it does not focus on specific and detailed recommendations for change. Instead, it is basically a very lengthy discussion of a number of relatively unsupported allegations of insufficient accomplishment and inadequate administration of the governmentwide EEO program. It attempts to indict the Government as a whole for its alledgedly poor record of achievement, and it condemns the Commission for asserted failure to fulfill our leadership and stewardship responsibilities in advancing equality of opportunity.

The same deficiencies found in the earlier report are often found in this latter one: selective and distorted use of findings, unsupported allegations, and conceptually faulty conclusions. Its content and approach, however, being less specific and pointed in terms of recommendations, require different treatment than the former report.

DETAILED ANALYSIS OF THE REPORTS

The following section of this paper discusses the four principal areas of concern addressed in these two reports: appeals, evaluation program, personnel investigations, and equal employment opportunity. In the first three areas, Commission comments are offered on each of the fifty-one specific recommendations contained in the first report.

Appeals

The fundamental thesis in the report is that the appellate function should be completely separated from the Civil Service Commission and lodged in a new Employee Rights and Accountability Board, which would have broad powers to protect employee rights and to apply sanctions against individual officials in order to influence official behavior. The specific recommendations are offered only as temporary palliatives: interim remedial measures while the appeals function remains in the Commission.

The overall thrust of the recommendations is toward an appellate system that will afford increased protection of individual rights, is more highly judicialized in its procedures, and is altered in its underlying philosophy. The report calls for different patterns and sources of staffing, new kinds of training, and greater independence in decision making by appeals examiners. Above all, it presses for a shift away from what it considers a management-oriented outlook, toward a process that is more open and guided by standards or precendent. Public hearings and published decisions are asked for, together with improved information, easier access and better administration. A major premise is that no activity is more important than the appellate area in determining what behavior will be rewarded and what punished, and that the Commission has overlooked the impact of its adjudications in this respect.

We have dealt with these recommendations in three ways: (1) we have indicated *agreement* with those which we consider appropriate and timely; (2) we have *rejected* those that are based on faulty or mistaken premises which we cannot accept; and (3) we have *deferred* decision on those that are so closely intertwined with the central aspects of our current study of adverse action and appellate processes that judgment should, we think, be withheld pending completion of the project.

In the following discussion, we have grouped related recommendations together for brevity and clarity of treatment, where appropriate.

Recommendations with Which We Agree

Recommendation 5.—This recommendation suggests that more and better statistical data and other kinds of information are needed in order to monitor and evaluate appellate operations.

CSC Comment: "Action is under way to design and install an improved management information system for the appellate function. Decisions made as a result of our current study of appellate processes will affect the content of the data system."

Recommendations 6, 8 and 10.—These recommendations call for the development of a case index (#6), the publication of appellate decisions (#8), and the recording and publishing of dissenting votes in BAR decisions (#10).

CSC Comment: "We already distribute significant appellate decisions within the Commission. The Board of Appeals and Review (BAR) has developed an index and had already planned to digest its significant decisions beginning this year. The Commission will now develop a system for indexing and digesting all significant or precedential final decisions. Dissenting votes are recorded and will be published as part of each decision. All decisions would be made available, with identifying information deleted."

Recommendation 12.—Transcription tapes of all Commission

hearings should remain in the hands of an independent third party who may certify their accuracy.

CSC Comment: "Transcription tapes should be handled systematically and cared for properly. It is not necessary that this be done by an independent third party. Action is being taken to set up the requisite system and procedures."

Recommendation 19.—The Commission should delineate the misuse and violation of personnel regulations for which agency officials will be punished and seek to make these regulations meaningful by their application.

CSC Comment: "It is entirely proper for the Commission to use its adjudicatory functions in appropriate circumstances to assure that personnel policies and regulations are enforced. We possess broad enforcement powers under the authority of Civil Service Rule 5.4, and it is incumbent upon us to take positive enforcement action, including requiring appropriate disciplinary measures, when violations are found. We are reviewing the extent to which our use of these enforcement powers needs to be strengthened, and to implement whatever further actions may be required to assure that the Commission acts promptly and affirmatively to correct and/or prevent misuse or violation of its regulations. Delineation of specific detailed offenses and penalties, however, is both unnecessary and infeasible."

Recommendations That We Reject

Recommendation 1.—William Berzak, Chairman of the Board of Appeals and Review, should be replaced.

CSC Comment: "The Commission has confidence both in the Board of Appeals and Review and in its Chairman. The past six years during which Mr. Berzak has served as Chairman have been difficult ones, involving significant changes in the nature and extent of appellate activity. Following several years of relative stability in the number of appeals received, appellate workload increased by a startling 70 percent in fiscal year 1971. Coping with this workload without sacrificing the quality of appellate review and decision making presented unprecedented management problems. In this situation Mr. Berzak and his staff did well, under a most difficult set of circumstances."

The report contains erroneous, misleading, and distorted information concerning the Board, that reflects a lack of understanding of the appellate system and its operations. The charge that Mr. Berzak withheld information and was less than cooperative is unfounded. The allegation that he instructed his employees that interviews with Nader's investigators would be conducted on their own time is totally false.

Recommendation 2.—In effect, this recommendation suggests that, as they retire, current members of the BAR be replaced from outside the Commission with attorneys who are not from the "federal personnel establishment."

CSC Comment: "Each member of the Board of Appeals and Review selected since 1965 has been recruited from outside the Commission, and all have legal training. Beyond that, however, there is an assumption behind this recommendation that is false. It holds that a personnel management background taints judgment and renders those who possess it incapable of fair and objective appellate decisions. The broad imputation that personnel management perceptions somehow deprive a person of the ability to make sound and objective decisions is just as wrong as the notion that the capacity to make proper decisions is the sole province of those trained in the law. Awareness of practical personnel management considerations would seem to have some relevance in deciding appeals from personnel actions. In fact, we should probably articulate more effectively than we do just how the principles of effective personnel management do apply in the situations presented by appellate cases; this could help to ensure that our decisions do, in fact, promote the efficiency of the service."

Recommendation 7.—The Commission should undertake a thorough and comprehensive study of the subsequent history of successful appellants, EEO complainants, and reinstated employees. Included in such a study should be a systematic review of coercion, reprisal, or retaliation which might have been taken against appellate witnesses or against agency employees.

CSC Comment: "The Commission's regulations clearly provide that appellants and their representatives shall be assured freedom from restraint, interference, coercion, discrimination, or reprisal. Mechanisms now exist for individuals who believe they have been coerced, retaliated against, or the subject of reprisal to obtain redress. The various appellate opportunities, Commission evaluation surveys, the complaint process, and correspondence generally reveal no indications of a problem of significant magnitude as is implied by the report. In fact, the allegation is itself illogical: successful appellants, EEO complainants, and reinstated employees, once having brought their dissatisfactions out into the open, would seem to have nothing to lose by complaining or appealing further, in the event that they considered themselves improperly treated subsequent to the resolution of the initial appeal or complaint. Rather than undertaking 'a thorough and comprehensive study,' to determine whether a problem exists when none is apparent, it would seem more appropriate and we will (1) assure that the proscription against coercion, reprisal, and retaliation is clearly reemphasized in policy issuances; (2) provide for effective dissemination of this policy to management officials and employees, so that violations may be brought promptly to the attention of the Commission; and (3) pursue rigorous enforcement, providing for effective disciplinary action whenever the violation is found."

Recommendation 14.—An expert advisory council of independent professionals should be established to aid in determining complex scientific or technical questions which might arise in an appeal.

CSC Comment: "There is no reason why appellate offices should lack expert scientific or technical services, when and if they are needed. Clear authority to obtain such services already exists, through a number of mechanisms that are readily available; these include reimbursable services from an appropriate Federal agency, short-term employment of experts or consultants selected for a specific purpose, and contracting for nonpersonal services from an authority in the field concerned. Accordingly, there is no need for the establishment of an advisory council; this would seem to be an unnecessarily elaborate step for accomplishing the intended purpose."

Recommendation 16.—Appellate review should be expanded when an allegation of coercion, reprisal, or retaliation is made concerning the action itself or any witness or potential witness. Reprisal against a witness who appeared should be considered within appellate scrutiny.

CSC Comment: "There is no question that the ability and willingness to act against threat or coercion in any form against an appellant, a witness, or a potential witness is necessary to ensure the integrity of the appellate process. Commission regulations provide that in presenting an appeal an employee shall be assured freedom from restraint, interference, coercion, discrimination, or reprisal. Any interference with the rights of an appellant or witness that comes to the attention of the Commission is within the scope of its authority to investigate and, if necessary, to prescribe corrective action."

Recommendation 20.—BAR should report directly to the Commissioners.

CSC Comment: "The Board of Appeals and Review already reports directly to the Commissioners. The Board is virtually an autonomous body within the CSC and has had an unhindered and direct reporting relationship to the Commission for more than twenty years."

There is no prior review of the Board's recommendations to the Commissioners by management officials or staff members of the Commission. The administrative relationships between the Executive Director, the Deputy Executive Director, and the Chairman of BAR are conducted in such a manner as to prevent any interference with the integrity of the direct-line relationship between the Board and the Commissioners.

Recommendation 25.—Commission hearings should be expanded in scope to allow a redetermination of matters decided in the agency hearing. Since the purpose of the agency hearing is to allow the agency to remedy its own mistakes, the primary hearing should be the Commission hearing and its conduct and scope should mirror this principal importance.

CSC Comment: "This recommendation may result from a possible misunderstanding of the scope of adverse action hearings before the Commission and of the wide range of discretion available to Commission hearing officers. Certainly there is no bar to the redetermination of relevant points of issue in a Commission hearing, notwithstanding that a previous hearing was held at the agency; and there are no limitations on a hearing officer's latitude in this respect. The observation that the Commission hearing should be regarded as the 'primary hearing' if the agency has not remedied its mistakes seems to be an unnecessary distinction, since the object of the Commission hearing (similar to one of the objects of the agency hearing) is to produce a fully developed record, and decisions are based on the record as a whole. Should any individual appeals examiner view the scope of the hearing too narrowly, correction can be readily made by the issuance of clarifying instructions, together with the remand of individual cases that rise to the BAR level. In short, the recommendation is unnecessary because it suggests practices that are already in effect."

Recommendations on Which Action Will Be Deferred

A full-scale review of adverse action and appellate processes is currently underway in the Commission. This is advantageous, because it permits timely consideration of the recommendations in the report dealing with appeals. The current study is a very basic and comprehensive one. It is examining the fundamental issues with which the appellate function is concerned, and it is evaluating both the effectiveness with which the system has operated and the needs for change and improvement. Since many of the report's recommendations relate to these basic issues, they will be dealt with as part of the overall system review. Accordingly, we are deferring action on these recommendations so that we may consider their merits at the time the overall systems study is completed. (An independent set of useful recommendations is also likely to emerge from a study of the system currently being conducted by the Administrative Conference of the United States.)

We are also deferring action on two other recommendations (#17 and #18) which are not directly related to the adverse action and appellate system study but which require further review prior to a decision. These are also discussed briefly in the following section.

Recommendations 3 and 4.—These recommendations speak to the career patterns and training of appeals examiners, including BAR members. The report suggests that separate career ladders be established for appeals personnel, and that their training be improved. Specific training recommended is an examiner's manual or handbook, and exposure in seminars to the views of employee groups and unions, civil liberties organizations, minority-group organizations, and others. Training should also include a clearly stated concept of the burden of proof.

CSC Comment: "Appropriate diversity, sound career ladders, and effective training are certainly valid objectives that the Commission has always sought to achieve. We question the common theme that seems to underlie these recommendations (as well as Recommendation 2), which alleges that a background in the Federal personnel establishment somehow taints judgment and renders those who possess it incapable of fair and objective appellate decisions. Professor Guttman's plan, which is suggested in the report as a model for implementing these recommendations, is predicated on the belief that experience in personnel management is looked upon in the Commission as more significant than legal experience, as far as the appellate function is concerned. The alleged result is a so-called 'personnel office approach' to the adjudication of appeals. We question the validity of this assumption. Nevertheless; the notion of a separate and independent career ladder limited to attorneys, who could move through a series of specifically identified appellate, legal, and other positions is a concept we had been exploring and working on several months prior to the visit of the Nader team. The intent of an independent career ladder would be to assure that the adjudicating functions are not improperly influenced, either consciously or unconsciously. The issues are so integral a part of the total systems concept of an appellate function that they are being treated as part of the current study."

Recommendation 9.—The Commission should now open its hearings to the public, in an independent decision, whether or not open hearings are ultimately judged to be a constitutional requirement of due process.

CSC Comment: "This is another question that has been under active consideration and involves the matter of protection of privacy. The issue of providing for hearings to be open to the public, either as a standard procedure or on a discretionary basis, stemmed initially from the Fitzgerald case. This issue is being considered in the current study of the adverse action and appeals systems."

Recommendations 21, 22 and 27.—First-level appellate offices should report to and be administratively responsible to BAR (#21), and appeals examiners should be empowered to make independent decisions without the concurrence of regional directors (#22). Voluntary action by the Commissions is urged to bring its appeals examiners and both Commission and agency hearings under the provisions of the Administrative Procedure Act (#27).

CSC Comment: "These recommendations call for greater separation of functions between first-level decision makers and management officials, but at the cost of increased formality of process. These recommendations question whether the Commission can decide appeals fairly and justly. We are certain it can."

Adoption of the formalized procedures of the Administrative Procedure Act would be, at best, a mixed blessing. Since the Administrative Conference of the United States is expert in this area, it may be wise to await its specific recommendations upon completion of its current study. In any event, the Commission cannot come under its provisions simply because it wants to. Personnel matters are specifically excluded from its coverage, and legislation would be required to bring Commission appellate proceedings and examiners under the Act.

We could, as a matter of policy, voluntarily adopt all APA procedures as those we would follow, except: we could not hire APA-type hearing examiners, nor could we acquire subpoena power in this manner.

At any rate, these are matters intricately related to the larger study, and should await its conclusion and, perhaps, the report of the Administrative Conference.

Recommendation 11.—Adverse action should not be taken against an employee (except in special circumstances) until he has had an opportunity for a hearing and a decision by the agency head or his designee.

CSC Comment: "We have examined this issue several times before and each time concluded that the policy should not be changed. The question of requiring postponement of the effective date of an adverse action until after a hearing and decision was a central issue at least as far back as 1961, when the provisions of E.O. 10987 establishing agency appeals systems were first being considered. The issue, as indicated in the report, was also explored as part of the so-called "Pellerzi Plan" in 1967, and figured in Judge Washington's report on his work at the Commission in the summer of 1969. It arose again in 1970, when the most recent changes in appellate regulations were made, and the question remains with us currently. (It is squarely presented in a district court case, still unlitigated, recently brought against the Government.)"

This is one of the thorniest issues to be considered in connection with our current review of adverse action and appellate processes. It is being reexamined again as part of the overall study. Because of the fundamental nature of the question, we feel it can be properly treated only in the context of possible revisions in the systems as a whole.

Recommendation 13.—The Commission should seek the power to subpoena witnesses in personnel hearings.

CSC Comment: "As the wording of the recommendation suggests, its adoption would require legislative enactment. Over the years, and linked to the growing occupational and geographical mobility of society in general, the instances in which the power of subpoena would be useful in resolving employee appeals have shown an increase. This question is being considered in our current study of appellate processes."

Recommendation 15.—The Board of Appeals and Review should clarify its procedures: (1) Stays at the first appeal level should only be granted in unusual circumstances; (2) the Commission should grant to the BAR the authority to reduce the penalties in adverse action cases; (3) the BAR should establish as its standard of review a review on the record. It should not act to substitute its judgment for the decision made by an appeals examining office.

CSC Comment: "Both the procedures of BAR and its basic role are central features of our appellate systems study. Each of the three suggestions in this recommendation is encompassed in that review. We know also that the Administrative Conference of the United States and the General Accounting Office are inquiring into some of these matters as part of their studies of appellate processes."

Recommendation 17.—Some review on the merits of dismissal of probationary employees should be allowed. This will reduce the absolute discretion of agencies and reduce the number of appeals alleging discrimination.

CSC Comment: "Since Part 713 of the regulations already provides for probationer appeals for agency and Commission review of actions taken on the basis of discrimination, the question here is whether probationers should have an opportunity to appeal separation actions against them on the merits of their cases under Part 752, and whether agencies should continue to have the broad discretionary power they now have to terminate probationary employees."

The concept of the probationary period as an extension of the examining and selection process derives from the Civil Service Act itself. Our consistent approach throughout the Commission's history has been to permit broad discretion to agencies in this matter, because we viewed this authority as no broader than the scope of discretion allowed agencies in initial selection for appointment. This principle was carried over in the Veterans' Preference Act of 1944, which did not confer even upon veterans a right of appeal to the Commission as probationary employees.

Action is being deferred on this recommendation, because a separate staff analysis and proposal treating this issue is currently being circulated within the Commission for clearance.

Recommendation 18.—Where a prima facie case is established that a reassignment or transfer has been made to circumvent an employee's appellate rights, the agency should have the burden of proof to show this is not the motivation for the action.

CSC Comment: "We agree. We are not aware, however, that this is a significant problem. Ruse or subterfuge may not be employed to accomplish what is prohibited. This principle was the basis of a recent court ruling (*Motto* v. *GSA*) holding that a geographical transfer could not properly be used to circumvent the rights of an employee whose removal was sought. We will be alert to this matter as part of the regular BPME survey coverage and take such action as may be needed.

Recommendations 23 and 24.—Agency appeals systems should be abolished, with all appeals made directly to the Civil Service Commission. No two-level appeal systems in agencies should be approved.

CSC Comment: "Adoption of the recommendation to permit employees to appeal *only* to the Civil Service Commission would require a radical shift in personnel management philosophy. We do not currently envision that our study now underway will lead to a recommendation that an employee be deprived of the right of appellate review of an adverse action by his employing agency. To the contrary, we believe that the further settlement of an appeal gets away from the time and place of the cause for action, the less useful the mechanism for resolution becomes to both parties. Although this specific recommendation is before the study group, other less drastic possibilities for resolving the two-hearing dilemma short of abolishing agency appeals systems are being thoroughly examined as part of our current study of adverse action processes."

Another factor in the equation is that certain unions have proposed to us that collective bargaining to establish negotiated grievance systems in agencies, culminating with binding arbitration, be authorized as an additional alternative to the Commission's appellate system. Eliminating appellate avenues in agencies would foreclose that possibility. And, while we are not suggesting a stance on the union proposal at this time, we see no signs that the report took alternative possibilities of this or other kinds into account.

The question of eliminating two-level appellate systems in the four agencies that currently have them is perhaps less fundamental, but our reaction is that a case for doing so is simply not established in the report. An employee is not deprived of any legal right by our regulations permitting an appeal after a first-level agency decision or the agency's second level. The provision does not diminish an employee's right of appeal to the Commission. It preserves it; and it is there to be exercised. What the provision does is to make a choice available; and there is nothing illegal or pernicious about a choice that expands the range of alternatives.

Nevertheless, this issue is being dealt with as part of the adverse action and appellate system study.

Recommendation 26.—The agency head or his designee should be bound by the decision of the agency hearing officer unless it is contrary to law.

CSC Comment: "This recommendation proposes a significant change in where the authority to decide an appeal should reside. It would confer this authority on an appeals examiner, instead of vesting it in a responsible management official."

We think it may be important to the interests of justice in deciding employee appeals that three distinct parts of the process be separated: (1) that the hearing examiner should make findings of fact and recommend appropriate disposition of the appeal; (2) that the management official concerned make the decision based on those findings, taking into account the recommendations; and

(3) that there be an opportunity for impartial review to provide for reversal when the management official renders a wrong decision.

While the findings of an appeals examiner must indeed be given weight, and they certainly are, there are good reasons for not making his recommendation binding. A very basic reason is that this could reduce, not enlarge, employees' protections by eliminating the additional level of review by the decision-maker, the manager.

This recommendation assumes the appeals examiner will always make a right and just recommendation (decision). Experience has shown, however, that the agency head as decision-maker frequently brings a balance and perspective to the process that results in withdrawal or reduction of the penalty recommended by the appeals examiner. In short, appeals examiners, too, can err. If the recommendation were adopted, this added protection would be lost to the employee.

Finally, the opportunity for impartial review by others outside the agency provides further assurance that the case, as developed by the hearing examiner and decided by the agency head, was fairly and justly considered and decided.

There are, in fact, real strengths in the independent check points in the three parts of the appellate process. Nevertheless, the issue of making the appeals examiner's decision binding is being studied in our review of the overall appellate system.

CSC Evaluation Program

There are two basic themes running through the analysis and recommendations concerning the Commission's "inspection" program. The first is the allegation that this program is far too management-oriented, with a resultant adverse impact on employee interests and protection of their rights. The second is an allegation that Federal managers are possessed of an overriding interest in self-preservation, and that they are unfair and vindictive in their treatment of subordinate employees who challenge them. We have carefully considered each recommendation in spite of these erroneous assumptions.

The report offers three kinds of recommendations for changing the Commission's evaluation program: (1) those dealing with public and employee access to the results of evaluation surveys; (2) those concerning improvements in inspection techniques used by the Commission; and (3) those dealing with agency influence on the evaluation program.

Regardless of the erroneous assumptions underlying these recommendations, not all suggestions are off point.

Recommendations 1, 2 and 3.—CSC should allow citizens, Congress, and employees to review its inspection reports (#1). Selected employees and employee representatives should be invited to attend close-out sessions conducted at installations (#2). More information concerning inspection results and planned follow-through should be provided by the Commission to employees and employee representatives (#3).

CSC Comment: "These recommendations are based on faulty premises concerning employee and public rights of access to the details of evaluation surveys, which are internal matters of personnel administration and, therefore, privileged."

In carrying out its evaluation function, the Commission is essentially an arm of the President. Its purpose is to evaluate personnel management effectiveness and to provide advice and assistance to agency managers to help them improve the way in which they carry out their personnel functions. As indicated in the report, this involves the Commission in a consultative role with agency managers, and the evaluation program is essentially a management oversight function designed to serve the needs of management.

Legitimate employee interest in the evaluation program is principally a function of how individual employees may be affected by the way agency managers carry out their personnel management responsibilities. Thus, individual employee rights and interests are adequately served by the current evaluation system. To the extent that evaluation findings reveal the need for corrective action with respect to individual employees, such action is prescribed and taken. On the other hand, the evaluation function is a management function, and the overall evaluation results are principally management's property and concern.

Members of Congress do have access rights to our evaluation reports, principally in terms of their legislative oversight function; consequently, we furnish them to members and to the GAO, upon request.

For basically the same reasons, selected employees and employee representatives have no right to attend close-out sessions, nor are they entitled to more information concerning inspection results and planned followthrough on evaluation surveys. Close-out sessions are for the purpose of communicating to management the evaluation results and the recommendations for appropriate action. The matter of followthrough planned by the Commission with respect to agency management action on the basis of evaluation results is principally a matter between the Commission and the agency managers concerned. To treat these matters otherwise would render less effective the corrective function they are advanced to enhance. The Commission, therefore, disagrees with Recommendations 1, 2, and 3.

Recommendation 4.—Greater employee involvement should be sought in the process of planning inspections. Interviews with employee groups might be conducted before a nationwide inspection plan is drafted.

CSC Comment: "The recommendation is understood as advocating contacts at the national level with such groups as unions and other appropriate groups representing substantial employee interests. In fact, we have done this on many occasions and will continue to do so. More importantly, there is an implication in this recommendation that only limited interaction exists between employee groups and our evaluation program. This is incorrect. Unions and minority-group organizations are not at all hesitant about bringing problem cases or other matters to our attention; we are not at all reluctant to conduct on-the-spot inspections to follow through on the allegations of poor personnel practices raised by these groups. We are in frequent contact with such groups concerning matters of interest to them, and a substantial amount of our inspection resources and effort go into these kinds of requests for special investigations."

Finally, and this cannot be repeated too often, the inspection program is not supposed to be a mechanism for employees to file grievances. It was never intended to function as a substitute for existing well-established channels set up for the resolution of employee complaints. In our evaluation process we do, indeed, solicit employee opinion and comment. This is one of many sources of information that give us a total picture of personnel management effectiveness; it is not a substitute for existing appeals and grievance systems.

Recommendation 5.—Employees should be informed of violations affecting them which are discovered during an inspection.

CSC Comment: "Action is already underway to develop improved guides on regulatory coverage and corrective action with respect to violations identified during evaluation surveys. This is part of the project to develop a new Evaluation Handbook. Included in this effort will be a specific assessment and determination whether current corrective action policy should be changed."

The essence of this recommendation is that an employee has a right to know when he has been the victim of an improper or illegal personnel action and, if he so chooses, to assert and defend his own interest in the matter. Under current policy, when we direct corrective action we do not specifically require that affected employees be informed. In some types of cases, this could mean some employees would not learn of what might be a grievable or appealable situation. The question is whether this policy is equitable to such persons adversely affected by violations of a personnel law, regulation or policy. This question is being thoroughly explored in our current review.

Recommendation 6.—New questionnaires should be drafted for employees. These new questionnaires should contain well-drafted questions dealing with EEO, the Federal Women's Program, and the appellate system.

CSC Comment: "Specific questions on these subjects are not currently included in questionnaires used on evaluation surveys. The previous employee questionnaire did include questions on EEO and the Federal Women's Program. Experience convinced the Bureau of Personnel Management Evaluation that these particular questions did not yield information or leads of significant value in evaluating these programs."

The decision to include items on any particular subject is not simply a question of its importance. We use a variety of fact-finding techniques; some are more effective or reliable or economical than others, in eliciting different kinds of information. We use interviews, review of complaint files, and analysis of various personnel management statistics, in addition to questionnaires, to obtain the requisite inputs for evaluation purposes.

The approach recommended in the report has been tried before. It was not productive of useful information not otherwise obtained, and therefore will not be reinstituted.

Recommendation 7.—A thorough review of personnel actions should be made during inspections.

CSC Comment: "We are developing more specific guidance to survey teams on the selection of regulatory samples and on extending samples when high violation rates are found."

This recommendation is based on a review of inspection statistical forms for FY 1969 and 1970. The report cites 30 instances in which either small samples of a given type of personnel action (e.g., promotions) yielded high rates of irregularity or violations where the samples were not extended, or small samples of adverse actions and RIF actions were examined. The conclusion is that we are not doing a thorough review of personnel actions. The 30 instances cited amount to only 6 percent of the total general evaluations (including Post Offices) conducted during FY 1969 and 1970. These 30 evaluations may not be representative, which could call into question the validity of the conclusions underlying the report recommendation. During each of these two years, survey teams examined about 8 percent of the personnel actions taken by all the installations under review. Each year, violations were found in 2 percent to 3 percent of the actions in the samples.

The recommendation appears to be intended as a sweeping criticism of our regulatory review. If so, it is not justified. We recognize, however, that better guidance to evaluators can improve regulatory review. This material is being given high priority, together with the additional guidance being prepared for corrective action in our new responsibilities for EEO evaluations under Public Law 92-261.

Recommendation 8.—In installations or agencies which have not been inspected within the last year, CSC inspectors should review personnel actions conducted during the period in which there was no CSC inspection or for at least three years. In separation actions, files or copies of the files should be retained at the agency for three years after a final administrative determination on the adverse action. Such files are now retained for only thirty days.

CSC Comment: "This is a two-part proposal. The first part

proposes extending the period from which we draw samples of actions for review. The proposal is based on an incomplete understanding of our policy and practice. Our handbook guidance on reviewing the processing of personnel actions and maintaining records states that coverage will include review of personnel actions taken during the twelve-month period preceding the visit; official personnel folders; supporting files and documents such as promotion program records, adverse action files, applicant supply files; and other records and files related to personnel actions."

Two points need clarification here: (1) in reviewing personnel folders we review all actions in the folder from the time the employee entered on duty, and (2) if total actions during the twelve-month period preceding the inspection visit do not provide an adequate sample, our instructions state that actions prior to the period should be included. So, our advisers are not limited to looking only at actions taken during the preceding year.

The second part proposes that we retain folders and files in adverse actions, including RIF separations, that were *not* appealed. This suggestion is based upon the fact that we do relatively few reviews of adverse actions, in great part because most of the pertinent files are at Federal Records Center at the time of a survey.

Both of these proposals are based on the assumption that we would find more faulty personnel actions by reviewing "off-year" records. Our policy is based on the opposite assumption: that "survey years" are representative of all years, including "off-years." The only way to determine the correct assumption is to test the recommendation to see if any useful purpose is served by extending the coverage period.

Recommendation 9.—Notification procedures should be reexamined and enforced to ensure adequate employee notification by agencies of planned Commission inspections.

CSC Comment: There is no evidence that what we require agencies to do in informing employees of a forthcoming CSC evaluation is inadequate. Accordingly, there is no need to reexamine our established procedures. We will, of course, continue to be alert in assuring that our notification procedures are complied with."

Recommendation 10.—Appointments for employees who wish to meet with CSC inspectors should not be scheduled by that agency's personnel.

CSC Comment: "Current practice is more than adequate. It provides three options to employees: (1) to contact the CSC office concerned before the survey; (2) to call our team office onsite directly; or (3) to make arrangements through an agency contact point."

If we required employees to arrange appointments through an agency contact only, there might be more basis for the recommendation. As it is, there is no basis for the suspicion that employees who have to deal through an agency contact suffer reprisals. As a practical matter, an employee cannot simply walk away from his work site without explanation. The supervisor has a right to know that the employee will not be on the job.

Typically, employees who contact us are not furtive or fearful about it. And if an employee relates a problem which we can only check by revealing he talked to us about it, we tell him this so he can decide for himself whether he wants us to dig into it.

Recommendation 11.—The CSC should use statistics gleaned from the 29-A forms more precisely to determine how inspection time is being utilized and how to redirect it.

CSC Comment: "We have recognized a need to furnish better guidance in this area and previously conducted preliminary analyses to serve as a basis for developing such guidance. It may be that statistically based samples and more specific review guides will give us a better base both for drawing conclusions and answering criticisms. We plan to provide improved guidance in a forthcoming section of the Evaluation Handbook."

We will be giving greater attention to the regulatory review of personnel actions, and we will use these statistical data as effectively as we can to improve the regulatory compliance aspects of the evaluation program.

Recommendation 12.—If the Complaint Office is to be used in the inspection process, greater publicity for the office is necessary. Reports should be given to employees of the inspection results coming from their complaints.

CSC Comment: "The essential purpose of the Complaint Office is threefold: (1) it serves basically as a check on the effectiveness of a sample of agency personnel offices with respect to handling employee complaints; (2) it is a limited source of information concerning complaint data that may be of value in planning evaluation surveys; and (3) it provides an opportunity for the Commission to directly and continuously "feel the Federal employee pulse." We see no need to expand the rule of this office, nor to give it greater publicity, because such efforts would tend to undermine agency counseling, grievance, and appeal mechanisms that are designed to deal with complaints. For the above reasons, we reject this recommendation."

Recommendation 13.—Survey directors should be periodically rotated every two or three years, to allow some familiarity with an agency and still avoid the development of relationships with agency personnel which could affect the objectivity of inspection reports.

CSC Comment: "Instituting a fixed rotation period for survey directors is neither necessary to provide fresh perceptions and viewpoints, nor is it desirable from the standpoint of effective personnel utilization. We will continue to review the effectiveness of survey directors, as we do now for performance appraisal and development purposes; and we will change survey director assignments, as we have in the past, whenever it is appropriate to do so. We see no useful purpose to be served, however, by establishing arbitrary time limits and inflexible assignment patterns. Therefore, we disagree with this recommendation."

Recommendation 14.—A complete reanalysis of the inspection agreements which have been signed with the armed forces should be made. These agreements should be abolished or be redrafted to assure that CSC inspections are not restricted.

CSC Comment: "The report is wrong; our agreements concerning the evaluation program with the three military services do not restrict us. Consequently, there is no need for redrafting these agreements, as suggested, and it would be inadvisable to abolish them."

The CSC has certain basic evaluation responsibilities which only the CSC can discharge, and we shall continue to conduct evaluations in carrying out these responsibilities. The newer responsibilities of leadership for agency internal evaluation systems, and such new methods as joint evaluations, are not substitutes for executing our basic evaluation mission. The report is in error, therefore, in referring to our evaluation responsibility as "quality control" of agency internal evaluations.

The report concludes that we had unduly circumscribed our independence of action in our evaluation agreements with Army and Air Force, and in our scheduling coordination arrangement with Navy. The recommendation is aimed at restoring what is judged to be the necessary degree of freedom of action. The report's basic assumption is simply not accurate. Nothing in the terms and conditions of these signed agreements effectively limits the Commission's authority or opportunity to act. The agreements are designed to eliminate unnecessary duplication of evaluations. Following are the essentials:

> *Air Force.*—The key current provision is based on a three-year cycle of nationwide reviews, which is obsolete. The agreement calls for limiting reviews between nationwide evaluations, and not conducting a CSC review at a base within one year of a previous Air Force evaluation. Discussions have already begun to update the current agreement.
>
> *Army.*—A new agreement went into effect in 1971. By March 1 each year, CSC regions are to propose Army stations for review in the following fiscal year, in priority order, with justification of the need for each. Army will schedule as many as possible of the stations listed by CSC, and we will schedule as many as possible of those listed by regions but not scheduled by Army.
>
> *Navy.*—CSC will not make general evaluations at installations where there has been a Navy personnel management survey in the preceding six months, or one scheduled in the next six months. This includes Inspector General reviews and Command reviews, which include coverage of civilian personnel management effectiveness.

As can be seen, these agreements do provide for certain "norms" on the frequency of evaluation visits under typical circumstances. But our right to act at any time in accordance with full scope of the Commission's legal responsibility and authority is in no way proscribed. Technically and practically we can go to any installation at any time to investigate and evaluate any aspect of personnel management we consider it necessary and appropriate to examine. In addition, should we find that any of the services are failing to adequately carry out their part of the agreement, we would not hesitate to end the arrangement.

Recommendation 15.—Followthrough on inspections should rely less upon agency evaluation of its own progress.

CSC Comment: "The report treats at some length one example of agency followthrough, or lack thereof, and represents CSC as uncritically accepting agency general assurances of proper corrective action and future good behavior. The implication drawn from this one example, reliance on responsible agency evaluations, is wrong. The example, as presented, does not fully reflect the situation and it is therefore misleading. Nor does this isolated example represent the general pattern of our relationships with agencies, on the matter of corrective action followup."

Where we require corrective action on the part of the agency, we also require specific and detailed reports of corrective action taken. In reviewing these reports, where we perceive a need for further followup on our part, we do it. It is a matter of informed judgment whether further on-site followup is necessary on our part, and we have no hesitancy in following up when our assessment of agency followthrough dictates a need to do so.

Investigations Program

The critique and recommendations of the Public Interest Research Group concerning the Commission's investigative program show many of the same themes common to their appraisal of other programs. These are alleged needs for (1) greater openness in all our investigative processes, (2) more stress on our accountability to the public, (3) greater exercise of our regulatory and agency oversight responsibilities under E.O. 10450, and (4) more concern for citizens' rights.

The report calls into question the basic need for and validity of personnel investigations. It suggests that a reexamination and redirection of the entire program is needed. And it offers some specific suggestions for changing the way we deal with applicants, the public, and agencies, as well as in the way we select and train Commission investigators.

Each of the nine recommendations is analyzed below, together with the CSC position in each case.

Recommendation 1.—The Congress and the Civil Service Commission should reappraise investigative programs and the standards used to judge employee suitability and loyalty. Such a reappraisal should consider the cost and benefits of the system and the predictive value of the standards that are used. In determining the costs and benefits, the losses to the Government and to individuals who are false-positives would be considered.[1]

CSC Comment: "We strongly disagree with the suggestion that the need for a personnel investigative program is questionable, as well as with the implication that the costs of such a program outweigh its benefits to the Government and to the people it serves. Further, we disagree with the suggestion that empirical testing is needed to evaluate the predictive value of investigative reports. Such a statistical study is neither feasible nor necessary. We are required by law to determine fitness and character of individuals for employment. Investigative information, both favorable and unfavorable, is essential to such determinations. To conduct an empirical test, trying to evaluate on some sort of statistical basis the relationship between the contents of these reports and successful job performance, would be an unnecessarily elaborate and costly way of proving what is already known.

Months before this report, we initiated a review and reappraisal of the standards used by the Commission to evaluate the fitness and character of applicants and employees. We anticipate that these standards may benefit from revision and further refinement. We recognize that the standards, as presently stated, have been criticized by some as too general and susceptible to subjective interpretation. We minimize subjective interpretations by training and supervision of those who are called upon to evaluate investigative reports and to make determinations with respect to the employment or retention of individuals based on fitness and character.

Recommendations 2 and 3.—The Commission should apply to itself the requirements of the Fair Credit Reporting Act. Federal agencies should be required to inform an applicant if he has not been hired as the result of information contained in an investigative report and to inform potential employees within three days of the time an investigative report is ordered.

[1]"False-positive" is defined as an individual who has been improperly identified as potentially dangerous or unsuitable.

CSC Comment: "The main thrust of these recommendations would require actions that are totally unnecessary to the fair treatment of applicants and employees, and would be administratively unworkable."

In the first place, the CSC investigative program is not governed by the Fair Credit Reporting Act, nor should it be. In any event, however, the objectives of assuring that accurate information is used as a basis for making employment decisions, and of preventing inaccurate or erroneous information from being used, are well-served by our current investigative program and practice.

The important issue here is the complete misunderstanding reflected in the report concerning the use of investigative reports in Federal employment decisions. Investigative findings basically are used in one of two ways: (1) *positively,* as a basis for comparing two or more applicants or employees being considered for a particular position, in order to select the best qualified among them; or (2) *negatively,* as a basis for disqualifying or otherwise ruling out from consideration an individual applicant or employee who does not meet the requisite standards of fitness and character. In the former case, the employment decision is not a negative decision not to hire those who are less well qualified; rather, it is a positive decision to hire the one who is best qualified. In the latter case, the reverse is true; the employment decision is a negative one: the individual either cannot be hired, or must be removed.

In the employee-removed case, the Commission makes available to the individual the basis for the proposed action and affords him the opportunity to reply; and our policy cautions agencies to act similarly in dealing with derogatory information that results in a deliberate decision not to hire, or to reject for security reasons. Thus, where the Commission or any employing agency acts negatively and specifically to deny an applicant consideration for employment, the intent underlying the report's recommendation is basically satisfied.

It is unnecessary and impracticable to follow this course in the other kind of cases. Where a number of applicants and/or employees are under consideration for a position, and the decision is a positive one to select the candidate judged to be best qualified, it would be wholly unnecessary, inappropriate, and administratively infeasible to extract all so-called "derogatory" information to disclose to each nonselected candidate, and to offer an opportunity for confrontation and rebuttal. Such action would serve no useful purpose either for the individual or the Government. The process now followed is not unfair, nor would adopting this recommendation result in any increase in fairness.

With respect to the matter of potential employees being informed when an investigative report is ordered, it is necessary to distinguish between two kinds of situations: (1) when applicants are being considered for appointment to nonsensitive or noncritical-sensitive positions, and (2) when applicants are being considered for appointment to critical-sensitive positions. In the latter case, there is no question that the applicant knows an investigation is being ordered at the time he fills out the required background information forms (SF 86). Personnel staffs in the employing agencies are well versed in this matter, and there is no question in our minds that prospective employees are well advised in advance that a background investigation is to be conducted, and are aware of the scope and nature of that investigation.

This may not always be the case in the case of applicants for nonsensitive and noncritical-sensitive positions. A national agency check and written inquiries normally constitute the scope of investigation for appointment to nonsensitive or noncritical-sensitive positions. If a national agency check or written inquiry identifies the possibility of derogatory information, a further investigation is usually ordered. In such instances, there is no direct notification to the applicant that such an investigation has been ordered, although applicants are often aware of this as a result of information volunteered by individuals contacted in the investigation. We agree that this practice should be modified. Rather than notifying individual applicants within three days of the time such an investigative report is ordered, as is suggested in this recommendation, we believe the more appropriate practice would be for all applicants to be notified, at the time they complete the SF 85, that the special investigation is standard practice in the event sufficiently derogatory information is uncovered as a result of the national agency check and written inquiries. In this fashion, all applicants would then be on notice with regard to this standard practice.

Recommendation 4.—The training program of investigators

should contain seminars dealing with civil rights and civil liberties. In addition, as part of their training, investigators should participate in seminars with representatives of minority groups, civil liberties organizations, employees, and young persons. Such seminars should be periodically provided for all investigators.

CSC Comment: "We agree that Commission investigators need to be broad-gauged, and our recruiting and training endeavors are designed to serve that objective. It is important that investigators be informed, knowledgeable, and sensitive individuals because of the importance of their work and the variety and sensitivity of their contacts. We take the training of investigators very seriously and we are continually improving both the quality of the training program itself and the results it is designed to achieve through more effective investigator performance. The report suggests certain specific approaches in training investigators to deal with and understand many of the diverse elements of our society that may be representative of current employees and applicants with whom investigators must deal. Acquiring a useful and appropriate degree of understanding and perspective in these and other matters is of concern in our current training program. We will consider the suggestions in the report, along with other alternative strategies for accomplishing the same training objectives as we continue to improve on training programs."

Recommendation 5.—The Commission should increase the representation women and minority groups have in the Bureau of Personnel Investigations.

CSC Comment: "For several years, the Commission has been engaged in aggressive affirmative action to encourage women and minority members to consider employment in the Bureau of Personnel Investigations. Of the last 25 investigators hired, for example, 14 were minorities and women. Essentially because of the nature of the work, and the availability of what are to them more interesting career development opportunities in other bureaus and offices of the Commission, very few women or minorities continue as investigators. Even when our affirmative-action recruiting has been successful, the percentage of minorities and women who are willing to remain in the investigative work force is extremely small. We will continue to give this our attention.

Recommendation 6.—More reinterviews should be conducted and any disciplinary action taken as a result made available to the public.

CSC Comment: "Essentially, this recommendation calls for providing greater assurance that the methods and techniques used by Commission investigators are sound, and that no investigative abuses are present. We seriously doubt that any such abuse is prevalent; our experience is that the American public is not reluctant about complaining when confronted with abuse of any kind from a Government entity, and the relatively few complaints we receive with respect to our investigative program would suggest that such abuses are not present in any significant degree."

The Commission's reinterview program is unique among the investigative agencies. The present practice is to conduct reinterviews in at least one case for each investigator once a year. If, through study of daily reports, production records, and reports of investigation, there is any reason to indicate that more reinterviews are necessary, they are conducted more frequently on the particular investigators of concern. The supervisory investigator also reviews the investigators' reports to make comparative analyses with the work of other investigators. Consequently, the Commission has a most advanced control technique already in operation, designed to ensure consistency in the quality of investigative reports

If disciplinary actions should be found to be appropriate, in the event of investigator abuse, certainly they should not be made public except to the extent indicated in our comments on Recommendation 8 concerning appeals. This would serve no useful purpose, and it would undoubtedly have a negative overall effect on morale and discipline.

We agree that it may be worthwhile to reexamine our reinterviewing efforts, to assure that they include a careful review of investigator technique, treatment of witnesses, etc. We reject the notion, however, that any disciplinary actions which may be appropriate, from time to time, should be made public.

Recommendation 7.—A procedure by which citizens may complain about investigative practices within the Government should be established. As a minimum such a complaint procedure would require an investigation of the complaint and a response to the citizen or employee stating what was found, the disposition of the complaint, and the reasons for any action taken or not taken.

CSC Comment: "Employees and citizens now have the right and opportunity to complain to the Commission on any matter, and acceptable procedures for investigating and disposing of such complaints already exist."

Citizens have the right as taxpayers to register complaints about public employee performance, and to expect remedial action when the performance is found wanting. There seems to be ample evidence that they are aware of and have no hesitancy in exercising that right. Complaints are received, investigated, and reported on. In addition, an appeal procedure for alleged violations of employment practices now exists for applicants, as set forth in Part 300 of the Commission's Regulations.

In complaint cases where disciplinary action is taken against investigators, we do not furnish such information in our responses to the complaint; nor does it seem appropriate for us to do so. A general summary of the action taken on a complaint should suffice without the internal disciplinary details.

Recommendation 8.—The standards for appraisal of agency internal security programs should be more closely defined and citizen and employee response invited.

CSC Comment: "The basic point that the report makes here is that the Commission has not been fully carrying out its security appraisal responsibilities under section 14 of E.O. 10450 on three counts: (1) visits have not been sufficiently frequent or comprehensive, (2) our standards are inadequate (the report argues that the Executive Order does not contain standards, only broad objectives), and (3) the Commission has not invited, in any systematic way, comment from those viewed as directly affected by federal security programs, i.e., the public and particularly employees.

We are conducting a review of the appraisal standards to see if additional criteria are needed, and in doing so we will solicit comment from appropriate groups affected by the security program. We believe the security appraisal function should be expanded, and months before this report we took action along this line by increasing staff and accelerating the frequency of appraisals.

Recommendation 9.—For those agencies to which the Commission has delegated investigative responsibilities for the competitive services, additional criteria and standards should be established. Improved oversight, including increased manpower assigned to appraisal and increased reporting requirements, should be provided.

CSC Comment: "The second part of this recommendation, dealing with increased staff, has already been discussed in the preceding recommendation. The first part of the recommendation, which calls for additional standards and criteria for agency conducted investigation, is directly related to the report's first recommendation that the Commission reexamine its own investigative standards. Since we are reviewing and refining our own standards, it follows that the outcome of that review will likely have an effect on the standards we prescribe for the agencies. We would also take steps to see that the standards are understood and consistently administered by the agencies."

Equal Employment Opportunity

Overall the report is a shallow and distorted assessment of this important program. The focus is almost entirely on the discrimination complaint system, and it touches only tangentially on the broader path to EEO progress through strong affirmative-action programs in the agencies. It makes some two dozen sweeping and largely unsupported allegations about the ineffectiveness of the federal EEO program and the Commission's leadership of it. The principal allegations are grouped and highlighted below.

The report charges that the program is run by whites, is structurally faulty because the EEO office cannot influence performance of higher graded bureau directors (partly because there are no structural links), and that our emphasis has been on "abdicating cooperation" with the agencies rather than a strict enforcement relationship over the agencies. This allegation, first of all, overlooks the fact that the Director of EEO, who is a black, plays an influential leadership role, as do the Director of the Spanish-Speaking Program, who is Spanish-surnamed, and the Director of the Federal Women's Program, who is a woman. Their activities are coordinated and given overall direction by a nonminority Assistant Executive Director; we disagree with the racist notion that there cannot be an equal opportunity program unless it is run by minorities. The allegation is also completely erroneous in the unsupported assertion that there is a lack of cooperation between the program bureaus and the EEO office. Finally, the implication that consulting with the agencies on EEO programs and policies is wrong, totally ingnores the fact that we share a clear and common interest and responsibility with agencies in furthering EEO objectives.

The broad allegations in the report directed at the discrimination complaint system fall into four categories: (1) delays in processing, (2) faulty procedures, (3) inadequate remedies, and (4) insufficient employee protections.

The charge is made that complaints are not processed within the sixty-day time limit set by Commission regulations, and that we do not keep adequate statistics on processing times. It is true that many cases are not and cannot be processed in sixty days; this was recognized in P.L. 92-261, which now provides a period of six months to handle a complaint administratively, before a civil action can be filed. There is no question that processing needs to be speeded up, however, and we have been doing so. Our statistical data on complaint processing can also be improved, for management information and control purposes. We have been working on this too, as part of our continuous improvement effort.

The procedural changes called for in the report include the following: (1) CSC should investigate all cases, (2) we should develop better guidelines for the evaluation of the merits of a discrimination complaint, (3) agency heads should not render final decisions, (4) open hearings should be provided, and (5) probationers should receive substantive review of an allegation of discrimination in connection with a separation.

The fact-finding undergirding these suggestions for procedural change is simply inadequate. The EEO Appeals Examiner Handbook explains in detail the evidence to be used in making a finding of discrimination; a probationer who alleges discrimination has the same rights as any other employee. The other allegations basically assume that agencies will not do an honest job of investigating and deciding complaints (despite final appeal to BAR). There is no support for this charge; in fact, agencies rarely disturb a recommendation for a finding of discrimination made by an independent complaint examiner.

On the matter of remedies the report alleges (1) that our statistics do not show whether complainants are satisfied, and that they are intentionally deceptive; (2) that not enough disciplinary action is taken against supervisors who discriminate; and (3) that the lack of disciplinary action is because the responsibility for taking action lies with the agencies. The allegation on statistics is inaccurate. Statistics will not show whether a complainant was fully satisfied; they will and do show the extent and kind of corrective action taken by agencies, and they are not deceptive. The charge about disciplinary action is primarily judgmental and unrelated to fact.

The final item relating to the complaint system has to do with the general category of employee protections. The report alleges (1) that the burden of proof is on the employee and, therefore, he should have subpoena powers; (2) that complainants have inadequate representation; (3) that counselors are inaccessible and at too high grades to gain employee confidence; and (4) that employees fear reprisal. Rather than developing his own case, which might require subpoena powers, it is the job of the investigator to develop all facts and then make them available to the complainant. With regard to representation, 87 percent of complainants have representation at the hearing stage. The remaining allegations are not supported by evidence in the report or through facts available to us.

The final major category of allegation of Commission ineffectiveness can be described as lack of overall EEO leadership (and therefore results). The principal charges here are: (1) affirmative-action programs have been ineffective and agency results uneven; (2) the CSC distorts statistics in a self-serving manner; (3) little progress has been made in increasing minority representation at upper grade levels; (4) we do not publicize enforcement efforts (i.e., BPME reports); (5) the Commission is not forthright on the issue of FSEE test validity; (6) our position on goals is too "liquid" and unrelated to minority representation in the population; and (7) we are protectors of agency management and the status quo, and do not wield our enforcement powers.

We reject completely the major thrust of the allegation that our affirmative-action programs have been unsuccessful. Solid progress has been made and we intend that more will be forthcoming. In fact, the record shows that the federal government is probably the best large employer in the land, as far as EEO is concerned. For example, during a period of overall staff reductions total minority employment has been on the increase. As of November 1971, there were 502,752 minority employees in the federal service. This figure represents 19.5 percent of the total federal work force; up from 19.2 percent in November 1969. Also encouraging is the upward trend in the better-paying white-collar occupations where minority employment increased, in the same two-year period, by 17,696 or 67.1 percent of the total increase in this category. The charge that we are less than honest about or distort statistics is false. Finally, we simply disagree that true equal employment opportunity can be achieved within or outside a merit system by adopting the employment-to-population ratios suggested in the report. For example, this simplistic approach fails to recognize the critical factor of availability of skills and knowledges in the labor market.

CONCLUSION

From the beginning and throughout the Nader study the Commission dealt openly with the Nader group, and we had expectations that an intelligent inquiry would result in constructive criticism and useful suggestions for change. We candidly discussed our problems with the investigators, sharing our ideas and the studies we were actively pursuing to solve the major problems of concern. Our hope was that the Nader reports—building, with their own independent fact-finding, on the work we had already done—would provide fresh insights into some of the difficult issues facing the Commission. We felt there were definite benefits to be gained by an outside review from the vantage point of a detached observer. Unfortunately, these expectations were not fulfilled.

The reports contained fifty-three specific recommendations. We agreed in full or in part with eighteen of these. It should be noted, however, that the Commission had already been working toward the same conclusions reached by the Nader investigators on almost all of these items, prior to or during the visit of the team. We chose to defer final action on another fifteen recommendations, because they involved issues that are identical to those that are being examined as a part of on-going comprehensive studies—principally in the area of appeals—that were initiated far in advance of the Nader review. Twenty recommendations were rejected as impractical, unnecessary, or unworkable; many of these, too, had been considered in previous analyses.

If the objective of these two reports was to prescribe an improved civil service system, they fell far short of the mark. They fell short because the research was either not original or, in the case of the rejected recommendations, was not thorough, objective, or analytical and therefore the conclusions and recommendations drawn were not based on clear perceptions of the issues. This is reflected in the many inaccuracies, distortions, generalizations, and misconceptions found in the reports. Because of their superficiality, tone, and lack of balance the reports contribute little to improving personnel practices in the federal government. They "call for civil service reform," but do not make a case for it. The net result of this effort, from the standpoint of the Commission, therefore, is essentially one of disappointment in the fact that so little constructive benefit has come of so much effort.

WRITTEN QUESTIONS FROM CONGRESSMAN JOHN ROUSSELOT, MEMBER OF THE POST OFFICE AND CIVIL SERVICE COMMITTEE, TO ROBERT VAUGHN

1. What do you understand to be the role of the Civil Service Commission as prescribed by the Congress?

In the 1883 Civil Service Act and in subsequent legislation the role of the Civil Service Commission has been to protect the integrity of the career service from political manipulation, to establish within the federal service an environment which induces the faithful performance of duties, and to represent the interests of the public, of employees, and of the Congress in overseeing the federal personnel system. In addition Congress has given to the Commission specific responsibilities and duties in areas such as the protection of federal hearing examiners (now administrative trial judges) and the control of the involvement in partisan political activities of state employees in programs supported by federal funds.

2. Are you suggesting that the Commission's sole function should be that of an independent regulatory agency within the strict definition of that term? If so, does it follow then that you are suggesting that the Commission should have statutory authority to intervene in, countermand, or overrule the decisions of agency managers on any and all personnel matters such as the right to hire, fire, or reassign their employees?

The report recommends that the Commission be revamped. Because of the Commission's oversight of important programs designed to protect the interests of the public and employees and because of the potential conflict of these programs with the interests of the executive, the report recommends increasing the independence of the Commission within the executive branch. "Give and take" between the executive and Commissioners who serve at the pleasure of the President does not always provide for aggressive representation of opposing interests. The report recognizes that such a revitalized Commission would still administer programs that were service rather than regulatory programs.

However, in the important area of employee appeals and the accountability of federal employees the report proposes an independent agency, the Employee Rights and Accountability Board. This Board would be a regulatory and adjudicatory agency to ensure the proper functioning of the appeals system. This independent agency would accept many of the assumptions of the present appeals program including the development of guidelines and standards to insure that the dismissal and disciplining of federal employees is done for the efficiency of the service and in the public interest. By its independence and its provision for citizen and employee complaints such an agency would ensure that the appeals process did act impartially to establish standards of performance that were enforced regardless of rank or influence.

3. Do you know of any other governmental or private organization of any size at all that has a similar centralized personnel authority structure?

As indicated in my testimony before the committee, certain functions of the Commission are more amenable to centralization than are others. The appeals process is already centralized in the sense that it should be developing uniform standards of behavior and procedure.

4. How do you see this as a workable structure for conducting the public business? Have you considered the broad implications of granting a Commission authority to question or police a manager's every move? What are the benefits to be gained from taking away a manager's authority to manage? Do you fail to see any disadvantages?

Applying guidelines and standards to the conduct and performance of federal managers is implicit in the concept of public employment. The meaningful application and enforcement of such standards is not a reduction of the rights to manage but rather a method of imposing responsibility for the abuse of that right.

The application of standards to the disciplining and removal of public employees has been a widely accepted concept. The Employee Rights and Accountability Board is not a central manager but a method of making the application of standards and the review of discipline effective as a method ensuring adequate public performance.

5. What evidence do you have that the vast majority of federal managers simply cannot be trusted to manage their employees and therefore an outside agent must do it for them? Would you care to mention the percentage of managers in a few agencies—say, the Cabinet agencies—that you consider cannot be trusted to deal fairly with their employees and indicate on what you base your figures?

Briefly I should like to repeat what was indicated in my testimony before the Committee. First the report does not say that all federal employees are dishonest or venal. In fact, one of the more heartening aspects of the study was the number of competent and capable federal employees who often went beyond what was expected often to the point of endangering their own positions in order to ensure that the public was adequately protected or the law properly enforced. The report itself is dedicated to these federal employees. Second, the report does say that the present personnel and appeals systems, by failing to provide for accountability at the highest levels, and by failing to establish standards applicable to all employees, and by failing to protect particularly dedicated and outspoken employees has created within each an isolated bureaucracy itself immune from responsibility but which can by application and definition establish the standards of conduct to be applied. In such a system it is not surprising that managers rarely bring charges against themselves, that they are unlikely to tolerate criticism from lower-ranking employees concerning shortcomings or incompetency in the administration of progress.

6. How much resources were devoted to the study, how many people, and particularly what were their qualifications and what other personnel and management systems have they studied?

Over a year and a half was devoted to the study. The report and my testimony outline the sources which contributed to the report. During the summer of 1971 two outstanding law students (whose educational backgrounds are mentioned in the report) from Harvard and the University of Oklahoma studied specific Commission programs. Because of the number of rules and regulations concerning Commission programs and the nature of the appeals process, their legal training was indispensable. These attorneys conducted their study against a background of research which included interviews with a number of experts in personnel administration and in the civil service system.

7. Your organization purports to be a "research group." What was your research plan and methods? How did you assure yourselves that your interview and data samples were, in fact, representative? What steps did you take to make certain that your questions were free of bias?

In my testimony I have referred to a number of ways in which we acted to ensure the accuracy and validity of our findings. At the very beginning of the report the research methods of the group were stated. In order for our technique of returning to question bureau directors to be most effective for the Commission and for our group, questions had to be probing, testing explanations and theories. Unfortunately the Commission's distaste for this type of exchange and for the conclusions of the report has been expressed as the unwarranted conclusion that the questioning was biased or the result predetermined. One of the grounds upon which the Commission draws such a conclusion is that not all official explanations were uncritically accepted.

Throughout the report are presented the positions of Commission officials in areas of policy disagreement or dispute. For example, the report calls for the public availability of inspection reports. However, the position of Mr. Schulkind, Chairman Hampton, and Executive Director Rosen that such availability would decrease the effectiveness of Commission inspection efforts is presented. The report recommends that the provisions of the Fair Credit Reporting Act be applied to the Commission's investigation program. However the position of Mr. Kimbell Johnson that such application was not intended and would reduce the ability of Bureau of Personnel Investigations to obtain information is presented. A statement of reasons explaining why such positions are viewed as sound or unsound, giving the reader an opportunity to judge the merits, is the approach which the report chose to adopt.

In these instances the policies and not the integrity of Commission officials is being challenged. However, the Commission for reasons of its own has chosen to embark upon the very course for which it erroneously castigates the report.

8. In the report you cite some dozen cases of employees who were disciplined for what you describe as doing their job, i.e., "whistle-blowing" on alleged illegal management practices. What were your sources of information on these cases? Did you look at both sides? Did you talk to the management representative in any of these cases? If not, why not? Did you really expect to get an unbiased account from someone who had been disciplined?

The source from which the case studies were obtained varied, including employees, employee organizations, and congressional hearings. In some cases a management official was contacted to seek an explanation for the agency's behavior. In other cases the position and arguments of agency management were already clear as a matter of record. For example, a Congressional hearing where management officials responded to charges, hearing records or testimony or the written response of management officials, provided such a record.

Your question is interesting because of the meaning which it gives to the term disciplined. Some of the case studies involve reassignments or Reductions-in-force which theoretically are not disciplinary actions but management decisions. However, as the report states and as the language of the question suggests, these actions often are "disciplinary."

9. How do you know that the cases you cite are representative? Do you consider these dozen cases sufficient support for your recurring theme that Government managers are self-serving and venal in their relations with their employees?

The recurring theme of the report is that unchanneled and unaccountable discretion can be detrimental both to employees and the satisfactory performance of public programs. My testimony discusses the importance of these cases. I would briefly like to summarize. The cases indicate the ways in which structural weakness can be utilized. The individual cases highlight the abuses possible. The system should be designed to handle the outstanding cases where political and agency pressures are the greatest. If there are failures in these highly visible cases, the resulting employee disillusionment and the discouragement of similar public-spirited performance can have impacts stretching far beyond an individual case. An individual case if occurring in an important regulatory program may have extensive adverse results on the public health and safety.

10. There are well-established procedures in government for employees to air their grievances or to appeal disciplinary actions taken against them. You are telling us, in effect, that the federal employee has no protections and the systems never work. Do you have data on the number of employees who have won grievances or appeals? Did you interview any of these successful appellants? If not, why not?

The report is saying that often the appeals system and the grievance system do not perform the functions that were intended. In other instances structural faults in the systems prevent the adequate resolution of particular types of disputes. For example, an employee who charges reprisal for his appearance as a witness in an appellate or grievance hearing may find the agency's grievance procedure the only forum available for the presentation of such complaints. If top management officials are charged with the reprisal, the effectiveness of such an internal process is doubtful.

The presence of successful appellants within the system should not foreclose criticism of failures or faults within the system. In the course of the study successful appellants were interviewed. (The report recommends that the Commission systematically interview more such appellants to determine what happens to them when they return to their agencies—how many win the battle but lose the war.)

11. You charge that the entire civil service, and the personnel system, are "spoiled" based on a review of only three programs: appeals, evaluations, and investigations. Why didn't you review other programs such as training, recruiting and examining, retirement, etc.?

These three programs—appeals, evaluations, and investigations—are programs where the Commission's responsibilities to interests beyond those of the management of federal agencies are most evident. Therefore the administration of those programs can most capably expose the Commission's ability to act as a representative of those interests—congressional, public, and employee—that may conflict with the needs of the executive.

The appeals program deals with the more basic aspects of federal employment—will an employee be removed? will he be disciplined? by what standards will such decisions be made? how fair and impartial will the decision-making process be?

The evaluation program is crucial to the Commission's ability to control the process of decentralization, to influence the performance of federal officials, to provide information about the operation of programs with which managers may disagree or resist.

The investigations program must carefully balance the requirements of federal agencies, the needs of the public, and the constitutional rights of citizens and employees.

Therefore these programs not only are intrinsically worthy of special study but also provide an especially effective way of evaluating the independence and performance of the Civil Service Commission.

12. What is the basis for your charge that the appellate system is promanagement, i.e., what percentage of cases do employees actually win on appeal? (1970 statistics show that the Commission's first-level appeals offices reversed the agency action in 31 percent of employee appeals filed directly with the Commission.)

A good portion of Chapter 2 of the report as well as a portion of my prepared statement to the Committee discusses the management perspective of the appeals process. Briefly, I would like to summarize the reasons for that view: (1) the service orientation of many Commission programs inclining Commission officials to see also the appeals program as a service program for managers of federal agencies; (2) the training of appeals examiners within the Commission—a training which stresses the personnel and management aspects of the appeals program; (3) the structure of the appeals process, which allows operating officials whose principal commitment is to the smooth functioning of agency-commission relations to participate in decisions of individual cases; (4) the history of the appeals program, in which the BAR has been seen not as an independent adjudicatory body but as an extension of the personnel office; (5) the lack of standards against which to test management assertions; and (6) practices and procedures which limit the ability to openly evaluate the perspectives of the appeals system including an inadequately defined burden of proof, failure to rely on precedent and to publicize dissenting votes, the holding of closed hearings, and the failure to publicly distribute appeals decisions.

Because of the ways in which the Commission has maintained statistics on the appeals program it is difficult to tell how many employees actually win on appeal. Of the 31 percent of appeals reversed by the first level of Commission on direct appeal, 22 percent were reversed on procedural errors which would allow them to be reinstated by the agency. Since the Commission does not maintain statistics which show whether such cases are recommended it is not possible to say how many employees in this category ultimately prevail.

(In fiscal year 1970 there were 841 adverse actions directly appealed to the Commission. However, 61 adverse actions were appealed to the Commission after an agency hearing. In these appeals the Commission reversed the agency in 10.5 percent of the cases on procedural grounds and reversed on the merits in 10.5 percent of the cases.) If the Commission in accepting Recommendation 5 of Chapter 2 has committed itself to maintaining statistics in this form, then in the future it may be possible to more thoroughly examine the issue raised by the question.

13. What would you consider or expect the employee success rate to be in a system that was not, as you say, "promanagement"? If the reversal rate of agency actions were any higher, could you not then turn around and charge that managers were incompetent or sloppy in their handling of disciplinary matters?

As indicated in response to question 12, the concern about the management perspective of the appeals process is based upon a number of factors. Among the disturbing aspects of the available 1970 appellate statistics is the striking difference in reversal rates of the BAR in cases initially decided by an appeals office in favor of an employee and in favor of the agency. The BAR reversed initial decisions in favor of the agency in 8 percent of the cases and reversed initial decision in favor of the employee in 37 percent of the cases. It is possible to see and appreciate the significance of appellate statistics without having to set a precise point where such statistics would have no significance.

14. How do you reconcile your recommendations for more highly judicialized appellate procedures, including APA-type hearings, with the widely held notion that it already is too difficult to fire a federal employee? Would not the type of system you are suggesting also slow down the appellate process?

Procedural protections do provide an initial obstacle which may cause a manager to refrain from investing the time and energy necessary to remove an employee. However, such procedures do not protect an employee to whose removal management is committed. Because top agency managers are not accountable, the application of standards becomes dysfunctional. A manager is more likely to be motivated to expend the effort to remove the outspoken rather than the marginal employee.

In many ways the proposal contained in the report would simplify and streamline the system. Only one hearing would be allowed rather than the two that are possible now. Agency personnel who must now often conduct hearings would be relieved to carry out their normal responsibilities, and an expert and independent corps of examiners would help to expedite the determination of appeals.

It is difficult to understand what delays might be caused by open hearings, the publication of decisions, the reliance on precedent, and the formulation of adequate standards, but to the extent that minor delays were caused, these delays would be compensated by increased efficiency in a personnel system where there was a meaningful application of standards to all government employees.

15. If due process is your objective, in what respect do the present appellate and hearings procedures fail to provide due process? What would imposition of APA procedures add that is already not provided for? In passing the Administrative Procedure Act, the Congress specifically excluded personnel matters. Are you suggesting the Congress erred and that new legislation is now needed?

A number of specific Commission practices are suspect on due-process grounds. For example, lack of proper standards of appellate review, opportunity for ex parte comment in appeals decisions, and the failure to hold open hearings. In fact, both the U.S. District Court and the U.S. Court of Appeals for the District of Columbia have found that in some instances due process requires an open hearing. (See *Fitzgerald* v. *Hampton.*)

In addition to the constitutional due-process problem, issues of due process or "fairness" are raised concerning the appellate process. My prepared statement to the Committee discusses at length these problems within the appellate process.

Congress in its provision for appellate rights and in its acquiescence and oversight of the appeal rights established by executive order intended to provide a fair and effective system of employee appeals. Congress has the prerogative to alter or change that system. Although the Commission can improve the appeals process, the report and my testimony state that new laws are necessary to establish a separate and independent appeals agency.

16. In a briefing of the full Committee last March, Chairman Hampton described, in some detail, a comprehensive study the Commission was making of the appellate system; the Commission has not been indifferent to the need for self-reform. Were your investigators aware this study was being planned and that most of the problems you cite had already been identified by the Commission for review? If so, does your report recognize this? If not, why not?

The report recognized that the Commission has studied or authorized a number of studies of the appeals process over a period of years. The Pellerzi plan and the Washington and Guttman reports are examples of these repeated evaluations of the appeals process. The report recognizes that the Bureau of Policies and Standards was conducting a review of the effectiveness of the appeals system (p.II—59); the nature of that Commission study was suggested in the prospectus: "Present procedures—adverse action and appellate—are highly protective. Because they are so protective a stigma attaches to the employee whose removal stands up under successive levels of appellate scrutiny."

Hopefully, the Commission study will generate proposals for significant change and improvement and will not become simply another study by the Commission of the appeals process. The mere existence of an ongoing study should not prohibit interested parties from commenting upon and recommending changes in the appeals process.

17. You looked at inspection statistics and your report lists about 30 inspections where you found the number of cases examined was too few in your judgment. From how many inspections did they draw those examples? Doesn't the Commission do hundreds of these inspections every year? (460 in 1970; 635 in 1971.) Are all the rest just like the ones cited in the report, or did you choose the ones that looked worse to you?

In addition to the samples of cursory review of personnel action or failure to extend review when violations are found, the report analyzes the coverage by examining the amount of time it was indicated for review of each personnel action. An average of about seventeen minutes for each personnel action.

Coverage during some inspections is better. However, the Commission's contention being examined was that Commission inspectors adequately covered personnel actions. The Commission admits that 6 percent of its inspections coverage of personnel actions in some areas was minimal, e.g., no actions in an area covered or a very, very small number covered. This alone should indicate that the adequacy of Commission review of such areas should be seriously questioned.

18. Did you obtain figures on the total number of personnel actions and files the inspectors examine every year, and the total violations they find? If so, why didn't you present these figures? (1970: 8,200 personnel actions, 4 percent violations. 1971: 9,800 personnel actions, 4 percent violations.)

The report was concerned with the adequacy of review of course; the adequacy and thoroughness of review may directly affect the number of violations discovered.

According to Civil Service Commission officials, adequate inspection coverage was ensured by the use of a number of inspection techniques. The examination of personnel action review was a part of an examination of a number of these techniques testing the Commission's assertion.

19. Your report says repeatedly that the Commission doesn't do enough inspections, doesn't examine enough cases, doesn't interview enough employees, etc. But your report never tells what is enough, never reveals what you're measuring them against. Just how much more, specifically, *should they do for the job to be adequate, in your judgment?*

The standard against which the Commission's inspection techniques are being judged is the Commission's contention that reviews are adequate to uncover trends and problems. In some instances such coverage can be a matter of debate with the establishment of a precise standard difficult. However, when no personnel actions are reviewed, when inadequate time is allotted to employee interviews or the review of such actions, the conclusion that the coverage is inadequate is more apparent.

20. Your investigators wrote that the Commission ought to go back further in time when they examine personnel actions, instead of one year as they now do. You argue they'd find a great many more cases where employees' rights were violated. What is the evidence for this?

The report argues that an extended review would give the Commission a broader sample from which to draw. The report's position is that a broader sample is more likely to be representative. In its response the Commission suggests it has not tested the assumption on which it has operated its inspection program. "The only way to determine the correct assumption is to test the recommendation to see if any useful purpose is served by extending the coverage period" (p. 22 Analysis of the Nader Reports).

21. Your study talks about some of the inspection work being "management consultant" work, and this is described as bad, because they could look at more cases and find more violations of the rules otherwise. Is regulatory review their only *responsibility under the law and the civil service rules?*

Rather the report speaks of the focus of the personnel evaluation program as being primarily a management consulting firm with principal emphasis upon agency cooperation. It is the effect of this orientation of the "new" inspection program that is feared will adversely affect the ability of the Civil Service Commission to carry out its regulatory responsibilities, to control the decentralization of programs and ultimately its ability to influence the direction of agency personnel systems.

Even in areas where it has not direct "regulatory" responsibility, the Commission's inspections should aggressively represent interests of the public, employees, and Congress which may often conflict with the interests of agency management. The Commission's stress upon results obtained by cooperation will draw it closer to the viewpoint of agency management. To justify its program, the Commission will be inclined to concede more to acquire such cooperation. The acquisition of such cooperation and the maintenance of good CSC–agency relationships upon which the success of Commission activity rests, inherently conflicts with other functions which the Commission should serve. There will be a tendency to overlook regulatory violations which might interfere with the relationship and to exclude areas in which it will be difficult to "motivate" agency management such as the application of the standards of conduct to high-ranking officials.

22. You describe the CSC investigative program as the function that has created more public concern and elicited more criticism than any other. In contrast to that, it's been my impression that the Commission program has been held in the highest esteem, even to the point of being excepted from the broad criticisms aimed at government investigative agencies generally in recent years. Would you please describe the expressions of public concern and criticism you documented to support this view?

The Civil Service Commission investigative program, including its responsibilities for the appraisal of agency investigative and security programs, its review of delegations to agencies, and the development and application of suitability standards, has elicited both public concern and public criticism. Indicating a long history of concern with investigative programs is Professor Rosenbloom's book, *Federal Service and the Constitution*. Among other recent expressions concerning investigative programs and the Commission's role are hearings by Senator Sam Ervin's Constitutional Rights Subcommittee and reports of that Committee.

The development and application of suitability standards by the Commission's investigative program has resulted in a number of litigated cases and comment in professional journals, e.g., *Comment,* "Government-Created Employment Disabilities of the Homosexual," 82 *Harv. L. Rev.* 1738 (1969). Chairman Hampton in an address before the Federal Bar Association in May 1970 alluded to the impact of this concern as expressed in litigation concerning the suitability program.

23. What is the basis for your recommendation that Congress and CSC should reappraise investigative programs and standards? Did agency officials furnish information leading to this recommendation? Employees? Subjects of investigation who were rated ineligible? How many of each category and how did you select those whose judgments you sought?

The basis of this recommendation was provided by Civil Service Commission officials who described the purposes and functions of investigative programs. From these descriptions a picture of these programs as essentially predictive systems emerged. Regardless of what old habits may indicate about the validity of such predictive systems, every predictive system must draw some lines; some decision must be made about factors to be considered in future behavior. Depending upon where the cutting line is set, the system must deal with the problems posed by individuals improperly identified as dangerous or undesirable but not identified as such. Because the burdens, often severe, which the investigative programs may impose upon the individual and because the Commission's obligation to screen individuals must be carefully balanced, such a predictive system must have some statistical or empirical verification upon which to base such a judgment.

The evaluation of a predictive system's trustworthiness must be made upon a statistical or actuarial basis. Without such testing, the establishment of cutting lines becomes arbitrary judgment. Any predictor must ask himself, "Am I doing better than I could by flipping pennies?"

24. Your report indicates that there are individuals whom the CSC has improperly identified as potentially dangerous or unsuitable. How did you go about making this determination? How many did you identify? What is the basis for your determination that the Commission's decisions were wrong?

The report concludes that in any predictive system, depending upon where the cutting line is set, some individuals will be improperly identified on the basis of chosen characteristics or factors to be dangerous when they will in fact not be. Without empirical testing of the effectiveness of the investigation program the number of such persons is not possible to determine and the costs imposed difficult to estimate.

25. You recommend that publicity be given to the disciplining of CSC investigators. How many instances of abuse of authority or discretion on the part of CSC investigators did you find? What was the nature of the abuses? Did you call them to the attention of CSC officials? Did they refuse to look into them?

In interviews Mr. Kimbell Johnson said that any complaints against Commission investigators were promptly investigated and, if appropriate, disciplinary action was taken. However, there was no record available of such complaints and no publicity of disciplinary action taken. Commission response to citizen complaints including a public record of such complaints and a publicizing of disciplinary action would, if the Commission program of responding to complaints is as successful as described, provide a record (1) to document the number and type of complaints; (2) to assess the propriety and adequacy of CSC discipline or lack of discipline in response to such complaints; (3) to influence the behavior of investigators and ensure compliance with guidelines; and (4) to reassure the public that complaints were meaningfully responded to. If the CSC investigative follow-up program for complaints is operating as described there are a number of positive values to the Commission of providing a public record of such complaints and subsequent action.

26. Your report suggests elimination or near-elimination of the program. Have you considered the implications of such an action? Does not the personnel investigation program protect the public rather than endanger it? Don't you think it is wise policy for the Government to be able to provide the public as much assurance as possible that its employees are loyal and of good character?

Rather than elimination, the report suggests ways of improving the program by analyzing its real effectiveness in protecting the government and in reducing the potential risks for improper practice within the program. Among these suggestions are (1) a review and analysis of the effectiveness of the program. (Is it protecting the government? Is it excluding qualified persons who do not pose a risk?); (2) procedures to increase public influence and confidence in the program, e.g., a public record of complaints and subsequent action; (3) provision of rights available to private citizens to ensure the accuracy of reports and to limit possible abuse in the employment process, e.g., application of the Fair Credit Reporting Act to portions of the Commission's program; and (4) a review and revision of standards. Ultimately, these suggestions will strengthen the program by ensuring its effectiveness and its proper operation within permissible boundaries.

THE REPORTS AND THE COMMISSION: AN AFTERWORD

Replies to responses can become tedious and muddled and are apt to mix defense and countercharge. However, the Commission's response did raise questions and charges upon which some comment is due. More importantly, that response illustrates the differences between the Commission's philosophy and the viewpoint of the report. A delineation of these differences is therefore a useful afterword to this report and the Commission's response.

The original reports, *The Spoiled System* and *Behind the Promises,* were released in preliminary form in June 1972. The intervening period has allowed some consideration to be made of the impact and efficacy of the effort.

Robert Hampton's description of the reports as inaccurate and distorted rested principally upon two pieces of evidence—(1) a statement purportedly made by a member of the study group during an interview with Commissioner Jayne Spain that the study group proceeded by reaching conclusions and then finding evidence to support them, and (2) the failure of the group to accept reasonable Commission explanations.

It is true that not all the Commission's explanations were accepted, but unless the Commission was seeking an uncritical evaluation, such acceptance should not have been expected. The Commission apparently confused approval with objectivity and criticism with bias. The Commission also misconstrued the concept of a "generic construct." In the Jayne Spain interview, Weldon Brewer commented that in studying an area one must use the evidence to build a "generic construct," a tentative conclusion which, if supported by additional evidence, could form a hypothesis that would be tested by posing it to officials responsible for a program. This explanation of research method became, in Chairman Hampton's testimony, evidence of bias.

The Commission, although castigating the report, chose to "take the high road" and glean what was usable from the fifty-three specific recommendations that the reports contained.

One of the principal differences between the reports and the Commission remains the concept of accountability. The Commission's response, by focusing upon its accountability to the public through a number of mechanisms including Congressional review and publicity, illustrates its misunderstanding of the concept. Even the existence of institutional accountability does not create the type of personal responsibility which can affect the direction of public programs. The report is not simply concerned with the protection of employees but rather with the development of a system whereby the standards for punishment will rest upon efficiency, honesty, and performance and will extend throughout the bureaucratic structure. At present an administrator who refuses to follow the law or who disobeys the law faces unpleasant news stories but very rarely a salary cut or removal from office. On the other hand, an employee who speaks out exposing corruption is guaranteed no protection. The imposition of meaningful sanctions and the protection of public-spirited employees are simply two ways of describing a revitalized civil service system.

Case studies not only indicate that abuses do occur but also illustrate the structural shortcomings which allow them to occur.

The reports and the Commission differ concerning the proper role for the Commission. For an agency as closely tied to the executive branch and the management of federal agencies as the Civil Service Commission also to regulate the behavior of employees in order to ensure compliance with law creates a conflict which will be resolved in favor of the executive management officials. The Commission does not believe that such a conflict exists. However, the Commissioners serve at the pleasure of the President and even in traditional areas such as the intrusion of partisan political manipulation into the Civil Service, offer an insufficient bulwark against abuse.

The Commission's viewpoint is understandable and, to the extent that it recognizes the political realities of the situation, it may be rational. However, the Commission has consciously moved (in the inspection program and in EEO, for example) to reduce friction with executive and administrative agencies, which must reduce the effectiveness of the Commission as an external force.

After almost two years of study leading to the report and after a year of discussion following the report, what has happened? Some very concrete and important changes have taken place. The Commission adopted eighteen of the recommendations. (The adoption was not always complete: for example, the Commission "accepted" the suggestion that third parties control transcription of hearings by saying that such control was unnecessary but that integral improvements in handling would be made.) The Commission also suggested that a number of the changes suggested by the recommendations would have been made in any event. Perhaps another Commission study was necessary to provide incentives for change and perhaps the public airing of problems with the appeals system encouraged these changes.

More discussion of the problems of public control of the civil service have taken place, and specific provisions have been included in legislation to create such accountability. Some concrete changes have occurred and these changes should improve the civil service, but in many ways the civil service is not significantly different than before the reports were issued.

The report and the effort connected with it are justified not only by these concrete changes but also by its wider consideration of basic philosophical issues. The civil service is different than it was seventy years ago. The problems and dangers are of a different character and magnitude; they concern the efficacy of Congressional actions, the control of large organizations, the interplay of management and legal systems, and the ability of citizens to influence a complex and technical federal administrative establishment.

Notes

Chapter 1, Institutionalized Boredom

1. The personnel crisis that exists in the State Department indicates the need to unify the federal personnel system. A number of recent cases have focused attention upon the lack of due process, the deception, and the bureaucratic insensitivity that has marked the State Department's personnel policy. Much of the information concerning the department's administration of its personnel system was presented in public hearings held on the confirmation of Howard Mace to become the Ambassador to Sierra Leone. Mr. Mace, who had been director of personnel at the State Department, and William Macomber, assistant secretary for administration, were mentioned in the hearings in regard to several personnel cases.

In the summer of 1971, an outside appeals examiner found that Allison Palmer, a thirty-nine-year-old Foreign Service officer, had been discriminated against because of her sex. The hearing also disclosed that the personnel office had kept secret a finding that it had acted illegally in discriminating against Ms. Palmer. In February 1969 a representative of the Inspector General's Office filed a report stating that Ms. Palmer had been discriminated against. Again in August 1969 the legal office stated in a memorandum its finding that the personnel office had acted illegally and recommended that additions be made to Ms. Palmer's personnel file to show that her career had been affected by prejudice against women officers. Unfortunately, portions of the memorandum, including the last page containing the conclusion of discrimination and recommending that the memorandum be placed in the file, were never placed in the file. In hearings on Ms. Palmer's discrimination charges, Howard Mace, director of personnel, insisted that the last page of the memorandum had been misplaced inadvertently.

At least once, Ms. Palmer received what she construed to be a threat concerning her discrimination complaint. On November

26, 1969, Ms. Palmer received a letter from Frederick Polland, equal employment officer, saying that she might well win a discrimination case but that her career prospects could be damaged by inclusion in her file of having invoked the grievance procedure.

The behavior of the department toward Foreign Service officers who do not fit official preconceptions of an officer underlines the significance of Mr. Polland's remarks. Murray C. Smith, III, was a young Foreign Service officer who was "selected out," or involuntarily retired. Mr. Smith was an antiwar activist and a civil libertarian.

In May 1968 Mr. Smith, along with other government employees who opposed the war, signed a petition appearing in the *Washington Evening Star.* The State Department threatened to include reference to Smith's signing in his personnel folder. The American Civil Liberties Union filed suit in U.S. District Court. In the face of the suit, the State Department agreed in writing that it would not include any mention of Smith's antiwar activities in his file.

In an article appearing in the November 1971 issue of the *Washingtonian Magazine,* Tom Dowling described how the department, under the guidance of the assistant secretary for administration, William Macomber, set about systematically to violate the spirit of this agreement. In the summer of 1969, Smith was transferred with twenty-four hours notice to the American consulate in Tabriz, Iran. Whereas documents favorable to Ms. Palmer were "inadvertently" not placed in her file, the department kept a ghost file on Smith's antiwar activities which was produced periodically to brief senior officials.

In his article, Dowling released State Department documents which he believes clearly demonstrate that John Burns, director general of the Foreign Service, and William Macomber "knew a great deal about the Smith affair, and were involved to the hilt in an effort to consciously pervert the standards by which State Department promotion policies and selection of procedures are governed." In a February 2, 1970, "eyes only" letter to Ambassador Douglas MacArthur, III, Mr. Burns wrote:

> We have again gone over this matter with Bill Macomber and what follows is our best current assessment of how to deal with what is assuredly, as you say, a messy case.

> First I should say that the Smith case is something of a type, i.e., we seem more and more to encounter FSO's [Foreign Service Officers] who, for one reason or another, are eager to have "confrontations" with the system in order to attack the promotion system service discipline, the time-in-class and selection out procedures, assignments, policies, etc. Some of these cases are very hard to deal with.
>
> Smith is three years in grade as of this year and if he is not promoted by the selection boards this fall, he will be forced to retire time-in-class in the spring of 1971. His file indicates that it is very unlikely, no matter what his next efficiency report, that a selection board will rank him high enough for promotion. I would say a 1970 report referring to those factors mentioned in paragraph 6 of Nick Thacher's most recent memorandum would in all probability eliminate Smith's last chance for promotion.

In a February 26, 1970, letter to Burns, Ambassador MacArthur commented upon Smith:

> Smith has not for many weeks discussed with him his preoccupations with his Constitutional rights nor any plans for further tactics to vindicate them as he sees them. Should there be any new developments our office would, of course, keep you fully informed, particularly should there be any that might threaten putting the whole business into the public arena where congressional action could be aroused.
>
> Philosophically, we have recognized that Smith's performance reflects many of the deplorable but recently fashionable excesses so often encountered these days . .
>
> With many thanks for all your thorough and careful backstopping and all the very best.

Murray C. Smith, III, was selected out of the Foreign Service.

Nor do the circumstances surrounding Smith's selection-out appear to be isolated. Stephen Koczak, a fifty-four-year-old former Foreign Service officer who is now an employee of the American Federation of Government Employees, was subject to a selection-out panel, where he was denied the right to an open hearing, to cross-examine witnesses, or even to communicate with other State Department employees during the hearing. A letter he wrote to the panel pointing out some of the discrepancies in his file was not entered into the official record.

John Hemmenway, a Foreign Service officer who was involuntarily retired, told the Senate Foreign Relations Committee under oath, "The department's personnel system is more than sick, Mr. Chairman, it is corrupt." Hemmenway also charged that "for two years documents directly relevant to the case have been withheld either totally or overclassified so as to make them unavailable in a fair and open hearing."

John Harter, a Foreign Service officer who involuntarily retired, told the Senate Foreign Relations Committee that a hearing on his grievance was held eight months after his request.

The most tragic case resulting from bureaucratic ineptitude and insensitivity was the case of Charles W. Thomas, a career diplomat selected out of the Foreign Service. With little money to support a wife and two children, and after three depressing years in which he had faced two thousand job rejections, Thomas killed himself in April 1971. Thomas was selected out because he had not been promoted from class 4 to class 3 within the required eight years.

The promotion board which passed over Thomas for promotion did not review a highly complimentary report by the Foreign Service Inspector, Ambassador Robert McClintock. That report was accidently misfiled under the name of another Charles W. Thomas. The report was filed properly two days *after* the promotion board had made its decision. The board, however, did not reopen the case. Even a special plea by Ambassador Fulton Freeman was not effective in causing the director general of the Foreign Service to express his concern about the Thomas case and what appeared to be a miscarriage of justice.

In testimony before the Senate Foreign Relations Committee, Mr. Thomas' widow told the committee that Mr. Mace was among those responsible for the attempt to characterize Mr. Thomas as a mediocre officer who was simply an unfortunate victim of a highly competitive system rather than a victim of an improperly handled personnel action. Mrs. Thomas told the committee that State Department officials "attempted to gloss over their own errors in this sorry handling of all efforts to have a review of circumstances relative to his involuntary retirement . . . Obviously my husband's career and his life was a matter of indifference to these personnel authorities."

2. The concept of obedience and acceptance of official action is implicit in the language used to state Commission regulations concerning the behavior of its own employees. Under Commission regulations, its employees may, in regard to official policy, "make an address explaining and interpreting such a program, citing its achievements, defending it against unjust criticism, pointing out the need for possible improvements or soliciting views for improving it."

The emphasis on discipline and obedience to superiors rather than to the mission of the agency as defined by Congress is justified philosophically by the concept of accountability. The theory holds that because of the President's political accountability, the managers of federal agencies have a right to expect obedience to the policies and practices supported by the executive. This, of course, would argue that the President's position gives him the authority to violate, or condone the violation of, the laws.

Justification of rigid obedience on the basis of efficiency is also doubtful. Efficiency can be confused with efficacy. Without a consideration of goals and purposes, efficiency can crush imagination and silence questioning. Efficacy, however, requires an understanding of the uses to which personnel techniques will be put. Without effective control, and without accountability, the personnel system becomes an instrument for the perpetuation of political and economic power in the hands of a few.

3. Despite charges by the California State Employees Association that the memo was an attempt to force workers to accept a political philosophy with which they might disagree, Mr. Johnson assured the Senate Committee that he would never "try to control anyone's thoughts about their beliefs or philosophy whatsoever." Mr. Johnson said that the memorandum was intended only for his immediate staff and that any broader interpretation placed on the memorandum by a staff member was in error. However, Mr. Johnson's memorandum was cast in more specific terms.

> Orientation sessions will be given new employees about the Administration's philosophy and policy. A special briefing concerning the Administration's philosophy and policy will be held for employees requesting that they include some of this information in their training programs for both state and county personnel. Each staff member should read the book *Reclaiming the American Dream* by Richard Cornuelle, which is the philosophical textbook

> of the Administration. Definitional sessions will be scheduled for Director's staff and Section Chiefs and groups of department employees. Division heads will include the philosophy and policy of the "Creative Society" in their staff meetings.

What would be the reaction in the federal government if a memorandum suggested that all employees must understand the "New American Revolution" or that all GS-16s should read *My Six Crises?* Unfortunately, California seemed to have no counterpart to Senator Ervin's Constitutional Rights Subcommittee.

President Nixon's desire to appoint a black man to the Civil Service Commission was understandable, but a black civil service commissioner might have been more than a highly visible appointment. A black commissioner with a sensitivity to the fears and concerns of black and minority employees might, for example, have helped move the federal Equal Employment Opportunity program off dead center.

Responding to criticisms made of the Commission's management of EEO, Commissioner Johnson replied, "From my study of the Commission's stewardship of the Equal Employment Opportunity Program and its results, it is clear to me that its critics simply select a few statistics or a narrow aspect of the program and don't bother to inform themselves of the whole story. . . . Efforts to paint a poor picture and put it at the door of the new Administration are foolish, if not downright dishonest."

He was quick to defend the undistinguished internal EEO record of the Commission: "The Commission has a highly specialized area of responsibility. Therefore, it should not surprise anyone that the best qualified person frequently is one with long years of varied experience in the Commission itself. We are a small old-line agency with a few top jobs and a history of stability—so there have been limited opportunities for selection of minority members for these highest jobs."

4. The post of executive director has traditionally been a powerful and influential one. The 1956 report of the House Committee on Post Office and Civil Service recognized the power of the position: "The executive director, acting under general policy and procedure as established and approved by the Commission and under direct authority of the Chairman, has almost complete responsibility for the conduct of all facets of the Commission's business."

5. Since this study was completed, two new members have been appointed to the Board of Appeals and Review: Virgilio Roel and Cameron Smith. Although both were selected from outside the Commission, they both represent the personnel establishment. Mr. Roel served as director of the Conciliation Division in the Department of Housing and Urban Development, and Mr. Smith was deputy director of personnel at the Department of Agriculture. They are not included in criticism based upon the performance of the Board prior to their arrival.

Chapter 2, The Management Monopoly

1. Kenneth Culp Davis in *Discretionary Justice* indicates that selective enforcement of rules and regulations is widespread in the administrative process. Professor Davis gives an excellent example:

> An Oakland ordinance, as interpreted officially by the district attorney, required holding every woman arrested for prostitution for eight days in jail for venereal testing. The ordinance conferred no discretionary power on the police. Even so, the police illegally assumed a discretionary power to be lenient to the girls who cooperated; only 38 percent of those arrested were held for venereal testing. One officer explained: "If a girl gives us a hard time . . . we'll put a hold on her. I guess we're actually supposed to put a hold on everybody so there's nothing wrong in putting a hold on her . . . but you know how it is, you get to know some of the girls, and you don't want to give them extra trouble." (1) The ordinance required holding every arrested woman, yet the police illegally assumed the power to be lenient. (2) The police converted the power to be lenient into an affirmative weapon: "if a girl gives us a hard time . . . we'll put a hold on her." (3) The innocent girl is more likely to resist and therefore less likely to cooperate and therefore more likely to be held. The discrimination seems clearly unjust. And the personal element as part of the motivation is even acknowledged: "You get to know some of the girls." (4) The usual specious reasoning that leniency for some is not unjust comes out with great clarity: "We're actually supposed to put a hold on everybody, so there's nothing wrong in putting a hold on her."

The dynamics of selective enforcement of personnel rules are quite similar. According to USDA regulations, for example, ready-to-cook products coming from meat and poultry plants are to be 100 percent free of processing errors. This standard, however, is not met in any poultry plant, and veterinarians who serve as inspectors-in-charge vary in the number of processing errors they allow. An inspector may, however, find himself faced with the charge that he is allowing excessive errors in the ready-to-cook product.

2. Commission regulations consider but fail to protect the employee effectively from the pressures that can be used to force resignation. F.P.M. Supplement Sl-la(3) provides that an agency may give an employee a choice between leaving his position voluntarily or having the agency initiate formal action against him. "It is also proper for the agency in the course of the discussion to advise the employee which of the possible alternatives will be in his best interests. . . . However, if the agency uses deception, duress, time pressure, or intimidation to force him to choose a particular course of action, the action is involuntary."

3. F.P.M. Supplement Sl-26c(i) provides that if, after an employee is influenced to separate voluntarily by his agency's assurance that the action will leave him with a clear record in his official personnel folder, the agency enters any unfavorable information on the separation form, the separation is faulty because the employee was deceived. An employee who accepts an agency offer to resign rather than face charges would be well advised to acquire letters of recommendation from his supervisors and the personnel officer *before* he submits his resignation.

4. Federal employees are asked on their employment applications about their willingness to change job locations after they are hired. This information is used, presumably, to evaluate the applicant for employment. If an employee is unwilling to accept geographical reassignments, this may well be a factor in deciding whether or not to hire. An employee who indicates his unwillingness to be reassigned on his application cannot be criticized, however, for feeling that the government has implicitly taken that to be a consideration of his employment. The Public Interest Research Group has received complaints indicating that employees who expressed an unwillingness to relocate on their job applications still face dismissal for refusing to do so.

5. In some agencies, employees are not necessarily faced with this Hobson's choice. For example, in the Department of Labor, Secretary's Order #2-62 provides that any proposed personnel action (transfer) which has been made the subject of a grievance shall not be taken pending settlement of the grievance. Such an action could be taken prior to the resolution of the grievance only if the Secretary determines that the action must be taken to prevent hazards to other employees, to preserve the reputation of the department, or for the best interests of the department.
6. This procedure is described in Harrison Wellford's *Sowing the Wind,* a Nader Task Force study of the Department of Agriculture published in 1972.
7. The FDA contended that the reassignment was to "beef up" the Division of Drug Advertising by placing an M.D. in it. This explanation, however, seemed somewhat bizarre—a recent reorganization of the Division of Drug Advertising specifically excluded medical personnel. (Both Commissioner Edwards and Elliot Richardson, then Secretary of Health, Education and Welfare, had justified the exclusion of physicians by emphasizing that the division could call on medical expertise within other divisions of the FDA.)
8. The federal courts rather than the Civil Service Commission have begun to restrict the ability of agencies to use reassignments to circumvent the appellate rights of an employee. A district court in Louisiana held that reassignments could not be used to force the resignation of an employee as an attempt to circumvent his appellate rights. *Motto* v. *G.S.A.,* 335 F. Supp. 694 (E.D. La. 1971).

Chapter 3, Behind the Promises

1. Other key staff members were Mr. James Scott, GS-14, assistant director; Mr. Higinio Costales, GS-15, director of the Spanish-speaking program (Mr. Costales replaced Fernando DeBaca, who was serving in the summer of 1971); Ms. Helene Markoff, GS-15, director of the Federal Women's Program.
2. To impress upon Commission employees that Mr. Frazier was the sole director of EEO, a letter was sent on December 18, 1970,

from the executive director to Commission employees stating, "Jim Frazier is head of the new [federal EEO] office and reports directly to the Executive Director who is governmentwide coordinator for Equal Employment Opportunity."

3. On October 7, 1971, for example, before the U.S. Senate Subcommittee on Labor of the Committee on Labor and Public Welfare, Mr. Kator testified on behalf of the Civil Service Commission, opposing removal of the EEO function from the Civil Service Commission to the Equal Employment Opportunity Commission. Mr. Kator was accompanied by Mr. Frazier, whom Mr. Kator introduced. Mr. Kator did all the talking before the subcommittee in defense of present Commission EEO programs. When the chairman of the subcommittee asked, "Now, Mr. Frazier, do you have anything to say?" Mr. Frazier replied, "No, sir." Several employees, technically on Frazier's staff, referred in interviews to Kator as their boss.

4. One EEO representative reported his lack of contact with the central EEO office or the bureaus in Washington: "Any EEO field representative has to deal through the deputy regional director. I write an annual report, but it goes through the deputy regional director. My real recommendations or reports are not heard, because they [the regional officials] will take out what they do not like. I do not like this system of reporting." The representative went on to explain that an EEO program was bound to suffer if the EEO representative did not have some independent contact with Washington, since some of the Commission's regional directors have less of a commitment to the EEO effort than is possessed by their subordinate EEO representative.

5. The total percentage of black representation in the supergrade work force throughout the federal service from 1967 to 1972 has risen from 1.2 percent to 2.3 percent—a 1.1 percent increase.

6. Spanish-surnamed citizens have not fared well in employment in the federal government. Although Spanish-surnamed employees comprise approximately 5 percent of the population, they hold only 2.1 percent of the total general schedule (while collar) jobs. The bulk of these positions are in lower-grade jobs. They hold only 3.0 percent of jobs in the federal government including blue-collar jobs.

7. The poor performance of federal agencies in California in hiring Mexican-Americans is highlighted by a report of Public

Advocates, Inc., undertaken under the sponsorship of the Mexican-American Legal Defense and Education Fund. The report found that the federal government is California's largest private or public employer. It employs 293,770 full-time civilians as of November 30, 1970. Only 16,506, or 5.6 percent, were Spanish-surnamed. The report also found that "Most Mexican-Americans employed by the federal government in California are in poverty-level jobs as defined for the U.S. Department of Labor for urban areas. For example, Spanish-surnamed persons constitute only *17.6 percent of all employees in the "Wage System" earning under $5,500 and only 0.6% of those earning $18,000 or more.*" [emphasis in original]

8. Public Advocates based their estimated salary loss on an average of $9,000 for the 27,265 jobs.

9. The President's Executive Order 11478 states that each agency and department head is responsible for assuring that recruitment activities reach all sources of job candidates. Chapter 250 of the Federal Personnel Manual states that each agency shall

> Identify and cultivate all likely sources of manpower, including, for example, participation in special manpower development programs such as programs for recruiting and developing disadvantaged persons and work-study programs...
>
> Assure equal employment opportunity in recruitment, selection, and placement for all persons, including the economically disadvantaged, members of minority groups, women, older workers, and the physically handicapped, by establishing and monitoring positive programs for this purpose...

In a memorandum to all agency and departmental heads accompanying his Executive Order 11478 on EEO, President Nixon wrote:

> There are several points in Chairman Hampton's report [to the President concerning federal EEO, a copy of which the President attached to his own memorandum] which I want to emphasize:
>
> In addition to assuring equal employment opportunity for all persons, the Government, as a responsible employer, must do its part along with other employers to provide special employment and training programs to those who are economically or educationally disadvantaged...
>
> I have asked the Civil Service Commission to work closely with

agencies and other interested organizations in the implementation of these programs' directions and *to keep me informed of progress.* [emphasis added]

10. The GAO Draft Report is of the opinion that not only the number and types of positions created or redesigned under "Operation MUST" (Maximum Utilization of Skills Training) should be reported by agencies to the Commission annually, but the number of disadvantaged persons and other persons placed in such positions should also be reported, so that "The Commission could ascertain how effectively the objectives of Operation MUST are being accomplished, and what additional steps need to be taken to accomplish these objectives." If the Commission does not know the effectiveness of present programs, how can it responsibly inform the President or the Congress?

11. In testimony before the Senate Subcommittee on Labor in October 1971, Irving Kator stated, "Overall federal employment of minority persons stands at over 505,000, or nearly 20 percent, with approximately 16.7 percent being nonwhite. Of the nation's total work force, only 10.8 percent is nonwhite." [Nonwhite population is 11 percent.]

12. Memorandum to the federal directors of personnel and directors of EEO, dated November 11, 1971: "Generally speaking, data on overall representation of minorities in the total population have limited value as a basis for establishing employment goals, inasmuch as these data do not reflect *the skills composition of minorities* in the labor market and cannot therefore be related directly to projected employment opportunities in federal agencies and installations." [emphasis added]

13. There were three major findings: the validity of the FSEE has not been established in accordance with generaly accepted standards and guidelines for employment tests; the use of the FSEE discriminates against black applicants; and the Commission considers "confidential" what limited materials it has available that might have some bearing on the issue of the validity of the FSEE. In the words of the Urban Institute Report:

> All attempts to find any comprehensive published studies showing the validity of FSEE scores have been futile. Inquiries at the Civil Service Commission produced the information that occasional

studies for selected positions have been initiated from time to time by the Commission or some government agency. These studies, however, are not available to the public for the following [alleged] reasons:

1. They are not sufficiently rigorous scientifically to be allowed public appraisal.

2. At the time of the Civil Service Commission move in 1964, many of the records were destroyed; the remainder are at the Records Center and it would be an impossible task to locate them.

3. The research done on the FSEE for the agencies is located in memos scattered in offices of the persons concerned at the time. Furthermore, it is not known if the individual agencies would release whatever research they may have on FSEE.

Chapter 4, The Appellate Lemon

1. The statistics used are from "Basic Appeals Data" compiled by the Appeals Program Management Office. These statistics are not consistent with the statistics on appeals contained in the Commission's 1970 Annual Report. The statistics in the Annual Report may fail to include cases on hand and do contain discrepancies. Even when corrections were made in the Annual Report (Appendix I), some inconsistencies still existed. "Basic Appeals Data" have been used because they are more detailed and include appeals to the agencies as well as to the Commission.

2. When asked about these statistics, members of the BAR responded that the agencies choose their appeals more carefully and, therefore, there was nothing striking about the disparity in the rates of reversal. Of the 808 Appeals Examining Office decisions adverse to employees, 605 (or almost 75 percent) were appealed to the BAR. One hundred five cases in which the decisions went against the agencies were reversed on the merits at the first Commission appeals level. The agencies appealed to the BAR in fifty-six (53 percent) cases. While this is smaller than the 75 percent of employee cases appealed, it is not sufficiently small to explain the difference between BAR reversal rates favoring employees and those favoring agencies. (The BAR does not indicate whether the agency appeals to the BAR were of cases reversed on the merits or on procedural grounds, but it is more likely that the majority of the cases appealed were those decided on the merits, since an action reversed on procedural grounds may be started anew by the agency without appealing further.)

3. The complaint, supposedly filed six months late, was filed by a job applicant. One wonders if the widespread lack of notice to applicants of their right to file a complaint could have been the cause of this one applicant's misfortune. Did the Commission consider how long he may have known of his right to file a complaint before doing so? Perhaps he never saw one of the (sporadically available) posters to inform him.

4. When Commission-appointed appeals examiners were substituted for the agencies' own appeals examiners, a clear indication of the benefits of increased impartiality ensued. In 1970, when 100 out of 116 hearings were held by agency examiners, 23.4 percent of all dispositions included an offering of corrective action before final adjudication. In the first part of 1971, however, when 107 out of 131 hearings were held by Commission examiners, corrective action was offered in 38.3 percent of all cases. Under the present system, however, a formal finding of discrimination does not necessarily result in the complainant's receiving more favorable "corrective action" that he might have received had he settled with the agency.

5. The Commission has favored Congress with similarly skewed statistics. In August 1969, the Senate Subcommittee on Labor of the Committee on Labor and Public Welfare asked the Commission: "What percentage of complaints of discrimination in government employment are upheld at the agency level on appeal to the Commission?"

In its reply, the Commission stated that findings of discrimination . . . are very difficult to prove, and substantiate. . . .

> Between April 1968 and March 1969 . . . the Commission's Board of Appeals and Review closed 267 appeals of agency decisions in discrimination complaint cases. The Board found discrimination in one of these cases, and recommended corrective action in six. *Agencies had already taken corrective action in a number of the complaints submitted to the Board, so that the overall corrective action rate on appeals closed by the Board of Appeals and Review between April 1968 and March 1969 was 27 percent.*

The Commission again misled the Congress when the Senate Subcommittee on Labor asked on October 8, 1971: "In response to complaints heard by the Commission itself, please provide information as to those which resulted in findings of discrimination, with a separate tabulation of each type of discrimination found, as well as the remedial action ordered by the Commission in those cases where there was a finding of discrimination."

The Commission's answer was another distortion. The covering letter to this answer was signed by Irving Kator, who also took part in a similar distortion on March 18, 1971, before the House General Subcommittee on Labor:

> By the time a complaint gets to the Board, it has been investigated and, in most instances, a hearing has been held and a recommended decision given to the head of the agency. The Board is thus in the position of reviewing a case which has already been reviewed several times, including once by a completely independent Appeals Examiner. You would not, therefore, expect the Board to uncover new evidence which would substantiate discrimination in a large number of cases. Nevertheless, 34 percent of the cases appealed to the Board during the same eighteen-month period resulted in corrective action affirmed or directed by the Board.

Kator is correct that "in most instances a hearing has been held." In fiscal year 1970, 116 hearings were held, not all of which were appealed to the BAR, while the Board received 362 appealed complaints. He neglects to point out, as well, that in 1970, 100 of the 116 hearings were before agency examiners—not "independent examiners," in spite of the inauguration of "new procedures" requiring a hearing before an independent rather than agency examiner—and that as late as the first half of 1971, more than a year after the "new procedures" were supposedly introduced, 24 out of 131 hearings were held before agency examiners under the "old procedures." He also fails to point out (1) that in the overwhelming majority of these cases, the Board, on the basis of old evidence, "affirmed" the alleged "corrective action" offered by the agencies but appealed by the complainant as inadequate to remedy his grievance; (2) that the Board rarely finds "evidence to substantiate discrimination," and it has done so only in 14 out of 1,306 complaints appealed from 1968–1972.

On August 23, 1971, William Berzak was asked how often the

BAR, and the BAR alone, had recommended "corrective action" after finding discrimination. In a letter dated September 1, 1971, he replied: "The Board does not keep statistics to show a breakdown between (a) corrective action taken only by the agency; (b) corrective action taken only by the Board; (c) corrective action taken by the agency and additional corrective action taken by the Board." Berzak's reply is curious, for just such a breakdown was given the Commission on Civil Rights on October 18, 1971, and to the Senate Subcommittee in August 1969.

6. Regarding 1970, Mr. Kator reported, in response to a questionnaire by the Public Interest Research Group, "In 176 cases the corrective action directly benefited the individual complainant and in 82 cases the corrective action was broader, resulting in actions to improve personnel management practices." Regarding the first half of 1971, "In 163 cases [out of a total of 198 cases in which agencies effected corrective action] the corrective action directly benefited the individual complainant, and in 35 cases the corrective action was broader, improving personnel management practices."

7. A final example of the inefficiency of counseling is seen in the following answer to a question posed on EEO dispositions to the Civil Service Commission by the Civil Rights Commission. Chairman Hampton signed the covering letter to the responses. A selection from the answer of the Civil Service Commission follows:

> During Fiscal Year 1971, 3,796 federal employees or applicants alleging discrimination on the basis of race had their employment problem *reconciled* at the equal employment opportunity stage. Of those females alleging discrimination on the basis of sex, 898 had their employment problems *resolved* at the counseling stage, as did 303 males who alleged discrimination on the basis of sex. In addition, 315 persons alleging discrimination on the basis of national origin had their problems *resolved* at the counseling stage. In total, approximately 15,000 persons were counseled in Fiscal Year 1971; 36.2% of those counseled received *corrective action* on the problem they presented. [emphasis added]

The term ''corrective action'' is inserted although the Commission does not know how many ''informal resolutions'' actually resulted in ''corrective action.''

8. The Commission's regulations also require each agency to develop plans, procedures, and regulations for affirmative action in EEO—including provision of sufficient resources; disciplinary actions against supervisors; maximization of the utilization of employee skills; maximization of on-the-job training and work-study programs; publicity of job opportunities to all sources of job candidates; cooperation with community groups to improve employment opportunities; evaluation, control, and training of managers and supervisors in regard to EEO programs; recognition of employees for superior accomplishment in EEO. The Commission also requires each agency to appraise, through "self-evaluation," its overall EEO efforts at regular intervals to assure their conformity with Commission policies and programs; and to establish a system which provides statistical employment information by race and national origin.

9. The office of the general counsel has submitted reports to the executive director of the Commission. Two law professors working for the Commission during a summer program have submitted criticisms of the appeals program. Professor Egon Guttman's thorough work was published in volume 19 of the *American University Law Review.* Judge James A. Washington's thoughtful critique was submitted to the Commission in 1968.

10. At one time the appeals examiner did indeed provide direct services to the management of agencies. Appeals examiners—trial judges as it were—routinely provided advice on procedure to management in the same cases in which they later sat as examiners. In one case, in fact, the BAR altered the date of service of notice of adverse decision to make it comply with procedural rules. Although this practice appears to have ceased, members of the Appeals Examining Office still contact personnel offices before a decision is reached in a case that is procedurally defective to suggest that it be withdrawn. (This is as if a football coach were to serve as both coach and referee in a championship game, stopping the game to tell his offensive team that it is lined up improperly for the defensive formation it is facing.)

11. The Commission's perspective not only affects the adjudication of employee appeals, but the performance of the Commission. A young attorney, an associate of a prominent Washington law firm who represented an employee seeking a temporary restraining order on a matter submitted to the Commission, wrote to the research group:

During argument the judges wanted to know what the status of proceedings before the Civil Service Commission is. Government counsel replied that proceedings have been stayed pending the Court of Appeals' decision. The Court wanted to know why the stay [delay] since the District Court's opinion did not preclude them from deciding, and, if they had decided, it would have mooted the issue. Government counsel agreed with that reading of [the] order and said the reason the Commission has stayed proceedings is that they [the Department of Justice] wanted to preserve the point for appeal. This business of the CSC taking action to accommodate the tactical needs of the Department of Justice did not sit very well with the court and didn't sit very well with me either. I am more than a little distressed at the idea that a quasi-judicial entity before which I am litigating an issue should be hand-in-glove with opposing counsel.

12. The Civil Rights Commission reports, regarding the IAG:

During fiscal year 1969, Directors of Personnel and Equal Employment Opportunity Officers from the score of agencies comprising the Equal Employment Opportunity Committee met four times. . . . The group's attention was directed primarily to the revised discrimination complaint procedures. Although the group also made suggestions regarding the agency equal employment opportunity actions plans, *there is no way of determining the extent of its influence.* In the final analysis, governmentwide policy decisions on equal employment opportunity are made by the CSC. [emphasis added]

13. The dangers of such conflict of interest and the dangers of the imposition of management bias is exacerbated by the practice of regional directors of consulting with the executive staff of the Civil Service Commission before some appeals determinations are made. Both the Boston and Philadelphia regional directors said that such contacts were made. Although consistency in the appeals program is desirable, this consistency is best supplied by the Board of Appeals and Review and by the Commission through the promulgation of regulations.

14. A small number of agencies have experimented with elected counselors, without the Commission's encouragement. Irving Kator, in an interview, stated views against *requiring* the election of counselors: "I've no objection to the election of counselors. The ultimate decision, through, I think ought to be a management decision. This is not a popularity contest. I've known people elected to such jobs that couldn't talk to management and that prevented a favorable case from getting an early resolution. It is important to have a guy who can do the job of counselor."

In a speech at an EEO conference, Kator also expressed the same viewpoint:

> An essential ingredient in an EEO counselor is his acceptability to employees as well as to management. He should be able to maintain the confidence and trust of all parties. Although it is management's responsibility to select the EEO counselor and to ensure that he is someone who can identify with all levels of the work force, unions and employees may have an input into nominating persons for counselors. Management, however, should make the final choice.

The fact that counselors are management-appointed and not employee-elected does not, of course, necessarily result in counselors able to "maintain the confidence and trust of all parties." Nor is it the case that any election of counselors need be what is called "a popularity contest."

15. Dr. Richard Weir, Professor of Political Science at Lindenwood College, St. Charles, Missouri, observed that "the EEO counselor usually has a relatively high grade. All of the EEO counselors encountered in this study [of upward mobility at two installations] had grades of either GS-9 or GS-11. Most complaints, however, come from employees from the lower grade ranges, with the bulk below GS-5. Thus the employee approaches an EEO counselor who, because of his relatively high grade, is identified with management, and it is management who is viewed by the complaining employee as responsible for his situation. The element of mutual trust, essential to any successful counseling situation, is, therefore, vitiated from the beginning by the selection of counselors with grades significantly higher than their clientele."

16. On March 9, 1954, the American Bar Assocation adopted a resolution which said that "the impartial conduct of cases by Federal hearings officers is not adequately safeguarded against agency influences by the regulations and practices which have been evolved under Section 11 of the Administrative Procedures Act."

In November 1954, Earl Kintner, chairman of the Committee on Hearing Officers of the President's Conference on Administrative Procedures, recommended the transfer of functions regarding hearing examiners from the Civil Service Commission to an independent Office of Administrative Procedure. In support of such a motion the committee said: "The Civil Service Commission has consistently failed to adhere to the provisions of Section 11 of the Administrative Procedures Act and has continuously violated not only the letter but the spirit of the section." The committee felt that the behavior of the Commission made it "constitutionally unsuited" to the tasks assigned it under the Administrative Procedures Act.

The behavior of the Commission that concerned the Committee included (1) solicitation of comments from legal practitioners who have appeared before the hearing officers being considered for promotion, (2) information in the Committee files which conclusively demonstrated that the requirement of rotation of cases had been disregarded by the agencies with the blessing of the Commission, (3) the failure of the Commission to undertake the tasks of establishing good cause for removal, (4) the failure of the Commission adequately to investigate and report upon the hearing-examiner program.

17. A formal hearing required by statute is governed by Section 1004 of Title 5 of the United States Code and requires notice of time, place, and nature of hearing, the legal authority and jurisdiction under which the hearing will be held, and the matters of fact and law asserted. In addition all interested parties must have the opportunity to submit facts and arguments. The hearing must be conducted by a hearing examiner. The bringer of the action has the burden of proof and every party has the right to conduct such cross examination as required for a full and true disclosure of the facts. Hearing examiners are specifically covered by Section 1004.

In the case of an ICC hearing examiner whose removal was sought on grounds of involuntary medical retirement, despite the statutory requirements, despite the fact that civil service regulations governing hearing examiners defined a removal for which a formal hearing was required as *"an involuntary change in status of a hearing examiner,* including discharge, demotion and suspension from the position of hearing examiner and demotion, reassignment, and promotion to a position other than hearing examiner" (emphasis added), the Commission allowed the case to be handled under the disability procedures rather than under the procedures applicable to the removal of hearing examiners. This ruling deprived the examiner of rights under the Administrative Procedures Act. In the oral hearings held under the disability retirement procedures, the Commission refused after a written request to provide for cross-examination of doctors upon whose written statements the involuntary retirement was based.

Not only did the decision of the Commission deprive the examiner of his rights under the Act, but methods of handling examiner cases under unsatisfactory procedures were encouraged. Equally disturbing was the attitude of the Commission's Office of Hearing Examiners, which allowed the case to be processed through the Bureau of Retirement and Insurance without formal protest.

18. Judge Washington thinks that when a probationary employee has made out a prima facie case of discrimination, the agency should justify its reason for separation, which the agency is not required to do in adverse actions against a probationary employee who does not allege discrimination. Judge Washington writes:

> Probationers are entitled to a procedural review but not a merit review in separation cases. Hence the general view of the Board is that it will not inquire into the reasons for separation. This view should not be carried over into cases where the probationer alleges discrimination as the reason for separation. While it is arguable that the Board in any such procedural review is at least required to determine whether separation was unreasonable or capricious, it would seem manifest, when the charge is that separation is the product of discrimination, that the Board has an obligation to review the reasons given by the agency for the separation; and if BAR finds them unreasonable, it should conclude that discrimination was the basis for the discharge. It is inconceivable that in such a situation BAR can separate the validity of the agency's grounds for discharge from the probationer's allegation of discrimination. The same situation could arise in cases of suspensions for thirty days or less.

[Judge Washington appends a footnote:] Cf. In the Matters of . . . , decided 11/22/67, the Board, it appears, did examine the reasons assigned by the agency for the discharge. But see, in the Matter of . . . , decided 8/18/67—the sufficiency of the reasons for separation [is not for evaluation in this review]. Rather, the scope of the Board's review encompasses only the question of whether considerations of . . . race entered into, or influenced, the decision to separate him.

19. Judge Washington, in his study of the appeals system, said, "Whatever the merits of the observation that the Board decides on a case-by-case-basis, it should be observed that the Board is constantly developing legal precedents which the Board, its examiners and appeals examiners in the regional offices will undoubtedly need for future reference." Judge Washington then cited three examples of such precedents. In a 1968 case the Board decided that a spouse incompetent to testify under state law is nevertheless considered competent to testify in administrative proceedings. In another 1968 case the Board decided it was not the role of the Board to determine agency compliance with union agreements; and in a 1967 case the Board decided that, where there was "strong evidence" that an employee's actions are due to mental disability, the agency is required to apply for disability retirement on his behalf. These are the types of decisions which the Board cannot escape making, and yet are the types of decisions which require that the Board look to its previous decisions for guidance.

20. The BAR does not circulate its decisions widely. Copies are sent to the appellant, the agency, the union (if the appellant was represented by the union), and that Appeals Examining Office which last considered the case. As a result of the limited circulation, a discrepancy is created between the decisions of different regions on similar cases, and the ability of the BAR to provide guidance to regional appeals offices is reduced. The establishment of the Appeals Program Management Office in the Bureau of Personnel Management Evaluation was a recognition of this discrepency. Although we were denied access to BAR decisons by the Commission, a number of employees have given us copies of the decisions they received in their cases.

21. Judge Washington commented upon the format of BAR decisions:

> It [the format] does not provide for the enumeration of the specific findings of fact. As it now exists, a decision compels the reader to search and find for himself the specific facts upon which the Board relies, and, as well, the impact of these facts upon the conclusion reached by the Board. Since every case decided by the

> Board is potentially one for court litigation, the failure to enumerate the findings of fact is a significant deficiency.
>
> By simply noting his agreement with the examiner's proposed decision, a Board member desiring to give only casual or even no consideration to the merits of a case can ostensibly fulfill his responsibility for in-depth review. This is a faulty mechanism and, although I do not intend in the least to suggest that any of the present Board members have ever professionally adopted such a cavalier attitude, the mechanism does exist within the system, and consequently there should be some assurance against the possibility of indifferent consideration of cases.

One attorney indicated that many of the photocopied documents in the case file upon which the decision of the BAR was based were illegible.

22. Very possibly because of fears of reprisal, the complaint system is rarely used by upper-level employees. Dr. Rosenbloom reports:

> The system is relatively unused by employees in grades GS-12 and above, where the stakes are substantial. A complaint would violate a cardinal rule of the bureaucratic culture against exposing the deficiencies of one's agency's leadership, and a complaint would almost certainly have a detrimental effect on a federal servant's career. Interestingly enough, most of the complaints at this level are on the basis of sex, which is probably more acceptable.

Dr. Weir feels that this shortcoming of the complaint system has a direct bearing on the failure of the Commission's "Upward Mobility" program for the promotion of lower-level employees.

Chapter 5, Waiting for Godot

1. A complete discussion of the case may be found in 38 *Geo. Wash. L. J.* 265, prepared by Marc L. Fleischaker, Steven Garfinkel, Nancy J. Kleeman, James R. Druse, Douglas J. McCollum, and James E. Nesland.

2. Before the Federal Executive Institute, EEO Conference, October 1970, Kator said:

> While the major thrust of the EEO program is affirmative action, an essential element of the total program is the complaint system. We must ensure that it is responsive in terms of *timeliness. We cannot minimize the value of timeliness in processing complaints of discrimination.* One poorly handled complaint can create bad publicity, and tends to compromise the credibility of the entire EEO program. *Prompt,* fair handling of cases will build confidence in the system. . . . Agencies should make every effort to process complaints of discrimination on a timely basis. The time frames established should be observed. If additional resources are needed, they should be provided by the agencies. Executive Order 11478 requires agencies to provide the necessary resources to get the job done. [emphasis added]

Nicholas Oganavic, former executive director of the Commission, in a May 14, 1970, memorandum to directors of EEO, stressed the problem of threatened credibility when complaints are overdue:

> Unnecessarily long delays in the adjudication of . . . cases can raise serious question in the public mind about the federal government's sincerity in this crucial area. Failure to process these cases expeditiously creates a *negative image* of the federal government's efforts in equal employment opportunity and negates the progress made under affirmative program activities. The federal government as an employer cannot afford to lose the confidence of significant segments of the population because some agencies are delinquent in resolving discrimination complaints filed by federal employees and job applicants. [emphasis added].

3. Withdrawal with corrective action, withdrawal without corrective action, decision on the merits with a finding of discrimination, decision on the merits without a finding of discrimination, rejection for lack of purview, rejection for untimely filing, dismissal because of complainant's separation from the federal service, dismissal because of complainant's failure to prosecute, showing the length of the alleged delay. The breakdown of processing time should also reflect whether a hearing was held: withdrawal with corrective action [hearing held], withdrawal with corrective action [hearing not held].

4. Concerning the number of overdue complaints, Irving Kator reported in a memorandum of August 12, 1971: "At the end of May

1971, 658 complaints were pending in agencies, of which 412 [62.6 percent] were more than 60 days old; of these 232 were more than 120 days old. A further breakdown of cases over 120 days old is not available.... These figures are exclusive of hearing time."

The Commission claims that it does not monitor extremely old cases pending in agencies and cannot distinguish statistically between a case 121 days old and one three years old, since both appear on its records as "more than 120 days old."

On September 8, 1971, several weeks after he claimed further breakdown was unavailable, Kator wrote a letter to the directors of EEO and the directors of personnel of all federal agencies in which he stated: "Chairman Hampton has informed me of his concern with delays in case processing. He plans to write personally in the very near future to the secretary or head of any agency which has cases over six months old." How was Hampton to know which pending cases were over six months old so that he could identify the agencies to write?

The Federal Personnel Manual requires agencies to report to the Commission processing times for pending overdue complaints. In Appendix C-3 of chapter 713 of the FPM appears the following: ". . . [W]here complaints have been in process over 60 calendar days...indicate the approximate number of calendar days of processing attributable to (1) investigation, (2) predecision review, (3) administrative handling and transit."

On January 11, 1973, Mr. Gerald K. Hinch, director of the Office of Equal Employment Opportunity, wrote in response to our question concerning this regulation: "Information on the number of days of processing due to investigation, predecision review, and administrative handling and transit of cases is not available. Since the Commission's program efforts are geared to expediting the processing of cases within 180 days of the filing date, cases which are lagging in various stages are handled on an individual basis. Our manual system does not allow for the compilation of this kind of data."

5. Information provided by Mr. Kator states, "For fiscal year 1970, agencies reported dispositions on 838 closed complaints of discrimination." This statement is somewhat misleading since in 1970 there were 1,153 complaints closed by agencies, but information was provided only on the 838 of those complaints which were reviewed by the Commission. Whether the other 315 dispositions closed which were not reviewed are similar in length of processing and nature of disposition is uncertain.

6. The 180-day limit is the same as the 180-day limit provided in the Equal Employment Opportunity Act of 1972. The act's deadline is the standard after which the administrative process may be bypassed by a direct appeal to the U.S. District Court. This is an outer limit and arguably should not be the standard by which the Commission judges the administrative process. This is particularly true since many employees must rely upon administrative fairness since they cannot afford a judicial remedy.

7. In 1970, out of 838 cases closed that were reviewed by the Commission, 406 were not fully processed, and were therefore probably closed quickly. Of these, 338 complaints were closed because of withdrawal of the complaint by the complainant, 36 cases were closed early because the agencies rejected the complaints as not within the purview of the relevant EEO sections of the Commission regulations, and 32 complaints were closed early after rejection by the agencies because of untimely filing.

The remaining 432 complaints were probably more time consuming, and closed later, especially since 379 were decided on the merits, which means that all the processing steps were necessary. Added to these 379 decisions are two smaller categories of complaints that would probably tend toward a longer processing time —those closed because of separation of the complainant from the government for reasons allegedly unrelated to his pending complaint (13 complaints) and those closed for the alleged failure of the complainant to prosecute his complaint (40 complaints), or a total of 432 complaints that would tend to consume more time in processing.

There were 412 complaints closed in 1970 after less than six months, a figure close to the number (406) of complaints withdrawn or rejected because of lack of purview or untimely filing. And there were 426 complaints closed after more than six months, a figure close enough to the number (379) of complaints reviewed on the merits to suggest that most of such cases meet with delays.

One might object to this conclusion by challenging the assumption that most withdrawals of complaints would tend to occur within six months, arguing that a significant number of withdrawals occur fairly late, after the employee receives some kind of corrective action from his agency (the usual reason for withdrawals) or tires for some reason of prosecuting his complaint (which would not speak well for the effectiveness of the complaint system). But it does not seem likely that informal resolutions and offers of corrective action would take longer than decisions on the merits. In fact, if this were the case, then the insidiousness of delayed complaints would even be greater than it is, since agencies would be delaying cases that they could settle quickly or intended to settle eventually, while processing rapidly those cases which they have no intent to settle; such a hypothetical pattern of processing would mean that the complainant whom an agency thinks to have a meritorious case receives the most delayed attention.

8. Few inequities in the Commission's complaint system are more obvious than the disparity between an agency's right to cancel and a complainant's right to wait.

Commission officials are not opposed to agencies using their power to close complaints when they think a complainant is going too slowly. On June 14, 1971, for example, Irving Kator stated:

> At the present rate, it is taking agencies an average of seven months to process a complaint. We realize some delays are due to the complainant's failure to move ahead with his complaint as requested. He should be encouraged to proceed on a timely basis. If he does not, agencies may cancel for failure of the complainant to actively pursue his case. The complainant will have a right to appeal to BAR from an agency's cancellation action. The same procedures apply at the hearing stage.

An appeal by the complainant to the Commission to take jurisdiction over an old complaint in a dilatory agency has never been granted, but in 1970 forty complaints were canceled by agencies for the complainant's alleged failure to prosecute.

How long the agencies waited on the complainants, or for what reason, is information "not readily available" in the commission's EEO office. Theoretically, if a cancellation for alleged failure to prosecute is not justified, a complainant may appeal to the BAR. This is a recourse of questionable effectiveness; BAR records do not indicate the total number of appeals on these grounds in 1970, but they do indicate that the BAR upheld an agency decision to cancel a complaint nine times. The basis for these cancellations is not given by the BAR, but, according to William Berzak, an agency takes this action when (a) complainant fails to prosecute his complaint or (b) complainant is separated from employment for reasons not related to his complaint. No record exists of the BAR overturning an agency decision within Berzak's (a) or (b) categories. (There were four remands in 1970 that could have been on these bases, but Berzak writes: "The common reason for remanding cases to the agencies are as follows: to hold a hearing or to hold another hearing; to further develop the evidence; to accept the complaint for processing where the agency ruled that the complaint was not timely filed or was not within the purview of Executive Order 11478.")

9. Bernard Rosen cited internal management studies to prove this contention. When the studies were requested he replied:

> With respect to the discussion on management studies that have been made on reasons for delay in processing appeals from employees, we do not have formal comprehensive studies on reasons for delay in processing appellate actions. We do have, of course, a *continuing management review* of case work load at the operating level. We periodically check cases which have been on hand *longer than a reasonable period of time* to determine the reason, and to *make sure that any delay within the Commission's control is corrected.* We are making a deeper management study of the reasons for delay because we agree with you that excessive time in acting on employee complaints tends to delay justice; this study is part of the comprehensive review of our appellate processes that Chairman Hampton advised you are making this fiscal year. [emphasis added]

Rosen disregarded Commission regulations that required sixty days rather than a "reasonable" period. Considering the number of overdue complaints, Commission review does not appear to have been uniformly effective.

10. The extent of delay in hearings contributed to or caused by agencies or the Commission may be understated. The flash report shows 86 percent of the hearing process still within the 60-day limit, 14 percent already overdue, *and all the cases are still being processed,* so that the eventual number that will go over the 60-day limit before being closed cannot be determined from the flash report. Before the flash report was provided, Mr. Kator wrote in a memorandum: "The average time spent in the hearing process during the first half of fiscal year 1971 was 66 days. These figures relate to hearings held under current regulations, under Commission jurisdiction. The majority of all hearings, including recommendations to agency heads, are now completed within 60 days of receipt in the Civil Service Commission."

Another source of hearing delay is indicated by the flash-report finding that thirteen out of thirty-eight cases sent to the Commission for a hearing were returned to the agencies because of inadequate investigation.

Chapter 6, The Bargaining Game

1. The term "inspection" rather than "evaluation" will be used throughout, because that term conveys far more clearly the real purpose of the function.

2. At one time, nationwide inspections were planned so that an agency would be reviewed every three to five years. Now the Commission has decided to emphasize more frequent examinations of the larger agencies. During these periodic reviews, not every field installation is examined. Therefore, some field installations may not have been examined for six to ten years; some may never have been examined.

3. The Civil Service Commission was to establish standards for evaluation systems, conduct research and develop methods for evaluating personnel management, ensure proper qualifications and training, assess the adequacy of agency evaluation systems, maintain its own capability to make independent evaluation, and collaborate and coordinate with the Office of Management and Budget responsibility for evaluation of organization and management in the executive branch.

The President's memorandum spawned a new series of euphemisms. The Bureau of Inspections became the Bureau of Personnel Management Evaluation; an inspection became an evaluation; an inspector became a personnel-management advisor or an evaluator.

Ultimately, the effect of the memorandum will be to place greater and greater responsibility on the agencies and to change the focus of the inspections that the Commission conducts. Gilbert Schulkind, director of the Bureau of Personnel Management Evaluation, stated in an article in the January–March 1971 *Civil Service Journal:* "As agencies make progress in establishing their internal programs, our long-range objective is to redirect the Commission's survey effort to concentrate more on problem solution through consultative reviews rather than on general reviews which duplicate agency evaluations."

4. Key Provisions of Commission Inspection Agreement with the Armed Forces.

The Commission's inspection agreement with the army stipulates:

> Approximately once every three years the Civil Service Commission will conduct a departmentwide inspection of civilian personnel management in the Department of the Army. Plans for the scheduling of inspections under the departmentwide plan will be developed to the extent possible, as a cooperative effort between the Commission's central office and Headquarters, Department of the Army.
>
> Selection of activities to be inspected . . . will take into consideration the operations and plans of the department's internal evaluation activity.
>
> . . . The Commission normally will not conduct inspections of Army activities in the years between the departmentwide evaluations.
>
> The Commission will take into account army plans for conducting future surveys.
>
> Every effort will be made to assure that off-year inspections are made only in those instances where a true need exists.
>
> Commission inspections generally will not be scheduled within one year of the previous Department of the Army survey unless special circumstances warrant a lesser interval.
>
> Plans relative to organizational and program coverage, subjects of special interest, sampling of actions, etc., during the departmentwide inspections will be developed to the maximum extent possible as a cooperative effort between the Commission and Headquarters, Department of the Army.

> In scheduling these inspections, the plans of appropriate office of Department of the Army for future inspections at the establishment involved should be taken into account to the extent to which plans are made known to or can be determined by the appropriate regional office.
>
> Commission inspections at Army field establishments should not be scheduled within one year of the previous survey by [Department of Personnel] unless special circumstances warrant a lesser interval.

The Commission's inspection agreement with the air force is substantially the same.

The Commission's inspection agreement with the navy stipulates:

> The Civil Service Commission will furnish Navy, one quarter in advance, a nationwide schedule of its planned inspections of Navy installations.
>
> Except as special circumstances warrant, the Commission will not make general inspections at installations where there has been a Navy personnel-management survey in the preceding six months if known.
>
> Where there has been a recent Navy survey of position management, MUST, (Maximum Utilization of Skills and Training) or some other program area, the results of the Navy survey may be used in lieu of intensive Commission coverage.
>
> In Commission inspections where there are serious negative findings, the regional director may wish to consider asking the Navy Regional Office of Civilian Manpower Management to conduct a follow-up survey.

5. An example of how the agreements may restrict the Commission's quality control is found in a summary of area inspection conferences held in May and June of 1969. Nicholas Oganavic and Bernard Rosen commented that experience had shown that military commanders who rotate every two or three years may be particularly reticent about telling Commission inspectors their problems because of their desire to establish a good record at a number of posts. They suggested that inspections be scheduled

in the early part of a new commander's tour of duty at the installation. However, this suggestion may conflict with the limitations imposed by the inspection agreements upon the selection of installations inspected.

6. In some inspections, such as special inquiry inspections, and in some program reviews, the regional office has a great planning role. However, for optional inspections outside the year of a nationwide inspection, Commission policy is restrictive. "Regional option inspections should be scheduled outside the year of nationwide review *only* in situations where it can be *clearly demonstrated* that a *critical* need exists and *immediate* action *is required.*" [emphasis added; from internal Commission regulations Federal Personnel Manual Supplement, 273-72]

7. As early as 1937 this conflict was recognized by the President's Committee on Administrative Management. In a report to the President, the committee commented: "The Commission is now obligated both to administer and to appraise and criticize its own administration. These functions are basically incompatible."

8. Indeed, because of these risks, the Bureau did at one time rotate assignments, but returned to permanent assignment because it felt the increased competence and efficiency gained clearly offset the risks. The attitudes of inspectors are similarly unacceptable. In interview after interview, the same phrases cropped up: "For some protections you must rely on the general goodwill of men." "Management has the right to manage." "Our Bureau has been management-oriented from the beginning." "Our job is to help management do the job."

9. During the first week of one installation inspection, Commission inspectors were put in an office next to the personnel office, and no one came. When the inspectors changed their location the following week, however, about forty employees sought interviews.

10. The employee questionnaire asked about job categories, attitudes, promotion, training, workload, performance evaluation, contained seven questions concerning the employee's relationship with his supervisor, as well as questions concerning the work environment and agency inquiries into personal matters.

The supervisory questionnaire contained questions concerning the helpfulness of the personnel and administrative offices, the availability of personnel manuals and regulations, the authority of the supervisor, and the attitudes of the supervisor toward his superiors. Supervisors were asked about labor-management relations and asked to compare the government with former private employers.

11. Question 22 had asked:

"In general, how are women treated as far as promotions, training opportunities, etc., are concerned in your installation? A. They are given more opportunities than men with similar qualifications. B. They are given the same opportunities as men with similar qualifications. C. They are given fewer opportunities than men with similar qualifications. D. I don't know."

Question 23 had asked:

"In general, how are members of racial minority groups treated as far as promotions, training opportunities, etc., are concerned in your installation? A. they are given more opportunities than others with similar qualifications. B. They are given the same opportunities as others with similar qualifications. C. They are given fewer opportunities than others with similar qualifications. D. I don't know."

12. This does not cover the contact with management officials at the opening conference and at the closeout conference, from which union representatives and employees are excluded.

13. In 1970 at the Naval Ammunition Depot in Crane, Ind., 1 of 179 removal actions was examined; at the Naval Air Rework Facility, U.S. Marine Corps Air Station, Cherry Point, N.C., only 12 of 604 promotion actions were examined; at the U.S. Post Office in Binghamton, N.Y., none of the 81 removal actions was examined; at the Naval Air Station, Chase Field, Beeville, Tex., none of 6 removal actions was examined; at the Naval Air Rework Facility, Alameda, Cal., 1 out of 61 transfers was examined; at the U.S. Post Office in Flushing N.Y., there was no record of examination of 422 removal actions; at the Philadelphia Naval Shipyard, only 2 out of 111 removal actions were examined; at the U.S. Naval Avionics Facility, Indianapolis, Ind., none of 45 Reduction in Force actions was examined; at the Southwest Regional Office of the FAA, only 32 of 1,768 promotion actions were reviewed; at the U.S. Post Office in Miami, Fla., none of the 20 removal actions was examined; at the U.S. Post Office in Washington, D.C., there is no record that any of the 519 removal actions was reviewed; at the Office of the Secretary of Health, Education and Welfare, Washington, D.C., only 6 of 535 reassignments were examined; at the Naval Ordnance Station, Forrest Park, Ill., only 1 of 41 changes to lower grades was examined; at the Military Sea Transportation Service Atlantic, Brooklyn, N.Y., only 9 of 310 removal actions and only 8 of 2,231 promotion actions were examined; at the Internal Revenue Service Center, Kansas City, Mo., only 14 of 576 promotion actions were examined; at the U.S. Naval Supply Center, Charleston, S.C., none of 6 removal actions was examined; at the U.S. Naval Academy, Annapolis, Md., none of 6 removal actions was examined; at the central regional headquarters of the Federal Aviation Administration in Kansas City, Mo., only 24 of 3,175 promotion actions were examined.

The few 29-A forms examined for fiscal year 1969 also indicate a cursory review of personnel actions. For example, at Region 3 of the Bureau of Sport Fisheries and Wildlife in Minneapolis, Minn., only two of 17 reassignments were examined; at the Goddard Space Flight Center in Greenbelt, Md., only 1 of 17 removals or separations was examined; at COPS of the Veterans Administration in Washington, D.C., only 6 of 456 reassignments were examined; at Sheppard Technical Training Center, Sheppard Air Force Base, Wichita Falls, Tex., only 2 of 400 reassignments were examined; at the Social Security Administration Headquarters in Baltimore, Md., none of the 21 removals, only 73 of 9,885 promotions, and only 31 of 4,852 reassignments were examined; at the Naval Air Engineering Center in Philadelphia, Pa., only 4 of 474 removals were examined; and at Region 2 of the General Services Administration in New York, only 1 of 607 Reductions in Force was examined.

At the Naval Air Station, Naval Air Test Center, Patuxet River, Md., the Commission examined 25 of 437 promotion actions. Despite the discovery of 6 violations (25 percent), no other actions were reviewed. At the Equal Employment Opportunity Commission, the Commission examined sixteen of 180 excepted appointments. Despite discovering 9 violations (about 56 percent), no other actions were reviewed. During the same inspection, the Commission found 10 violations (about 40 percent) in the 24 promotion actions examined; but no other actions were reviewed. At the U.S. Naval Academy the Commission examined 20 of 166 promotion actions. Despite finding 3 violations (15 percent), no other actions were reviewed. At the U.S. Naval Weapons Station, Yorktown, Va., the Commission examined 55 of 636 promotion actions. Despite finding 6 violations (about 10 percent), no other actions were examined. At the Atlanta Region of Housing and Urban Development, 2 violations were found in the 15 promotion actions reviewed (about 13 percent), but no other actions were reviewed.

14. Fifty-six percent of separations are appealed to a first-level appeal within the agency.

15. Delay in report writing is continuing. The inspection report on the National Institutes of Health took six months. The report of the Chicago Payments Center of the Social Security Administration was completed in January 1971, but it did not reach the installation until June 10, 1971. An inspection of the Social Security Administration was conducted in July 1971. In June 1972, the Civil Service Commission contacted the agency saying that in the middle of June the Commission would orally summarize its findings.

16. Included in the attachment, referred to as the BPME memo, are: (1) assessment of the caliber of the personnel officer (if done, *required* to be placed in the BPME memo); (2) problems at the local level which have been created by headquarters policy—this is placed in the memo, we were told, "because we [the Commission] don't want the child to know when the father has erred" (copies of nationwide inspection reports are not given to local installations); (3) assessment of what the inspection impact and its results will be; (4) findings which will have a nationwide impact, i.e., action at one installation which suggests similar nationwide action is necessary; (5) sensitive or confidential matters; (6) a recommendation of a withdrawal of authority; (7) areas of special coverage in nationwide inspections which do not belong in the report.

Until recently, regional offices received little information about action taken on items included in the memo. As the head of inspection in one region said, "Often we do not know what negotiations may have taken place in regard to some of our [memo] findings or recommendations." Field inspectors still complain of the lack of feedback on the BPME memo. A field inspector in a regional office reported returning to an installation which he had inspected two years previously and found that a situation which he had reported in the BPME memo was unchanged.

One survey director told us that when a particularly bad EEO problem was detected, a regional office would paint a rather optimistic picture in its report to the installation but would include the damaging information in the BPME memo. The BPME memo concentrates decision making on major controversial issues in the Commission's central office, which is more attuned to the political pressures that may be brought to bear. However, Gilbert Schulkind felt that the Bureau could destroy the inspection system if lower levels were allowed to reveal everything in their reports.

17. Some inspectors felt that the primary purpose of inspection reports was to allow the Commission to evaluate their work.

18. One of the Commission's principal tools to improve minority-group and women employees are agency affirmative-action plans. The Federal Personnel Manual requires each agency to submit to the Commission its current plans and "commitments" for the accomplishment of EEO objectives, with revisions of the plan required at least once each fiscal year. The manual requires that "target dates" for each "action item" be listed in the plans.

The manual states, "Action plans shall reflect consideration of identified problem areas or impediments to equal employment opportunity in all organizational units, occupations, and levels of responsibility." Also, the manual requires that eight topic areas with the objectives of the coming year for each topic area be included in each plan. The manual also indicates that there "should" be an "Appendix" to each action plan . . . reflecting agency plans for participation in programs for the disadvantaged and the hard-core unemployed. . . . These are: (1) Sufficient resources and staff to administer an adequate EEO program; (2) Recruitment activities; (3) Full utilization of the present skills of employees; (4) Opportunities provided to employees for training, development of potential, and advancement; (5) "Training, advice, incentives, performance evaluation, to assure program understanding and support by supervisors and managers, and positive application and vigorous enforcement of the EEO program, including disciplinary action, when appropriate"; (6) "Participation in community efforts to improve conditions which affect employability, including support of fair housing, adequate transportation, quality education"; (7) "Systematic internal program evaluation and periodic statistical and substantive progress reports to Civil Service Commission"; (8) "Prompt, fair, and impartial processing of complaints of discrimination, appropriate remedial action, and disciplinary action, when indicated; and provision for precomplaint counseling by trained, accessible EEO counselors."

19. As in the case of the Maritime Commission report, grave inadequacies appeared in the Civil Service Commission's "action plan" program. If other evaluation reports could be seen, what might they reveal?

The Department of Labor, alone among the government's larger agencies, lacked an "action plan" for the period preceding the March 1971 EEO evaluation report. One would not be likely to find the Commission admitting this incredible lapse in its public statement about "action plans." It is to be hoped that *some* time before March 1971 the Department of Labor did have an EEO "action plan," since the Commission would otherwise have been caught in an unfortunate misstatement. In an FPM Bulletin (No. 713-12) of December 30, 1969, the Commission stated: "The Civil Service Commission first issued guidelines for developing agency plans of action in CSC Bulletin 713-5 on September 1, 1966. *Since that time, all agencies have published overall EEO plans,* and the plan of action concept has been applied to installations of agencies and tailored to meet the needs of such installations . . ." [emphasis added]

Further concern about the lack of a Department of Labor "action plan" preceding March 1971 arises from an examination of certain information furnished by the Civil Service Commission in October 1971 to the Senate Subcommittee on Labor at the request of Senator Peter Dominick. The question to the Commission was the following: "Does the Commission require federal agencies to have specific affirmative-action programs for equal employment opportunity?" The Commission's answer was, "We require each federal agency to have a specific affirmative-action program for equal employment opportunity. This is spelled out in an Action Plan which each agency is required to submit to the Commission."

A good question is why the Department of Labor's lack of an EEO "action plan" had not come to the attention of the Com-

mission's EEO office and was not immediately remedied by that office long before the BPME evaluation team got on the scene.
20. Violations included not only procedural and program violations but also regulatory violations. Employees were promoted and within a short period of time were reassigned to other positions; in many instances these were positions to which the individuals could not have been promoted. In several cases employees never reported to the positions to which they were promoted.
21. Charles Johnson, president of the local of the union that had alerted the Commission, summarized the Commission's follow-up, "We got no response from the Commission. We heard nothing from them."

Chapter 7, Merit and the System

1. Among the jobs listed as confidential or policy-determining are four secretaries for the director of the Office of Management and Budget and two chauffeurs for the Secretary of Defense, and one public affairs officer to the President's Commission on Consumer Interests. 5 C.F.R § 213.3301
2. According to Mike Causey of the *Washington Post,* during the Kennedy and Johnson years federal job seekers were rated on a secret three-point political scale that determined, even before interviews or security checks, whether they would ever work for the government. The endorsement of the White House fell into three categories. Category one required courteous handling and follow-up, but a job offer was not mandatory. Category two included applicants where local considerations were involved. This required that an applicant be viewed with greater favor. Category three meant that some job had to be found for the bearer. The *Post* story was based upon documents that outlined the procedure. Mike Causey, "Federal Dairy," *The Washington Post,* (June 21, 1971) p. B9.
3. The Watergate hearings have demonstrated that loyalty of public officials to superiors can overcome conscience and duty. Although employees are admonished to put loyalty to the highest moral principles above loyalty to person, department, or party, such admonishments must become meaningful. Methods must

be found to encourage employees to perform their public duties and to protect those who do.

The illegality and notoriety of Watergate, however, should not obscure the trends in the civil service which, while not necessarily leading to Watergate, helped to make it possible. The politicization of the civil service is one of these trends. Another is the immense special-interest pressure exerted upon executive and administrative personnel.

4. The companies most heavily represented in these revolving-door interchanges read like a "Who's Who" of defense contractors, including some of those best known for cost overruns, or "cost growth" in Pentagon terminology. Seventy-seven employees of Boeing were involved in these lateral transfers; fifty-three of Computer Sciences Corporation; forty-eight of General Electric; forty-three of Litton Systems; twenty-seven of Lockheed Aircraft Corporation; twenty-one of Lockheed Missiles and Space; thirty-two of LTV Aero Space Corporation; seventeen of LTV Electrosystems, Inc.; forty of Martin-Marietta Corporation; sixty-two of McDonnell-Douglas Corporation; thirty-two of North American Rockwell; thirty-eight of Northrop Corporation; twenty-six of Raytheon Corporation; and forty-four of Westinghouse.

5. There have been twenty-three more corporate participants than government ones. Assuming a salary of $20,000 and only one year of service for each additional corporate executive, the additional cost to the government is $460,000.

6. Among the companies that have sponsored participants are American Telephone and Telegraph, Bank of America, GTE Sylvania, IBM, General Electric, Mobil, Humble, Westinghouse, McDonnell-Douglas, LTV, and North American Rockwell. Among the host corporations have been IBM, Consolidated Edison, Atchinson, Topeka and Santa Fe Railroad, and Standard Oil of California.

The companies contacted for 1972, according to Neil A. Stein, deputy director of the President's Commission on Personnel Interchange, were similar. Of course, he added, other companies could contact the Commission. They could, that is, if they learned of the program by reading a business magazine and, despite the publicity that centered around large corporations, decided to inquire about participation.

The private-sector members of the Interchange Commission

hardly represent small business; among them are the chairmen of the boards of Cluett, Peabody; Atlantic Richfield; North American Rockwell; Norton Simon; and Kidder, Peabody and Company; the vice-chairman of the board of General Electric; the manager of governmental and public affairs of Pacific Gas and Electric Company; and the president of the National Association of Manufacturers.

7. A broad legal attack by the American Civil Liberties Union has led to several reversals of dismissals on the grounds of immorality; partly because of these reversals, changes have been made in the Commission's application of the suitability standard. In an article in the *Civil Service Journal,* Kimbell Johnson indicated that immoral behavior must have some aspect which makes it more than simply private conduct. "Above all we take into account whether or not notoriety, scandal and censure was involved in the misconduct . . . . [The immorality of an act is determined] in light of today's attitudes on morality, not those of the distant past." The duty of judgment which the Commission places upon itself is indeed great.

To begin to determine "generally acceptable moral standards" or conduct "truly offensive to the sensibilities of the average person," the Commission would have to conduct a massive sociological review of the United States. Since this has not been done, the generally acceptable moral standards of the Commission or that which is truly offensive to the sensibilities of the Commission becomes the standard to be applied. In December 1973 the Commission proposed new standards in response to court decisions interpreting Commission standards. The new standards focus on the relationship of the applicant's misconduct to his/her job performance.

8. Professor David Rosenbloom notes that, in theory, loyalty and security are distinct. Disloyalty implies a conscious effort to destroy the government while security is based on a determination of trustworthiness and reliability involving an official estimate of the civil servant's susceptibility to coercion by subversives.

9. The competitive service includes the majority of civil service positions for which testing or other qualification requirements are imposed. The excepted service includes positions specifically exempted from the competitive service by statute and positions to which appointments are made by nomination for confirmation by the Senate. Political appointees are within the excepted service.

10. The National Agency Check uses the following government records: FBI name files; FBI fingerprint files; Civil Service Commission security files; Civil Service Security Investigations files; the appropriate military intelligence files if there has been military or civilian service with the armed forces; the files maintained by the House Internal Security Committee.

11. In agencies with their own investigative apparatus, limited suitability investigations are not conducted by the Commission for excepted positions. The adverse information is referred to the agency for investigation. Cases involving less serious suitability matters or persons in lower grades are also referred to the employing agency. In cases in which the results of the National Agency Check and Inquiries are clearly favorable, no investigative report is furnished to the agency. Unless the agency has requested the file of the case within three months, the file is destroyed.

12. By special arrangement, the Commission conducts investigations of noncompetitive positions for some agencies; the Commission has given to the Armed Forces, the Departments of Treasury and State, and the Postal Service the right to conduct full field investigations in competitive service. The FBI, the Justice Department, the National Security Agency, and Central Intelligence Agency conduct their own investigations. A number of full field investigations are of contractor personnel for the Atomic Energy Commission.

13. These reimbursable investigations are assigned and controlled by the Bureau of Reimbursable Investigations in Washington, which reviews every report of a reimbursable investigation and returns those which are seriously lacking to the regional offices.

The Bureau establishes a sixty-day time limit for agency-funded full field investigations. An agency may request that 10 percent of its cases be conducted on an expedited basis. Most of the investigations of Commission employees are conducted on an immediate five-day basis.

14. The Bureau, according to Mr. Johnson, has been able to limit recruitment to the top of the register.

15. In order to extend an investigation, an investigator must seek special permission. Commission instructions emphasize that extensions must be used "judiciously" because extensions add to the cost of the case and often make it impossible to meet deadlines. A copy of internal Commission instructions to Commission investigators was provided by Mr. Johnson.

16. Commission instructions to investigators require that derogatory information obtained from a witness must be supported by corroborative evidence either of record or from additional witnesses.

17. Confidential information contained in Civil Service investigative reports might also be used by agencies to establish the basis of an agency adverse action. The Federal Personnel Manual Supplement provides: "If the agency wishes to use information in a Civil Service Commission investigative report which cannot be made available to the employee because it would violate a pledge of confidence, the agency may obtain the information independently in a form that can be disclosed." [F.P.M. Suppl. S4-la (3) (1972)] Among suggested techniques of "independently acquiring" the information are interviewing the employee or contacting other sources.

18. A former Commission employee reports that investigative reports on community leaders applying for EEO positions that showed only the most innocent connection with the Communist Party invariably had the words COMMUNIST PARTY OF THE UNITED STATES on the front of the report in capital letters.

19. This is not as ludicrous as it appears at first glance. Reporter Robert Sherrill reports a case in which the Commission ruled that an applicant had falsified his application for federal employment and ruled that he would have to stand aside for a year before reapplying. According to the investigative report, the applicant had lied by saying that he had never been a member of the Communist Party. The investigative report accused him of belonging for three months in 1943 and attending Communist social functions in Pennsylvania. This was bizarre, considering that for seven years he had been an investigator for the House Un-American Activities Committee.

20. According to a former Civil Service Commission employee, a report on a speaker to appear in government training courses said that six years earlier the speaker's sister had traveled to Sweden to attend a world youth conference supported by the Communist Party.

21. One Commission letter of interrogation questioned the applicant's living in a house owned by a Communist group. At that time, the applicant was ten years old and was living with his parents.
22. A letter to one clerk-typist from the Commission commented that while she had been in college she reportedly had poor habits of personal hygiene, and openly used profanity.
23. Kimbell Johnson, director of the Bureau of Personnel Investigations, said in an article appearing in the *Civil Service Journal* that the Commission's position of disqualification for use of marijuana was based neither on medical grounds or on public opinion, but on the law. "Persons who currently use narcotics . . . in violation of law are disqualified for employment in the federal service." In most states use of marijuana is a misdemeanor.
24. There is no evidence that such information has appeared in a Commission report, although information about credit and debts does appear. However, the air force investigators probing Ernest Fitzgerald, following his congressional testimony on cost overruns on the C-5A, referred to Mr. Fitzgerald as a "cheap skate" because, despite his salary, he drove an old Rambler.
25. Other investigative reports may be included if they have led to full field investigations.
26. Except in the Washington area, where the decision is made by the chief of the Division of Appraisal and Adjudication, the decision is made at the regional level by the chief of the investigative section. The employee need not appear if he wishes the case decided upon the information presently in the Commission's hands. (An employee of the executive branch may under special circumstances be required to respond under section 5.3 of Civil Service Rule 5.) The employee may bring a representative with him.

Chapter 8, Toward a New Civil Service

1. One way the Commission could sensitize itself to a new role would be to issue "an environmental impact statement" to accompany new rules, regulations, and major policy directives. This action would force the Commission to determine the specific impact of its regulations upon employees and their public performance.

If, for example, it had been forced to consider the impact of its decision upon the conduct of agency hearings, the Commissioners might not have overruled a Bureau of Policy and Standards' recommendation limiting the discretion of agency officials to reverse the decision reached in agency hearings.

2. Section 210 of the Labor Law of New York provides "that any officer, agent, or employee of this state or of a municipal corporation therein having a duty to act in the premises who violates, evades, or knowingly permits the violation of any provisions of this chapter [of labor laws] shall be guilty of malfeasance in office and shall be suspended or removed by the authority having power to remove such officers."

The statutes of some states allow the governor, county executive officer, or other executive officers to remove an employee for malfeasance. Section 210 contains a provision that could make a law truly effective in curbing bureaucratic lawlessness. "Any citizen of this state may maintain proceedings for the suspension or removal of such officer, agent, or employee who knowingly permits the violation of any of the provisions of this chapter."

Adam Walinsky, a New York attorney representing New York workers exposed to hazardous working conditions, brought suit under this statute seeking the removal of the Industrial Commissioner for failure to enforce sections of the labor laws of the state of New York. Mr. Walinsky contended that this statute was a mandatory accountability statute.

No inspections of working conditions had been conducted even though workers had complained. The results of previous inspections were withheld from the public. Internal reports of the Labor Commission showed that 41.4 percent of fatal accidents were contributed to by violations of the labor law.

Despite a series of severe physical injuries to persons employed in the manufacture of molecular sieves in the Union Carbide Company's Tonowanda N.Y. plant, and despite continued efforts by workers to bring these conditions to the attention of state officials, little was done to reduce the health and safety hazards as required by law. The malfeasance with which the Industrial Commissioner was charged caused men to be exposed to conditions from which workers developed sores on their legs, pulmonary fibrosis, acute bronchitis, and emphysema. Because officials control information and are obligated to inform themselves about their responsibilities, Mr. Walinsky contended that ignorance of violations was no excuse. After the suit was filed, the Industrial Commissioner resigned, preventing the case from being tried.

3. Senator Paul Douglas aptly remarked in his book *Ethics in Government,* "The bureaucracy is defective in imagination and somewhat wanting in sympathy."

4. *Driscoll v. Bulington Bristol Bridge Co.,* 86 A. 2d 201, 221 (N.J. 1962)

5. *Association of Data Processing Service Organizations, Inc.* v. *Camp,* 397 U.S. 150 (1970); *Bralow* v. *Collins,* 397 U.S. 159 (1970); *EDF* v. *Hardin,* 428 F.zd 1093 (D.C. Cir. 1970)

6. *U.S.* v. *Carter,* 217 U.S. 286 (1909); *U.S.* v. *Mississippi Valley Generating Co.,* 364 U.S. 520 (1961); *Bishop* v. *U.S.,* 366 F.zd 657 (5th Cir. 1961); *Smith* v. *U.S.,* 305 F.zd 197 (9th Cir. 1962); *U.S.* v. *Goldfield Corp.,* 384 F.zd 669 (10th Cir. 1967); *U.S.* v. *Drisko,* 303 F. Supp. 858 (E.D. Va. 1963).

A

D

E

L

M

N

O